BEING
<u>THERE</u>

All of the photographs in this book were taken by the author.

BEING THERE

THE NECESSITY OF
FIELDWORK

DANIEL BRADBURD

SMITHSONIAN INSTITUTION PRESS

Washington and London

Library of Congress Cataloging-in-Publication Data appears on the last printed page of this book, following the index.

Permission has been generously granted to use material from the following copyrighted works: From "Hermes' Dilemma: The Masking of Subversion in Ethnographic Description," by Vincent Crapanzano, "Fieldwork in Common Places," by Mary Louise Pratt, and "Post-modern Ethnography: From Document of the Occult to Occult Document," by Stephen A. Tyler, in James Clifford and George Marcus, eds., *Writing Culture,* © 1986 by the Regents of the University of California, reprinted by permission of University of California Press; from "On Ethnographic Authority," by James Clifford, in *Representations* vol. 1, no. 2 (1983), © 1983 by the Regents of the University of California, reprinted by permission of the author and University of California Press; from *Works and Lives: The Anthropologist as Author,* by Clifford Geertz, © 1988 by the Board of Trustees of the Leland Stanford Junior University, reprinted by permission of Stanford University Press; figures 15 and 23 from *The Cambridge History of Iran,* edited by W. B. Fisher, © 1968 by Cambridge University Press, reprinted by permission of Cambridge University Press; from "My Worst Journeys," by George Woodcock, in Keath Fraser, ed., *Bad Trips,* © 1991 by Random House, Inc., reprinted by permission of Random House, Inc.

Copy editor: Susan A. Warga
In-house editor: Ruth Spiegel
Designer: Kathleen Sims
Composition and map production:
    Blue Heron Typesetters, Inc.

For those who made this possible:
Ann Sheedy Bradburd,
and my parents,
Dorothy and Ervin Bradburd

CONTENTS

PREFACE

I intend this preface to be brief. The introduction sets out my primary goals for this text and my reasons for writing it. Some of those reasons and goals stem from recent intellectual debates in anthropology or the academy as a whole. I doubt they are particularly engaging for most people. There are, however, other reasons I have written this book.

First, by focusing on the relationship of fieldwork and understanding, and by centering my discussion on concrete events and my responses to them, I have tried to convey to people who have not done fieldwork something of what it feels like to do it. If I have succeeded, readers will know a bit better how it feels to be confused, fascinated, upset, and exhilarated at nearly the same time—how one can watch something and have part of one's brain say, "Wow, that's fascinating," while another part of one's brain is livid with rage because the "fascinating" event is repugnant or has radically diminished the value of days, weeks, or even months of careful planning or hard work, or both. In short, I hope this book provides the reader with some feeling for what it is like to attempt to understand something so complicated, fast-moving, and personally involving that one knows one can never come close to getting it all and can only hope to get some parts of it (ideally, the important ones) mostly right. I hope the book will also help people understand how anthropologists come to be nearly totally embedded in the cultures they are trying to understand, and as a result are not simply confused by what they see, but are buffeted by their emotional responses to their experiences. We anthropologists are our own tools, and the chips, cracks, and dents we pick up during fieldwork are manifest not only in and on our bodies, but in our psyches as well.

Second, if what I have suggested above is true, if gaining anthropological understanding through fieldwork is so hard to do and comes with an inevitable personal cost, one ought to be able to answer the question "Why are people stupid enough to become anthropologists?" I suppose one answer is that most of us didn't really know what we were getting into until we got off the plane, boat, or camel that brought us to where we were going. A better answer is that doing anthropology is one of the most intellectually exciting things a person can do. Being there and trying to understand what is going on is like being the detective in the biggest, most complicated mystery ever. So one reason to do anthropology is the sheer intellectual challenge. That, coupled with intense emotion and, often, exotic locations, makes doing anthropology real fun. Fieldwork is hard and it often hurts, but it is also about as much fun as one can have and still be doing something called work. I hope this book conveys some of the joy that there is in doing that work.

Third, I have written this book to argue for the value of fieldwork and of sustained experience of and contact with the lives of other people in other cultures. We live in a world full of divisions, many of which are exploited in situations of horrific violence and human cruelty. Anthropology has a long and very positive tradition of attempting to use knowledge to create understanding in the hope and belief that understanding is valuable, that it somehow helps prevent the dehumanization of others that is so central to mass violence. If doing anthropology is fun, providing anthropological understanding is important. Reading this book should provide an increased anthropological understanding of one people, the Komachi, in one country, Iran (which is generally badly misunderstood in the United States). It should thus also give people the opportunity to gain greater insight into the nature of anthropological understanding.

Finally, and not entirely trivially, I have written this book so that my children will have some idea of what my life was like twenty-odd years ago. They have lived with my choice; they should know what helped me make it.

ACKNOWLEDGMENTS

Many people provided me with valuable comments and, sometimes, even more valuable encouragement as I worked on this text, and I owe them all a great debt. Bahram Tavakolian read an early draft of the manuscript and, as always, his comments were enormously helpful. Three of my colleagues at Clarkson, Ellen Caldwell, Joe Duemer, and Dennis Horn, also read early versions, and their assurance that the work was of interest to them even though they are not anthropologists provided incentive to keep on working. Joanne Passaro, my one colleague at Clarkson who is an anthropologist, provided very helpful comments, particularly on the book's last chapter. Dale Eickelman took on the burden of reading the manuscript at a later stage, and I greatly appreciate his comments and encouragement. Audrey Shalinsky's comments on an early version of my last chapter were trenchant and helped point me toward making a significant modification in its tone. I similarly profited greatly from discussions with Greg Starrett about both my text and other recent takes on anthropological fieldwork and theory. Tracey Heatherington gave the text a very careful reading, and she provided very helpful insights into how the book might look to someone at a very different stage of their career. Bill Merrill took valuable time from his fieldwork to help me with revisions of the last chapter. Bill was equally generous in his general support of the project, and I greatly appreciate all he has done to make this a better work.

I must also thank various institutions for the part they played in this project. My original fieldwork in Iran was supported by the National Institute of Mental Health and the National Science Foundation. A National Endowment for the Humanities Fellowship for College Teachers provided support that permitted me to spend time in London at the British Library, the India Office Records Library, and the Public Record Office at Kew, where I was able to become deeply familiar with the style and nature of reports produced by travelers to Iran in the eighteenth, nineteenth, and early twentieth centuries. The first draft of this text was written during a sabbatical provided by Clarkson University. I greatly appreciate the freedom to simply concentrate on my writing that the sabbatical provided.

Others have played a less direct but nonetheless very important role in this work. In particular, I wish to mention Philip Salzman, who generously arranged my participation in a field project on Sardinia. In the course of preparing for that project and during work there, we shared many, many vigorous— or at least loud—explorations on the whys and wherefores of fieldwork and the current state of anthropology. In ways too numerous to recount, both that field experience and our discussions are reflected here.

In the end, of course, whatever help and encouragement I have received, I take full blame for all the faults the work has. Those to whom my thanks are due have only improved what they generously agreed to read.

Finally, and as always, my greatest debt is to my wife, Ann Sheedy Bradburd. Not only was she there with me for the fieldwork, she was also there over and over again to help me hammer out my thoughts and my prose. For her patience, support, and great good sense, I am eternally in her debt. My children, Nat and Kate Bradburd, also helped, largely by being themselves. The experience of having and raising them has certainly helped me come to a deeper understanding of others—which is, I hope, reflected in this text.

INTRODUCTION

This book began as an attempt to show how my understanding of the culture of Komachi pastoralists in southern Iran was shaped by the cumulative impact of the unexpected, unprogrammed, sometimes exhilarating, sometimes uncomfortable events my wife, Ann Sheedy, and I experienced over the course of nearly two years in the field. It was motivated by my growing annoyance with both postmodernist criticisms of ethnography and responses from the anthropological community that stressed greater methodological strictures and scientism as the bulwark against those criticisms. To that end, I sought to link together a collection of anecdotes recording some of the serendipitous happenings I encountered, observed, or participated in as I lived among the Komachi in 1974 and 1975 and, by describing and explicating them, to show how this kind of experience is central to the formation of anthropological understanding. In a sense, then, this book is a kind of backdrop to my earlier ethnography, *Ambiguous Relations,* which provided a more formal and structured view of the Komachi.

I am not entirely certain what initially drove me to frame this work as a series of anecdotes about the out-of-the-ordinary, unplanned elements of my field experience. Certainly I was aware that discussions of the anthropologist's own experiences effectively ground such diverse but fundamental works as Clifford Geertz's "Deep Play: Notes on the Balinese Cockfight" and Richard Lee's "Eating Christmas in the Kalahari." I knew too that my students always respond strongly to discussions of my field experiences (and, indeed, others' experiences as well).

While this project moved forward in fits and starts, I was also working on a second project, analyzing the political and economic structure of Iran's larger pastoralist populations. I began rereading accounts of tribal Iran written by European adventurers, diplomats, travelers, and spies during the nineteenth and early twentieth centuries. It was not long before I began to have the haunting feeling that my narrative echoed those written 90 to 150 years ago. As I noted information on the prices of commodities and the details of tax farming schemes, I found myself adding new marginal notes with cryptic messages such as "parallels 'census'" or "'bury dead' question." Soon it became clear that I was fast accumulating a large stock of passages that in one way or another struck me as helpful in illustrating and thinking about portions of my own narrative.

In the text that follows, not only do I attempt to show how the impact of singular, salient events, combined with the accumulation of experience during fieldwork, shaped my anthropological understanding, I also try to use material drawn from earlier travel writing to explore some of the similarities and differences between life in tribal Iran in the mid-1970s and life there in the mid- to late nineteenth century. To a lesser degree, I also attempt to note the ways in which the vision of Iran and tribal Iranians embodied in that travel writing differs from my representation in the ethnographic narrative I have produced here. In drawing on travelers' accounts, I have made only the barest attempt at systematic sampling. The four authors whose work I most commonly cite are Sir Henry Layard, Lady Mary Leonora Sheil, Mrs. Isabella Bishop, and Sir Arnold Wilson. They traveled in Iran at times between the 1840s and 1914; Layard, Bishop, and Wilson all spent time among tribal peoples. Layard, who was the earliest of the travelers, lived among the Bakhtiyari, and the central portion of his text is a passionate account of the lengthy and ultimately unsuccessful struggle between Mohammed Taqi Khan, perhaps the dominant political leader of the Bakhtiyari at that time, and the powers of the Iranian state. At the time of his travels, Layard was in his early twenties and largely seeking adventure, though he kept a sharp eye out for the commercial potential of the regions he traversed; he later "discovered" the ruins of Ninevah and then undertook a career in the British Foreign Office, culminating in positions as undersecretary of state for foreign affairs and Her Majesty's ambassador at Constantinople.

In the period recorded in his diary, 1907–1914, Wilson was in his mid- to late twenties, a junior officer in the Indian army seconded to the political department during his tour in "S.W. Persia." He too later moved on to a substantial career, first in the political office in Iraq and then in the early 1920s as resident director of the Anglo-Iranian Oil Company. If Layard was an adventurer, moving on his own, Wilson was an agent of the British government, traveling to collect intelligence information on the region and its tribes in the immediate pre–World War I era. In a very real sense, therefore, he was engaged in the profession of collecting and analyzing information about tribal Iran, generally with a political and economic focus.

I have chosen to draw on Layard and Wilson not only because they both worked at understanding the political and economic structures of tribes, but also because they were roughly the same age Ann and I were when we did fieldwork among the Komachi. Thus I felt that in some ways their experiences and outlooks might parallel ours.

Bishop was also a professional at gathering information, for she was an author of travel books on faraway and exotic places, which in addition to Iran included Japan, Tibet, the Rocky Mountains, and India. In some sense, I include Bishop as a straw woman. She was interested in the activities of Protestant missionary groups, and she had a very sharp, critical eye for the moral as well as political and economic weaknesses of the places she visited. She was observant and intelligent, but not a relativist. Because she made her living reporting on the ways of others, Bishop had a particularly keen eye for the colorful or striking situation.

I think I have chosen Sheil because I like the slight tone of irony and self-deprecation in her book. Her husband, Sir Justin Sheil, then a colonel, later a major general, was Her Britannic Majesty's plenipotentiary ambassador to the court of the shah from 1844 to 1853.[1] Lady Sheil came to Iran in 1849 and left with her husband at the end of his appointment, four years later (Wright 1977, 22). Thus, while Layard, Wilson, and Bishop (and Ann and I) voluntarily roughed it in one way or another, Sheil's view of Iran was filtered through layers of ceremony and privilege. She moved at the highest levels of society, and her rank and station meant she always received special treatment. She was not doing fieldwork. Nonetheless, she was observant and, it seems to me, unusually reflective. From evidence in her text it seems that she and her husband were Anglo-Catholics, and I suspect that was the basis of the religious relativism that provides the tone for her book.

Finally, as I have worked and reworked this manuscript it has become increasingly clear to me that in addition to examining how my encounters with the Komachi shaped my understanding of them, and considering how my encounters and understandings were similar to or different from those of earlier travelers, a third element has crept in. Over and over I find myself commenting on how encountering one or another circumstance among the Komachi brought into sharp relief not only elements of their culture but also parts of my own. As a result, throughout the text I find myself not just describing the Komachi, but also musing on elements of American culture (and Western culture more generally) and the powerful ways it shaped Ann's and my actions and understandings in the field.

FIELDWORK AND ETHNOGRAPHY

Lately a great deal of critical attention has been paid to writing ethnography and, to a lesser extent, to doing fieldwork. Reading that material with what is, I freely admit, a jaundiced and biased eye, I occasionally feel that I am witnessing the scene in Canto XXV of Dante's *Inferno* in which the damned are caught in a never-ending cycle of alternately being eaten alive by giant lizards and then themselves becoming these monstrous consumers of human flesh. I am not certain the spectacle needs to be more broadly displayed. But there is a second reason I am uncomfortable about directly entering this dialogue. When I was in graduate school, one of my professors threw out as a rule of thumb (he was talking about sex) the proposition "If you're talking about it, you're not doing it." Over the years, I have found this principle remarkably accurate. So rather than focus here on how my choice of tropes does or does not effectively create an authoritative authorial voice for my narrative, I concentrate on another question: What, in the process of fieldwork, most shaped my understanding of the Komachi?[2]

Part of my understanding derives from systematically collected data: surveys, censuses, genealogical charts and interviews that Ann and I sorted and tabulated, pondered, argued about, and obsessed over. But the literature on writing ethnography and doing fieldwork, in addition to discussions with my empiricist friend Philip Salzman, compelled me to think more and more about fieldwork and our stay among the Komachi. I came to feel that I was right to think that our understanding of the Komachi and Iran was forged as much by a series of unplanned encounters unfolding over our nearly two years there as by reading or systematic data collection. It is these encounters, some striking, some cumulatively powerful though individually almost imperceptible, that I try to present below, along with a reflection on how these particular experiences shaped our view of the Komachi.

I intend this account of cumulative, serendipitous encounters to be quintessentially an account of "being there"—to illustrate how important "being there" is and to show how it shaped my understanding of the Komachi, and therefore my representations of them.[3] To that end, this text is far more a personal narrative than is other work on the Komachi.

In "Fieldwork in Common Places," an essay on fieldwork and ethnographic writing that helped inspire this project, Mary Louise Pratt identifies two styles found in both ethnographic and travel writing, "personal narrative" and "impersonal description," that are variously employed to create authorial authority. Pratt argues that

> personal narrative is a conventional component of ethnographies. It turns up almost invariably in introductions or first chapters, where opening narratives commonly recount the writer's arrival at the field site. . . . These conventional opening narratives are not trivial. They play the crucial role of anchoring that description in the intense and authority-giving personal experience of field-work. (Pratt 1986, 31–32)

In small doses and in opening chapters that well may be. In this book the intent of the personal narrative is not to buttress the "objective" or to "set . . . up the initial positionings of the subjects of the ethnographic text" (Pratt 1986, 32), for here the ethnographic text *is* a personal narrative. If I have been successful, my narrative does two things: First, its very disjointedness—the fact that it is "one thing after another"—permits a representation of the Komachi that expands upon the one presented in *Ambiguous Relations,* recounting material that was hard, if not impossible, to effectively discuss within the structure of that work. Second, its sharp focus on how the combination of singular events and cumulative experience affected our perceptions and analysis shows how "being there" creates ethnographic understanding.

In a more recent work, Pratt labels "sentimental" narratives that center on the authors' "trials, challenges, and encounters with the unpredictable," arguing that "sentimental writing explicitly anchors what is being expressed in the sensory experience, judgment, agency, or desires of human subjects. Authority lies in the authenticity of somebody's felt experience" (Pratt 1992, 75–76).

My intention in highlighting the sources of my understandings is not to claim that my felt experience provides authority; rather, it is to reveal, as well as possible, the bases for my claims about the Komachi, permitting readers to evaluate appropriately the authority of my representation. To that end, in setting down my experience I have attempted to keep in mind Vincent Crapanzano's critical assessment of the ways ethnographers have recorded ethnographic encounters:

> In traditional ethnography the ethnographer's encounter with the people he has studied is rarely described. Often, as in the case of Geertz's "Deep Play" . . . even the activity that is described and interpreted . . . is not presented in its particularity as a single, and in some ways unique performance. We are usually given a general picture. . . . It gives the illusion of specificity when there is no specific temporal or spatial vantage point. It attests to the ethnographer's having been there and gives him whatever authority arises from that presence. (Crapanzano 1986, 75)

I have therefore tried to describe encounters fully, to eschew the general, and to be as specific as possible.

That said, I am not unaware that the text I have created to counter the claims of postmodern theory has more than a few postmodern aspects. Rather than a single, totalizing voice, it has several, including voices of informants and previous travelers; it is episodic; it does not aim to present a single, overarching vision of the Komachi. It is instead an attempt to show, by describing my encounters with various Komachi and also their encounters with each other and the non-Komachi world, how and why I came to my understandings of them.

THE REPRESENTATION

The account that follows is almost entirely anecdotal. In its broadest outline it is chronological, beginning with our arrival in Iran and ending with our departure from the Komachi. However, within that broad chronological progress, many of the chapters include anecdotes that are far out of chronological place. Their placement arises from my feeling that they help illustrate or clarify the more chronologically bound pieces with which they are associated. One inevitable effect of this technique is that people and places appear and reappear in anecdotes with no particular pattern. I attempt to fully identify significant people and places when they first appear, and I try to provide periodic reminders of who is who and what is what as I go along. I occasionally make cross-references from one chapter to another, though I have tried to avoid the loathsome device of promising fuller explanation "later" or "below." Above all, I have endeavored to make this account both readable and informative.

I

PEOPLE AND PLACES

I arrived in Iran on December 4, 1973, accompanied by Ann Sheedy. We were both graduate students in anthropology at the City University of New York Graduate Center, and we intended to stay in Iran for at least a year to study aspects of decision making and household economy among pastoralists. I went to study pastoralists because I found the Middle East and its culture interesting, because I found that aspects of pastoral life provided a good arena for examining theoretical issues that were important to me, because I was able to write a sharply focused, fundable research proposal around those interests, and because I found the idea of living in a desert with nomads emotionally attractive. Perhaps I had watched *Beau Geste* too often when I was young. I went to Iran because, in the 1970s, it was one of the easiest places in the Middle East for an American to conduct research. Ann, who is now a certified public accountant, did not share my interest in or my affection for the Middle East—owing, she says, to having seen too many maps of Canaan in Sunday school. She went to Iran because I did. However, she was able to draw on her interest in the domestic cycle among pastoralists and an abiding interest in playing house. Although we worked together as a team and were fully engaged in the process of collecting, analyzing, and thinking through our data, ultimately I continued a professional career in anthropology while Ann became an accountant. She still studies the domestic economy, this time from within a bureaucratic theoretical framework in which the distinction between public and private is replaced by the distinction between business and personal.

We lived with a small tribe known as the Komachi from April 1974 until October 1975, when our stay drew to a close. The Komachi were nomadic pas-

Map 1. Iran.

toralists who lived in southern Kerman province, located in south-central Iran
(see maps). Kerman city, the capital of the province, is about five hundred air
miles from Tehran. The Kerman area was something of a backwater and had
been one for quite some time. Thus, although Iran was experiencing the burst
of development that came with the tremendous surge of oil revenue arising
from the 1973 Arab-Israeli War, Kerman province and its capital experienced
less rapid growth than many other areas of Iran.

The Komachi spent their summers in the mountains about a three-hour drive
from Kerman city. Though they spoke of themselves as living in Kerman, they
also migrated to winter quarters that were about 150 miles farther south, near
the Persian Gulf. Komachi winter quarters were about half again as far from
the port city of Bandar Abbas as their summer quarters were from Kerman city.
Kerman was an older, quiet city; its bazaar was well preserved, and there were

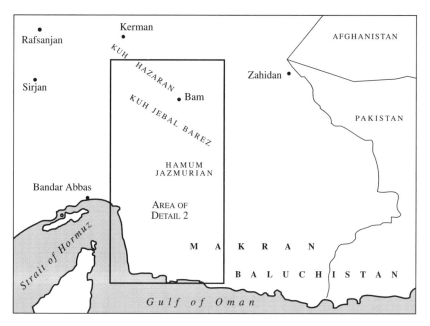

Map 2. Area of detail 1: eastern highlands of Iran. After Fisher, *Cambridge History of Iran,* vol. 1, with permission of Cambridge University Press.

attractive shrines and mosques in the city and the surrounding countryside. The Komachi knew many people in Kerman city, and several had teenage sons living there while they attended high school. Bandar Abbas, by contrast, was a nearly new city. Although it had once been a significant port, it had fallen into great decline until, shortly before we arrived in Iran, Mohammed Reza Shah decided to make it the home port for his Persian Gulf fleet. Bandar Abbas had all the charm one associates with a city built around a large military base. Most older buildings had been knocked down, and most newer buildings looked as though they belonged in a shabby strip mall. Even the "luxury" hotels that catered to expatriate American and British military advisors had a somewhat seedy aspect. While it was a great place for us to shop, neither we nor the Komachi really liked Bandar Abbas, and the Komachi rarely went there.

The period that Ann and I spent in Iran preceded the Iranian revolution. While we had heard of political unrest, we would not and could not have predicted that the shah would be overthrown within five years of our departure. On the one hand, visitors to Iran were constantly aware of the conspicuous presence of various police and armed forces. Within the American community, there was also constant discussion of SAVAK, the shah's secret police. On the

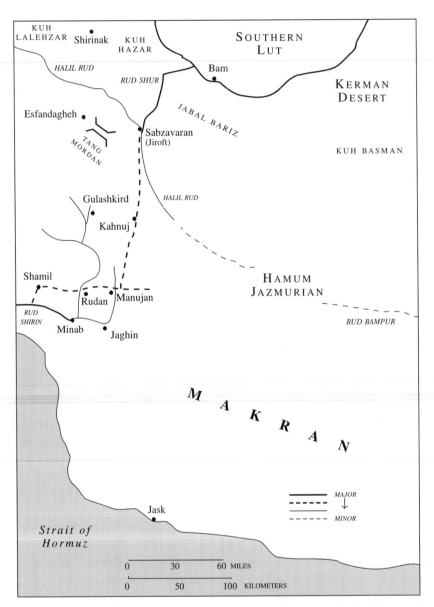

Map 3. Area of detail 2: Hamum Jazmurian basin. After Fisher, *Cambridge History of Iran,* vol. 1, with permission of Cambridge University Press.

other hand, during the twenty-two months of our stay in Iran, the flow of oil wealth coming in was so great that even the enormous inflation and corruption that it promoted could not prevent some of that wealth from trickling down. By the time we left, this was no longer true. Nonetheless, during most of the time that Ann and I spent with the Komachi, they were able to demand good prices for their pastoral products, and they felt they were doing well.

During the time we lived among them, there were approximately 550 Komachi living in about 110 nuclear family households. Almost all Komachi dwelt in black goat-hair tents and were involved in pastoral production. They migrated twice a year, and most of their spring migration was conducted on camelback. While the Komachi claimed to be "all kin," the tribe was in fact an unstable social body, formed from the intermarrying of several smaller groups, and was to some degree unraveling even as it was being knitted together. Although the tribe was small, it was not socially homogeneous. The wealthiest Komachi owned more than fifty times as many animals as the poorest; wealthy Komachi also owned land and gardens, which merely accentuated the basic economic difference in animals owned. Differences in wealth were, generally, matched by differences in class. Wealthy Komachi hired shepherds, who did almost all of the actual work needed to care for the animals. Poor men worked as shepherds. Relations between employer and shepherd were often tense, and the tribe as a whole was anything but a small group of kin living in peace and harmony. The differences in wealth and class are among the most striking features of the Komachi social order, and these features form a constant backdrop to both the descriptive and the theoretical sections in subsequent chapters.

Ann and I were relatively young—Ann was twenty-seven and I was twenty-eight—when we arrived in Iran. In hindsight, we were also relatively inexperienced, either in fieldwork or in life. Youth provided us with the freedom to take two years to do our fieldwork, the resilience to sleep on the ground for eighteen months, and the optimism to embark on the project.

I would close this by noting that neither of us expected that it would be more than twenty years (and counting) before we returned to Iran. We looked on the fieldwork I describe below as a beginning, not as an end. We regret not being able to return; we have never regretted going.

CENSUSES AND THE REAL TRUTH

From the very beginning of our stay, Ann and I knew that we wanted to do a complete census of the Komachi. After some time there, we came to realize that getting accurate data was going to be harder for some topics, largely economic ones, than for others. As a result, we decided to split the census into two phases. Early on, we did a household census, collecting people's names and their genealogies. Many people were as interested in this data as we were, and, as we had hoped, this part of the census went quickly and easily. At this point we did not try to systematically conduct an economic census. Instead we tried collecting information directly, by counting heads when the mobile veterinary team visited to inoculate the animals against liver fluke. After counting two or three herds this way, we realized that the process was not efficient, so we also asked Reza, a young man whose government job involved supplying veterinary medicine to other Komachi, for his estimate of how many animals people owned. He gave us his figures on how many doses of medicine he had given each owner. He told us that in some instances the animals included those bought from other tribes for resale, so the numbers were a bit high, but, he assured us, they were basically accurate. We were confident that these numbers gave us ballpark figures on people's holdings, and with them we were able to begin to figure out who had what. We still wanted and needed better numbers, including a breakdown of herds by type of animal, age, and sex, but we decided we would wait till near the end of our fieldwork to do our own economic survey. We hoped that by then we would know everyone, they would know us and trust us, and we would therefore be able to get the accurate information we wanted. In the meantime, we would look, listen, and count, and attempt to build up profiles of wealth against which we could match our figures when we collected them.

Given that strategy, late fall and early winter was a busy time for us. We visited households and counted sheep (and goats) as lambs and kids were matched with their mothers. We listened as people discussed how many of their animals had or hadn't given birth, and we tried to keep track of how many animals were lost or died. We also tried to visit the irrigated gardens some Komachi had, and to find out who owned what there. We did not do this secretly, and some people were quite helpful. Still, we felt that this was hard information to gather. We were therefore very excited when we learned that the government census enumerator was coming to the area and would visit the Komachi camps. We hoped that, with his permission, we would move with him from camp to camp, record people's responses, and thus have a reliable set of data.

In this case rumor was accurate, and in midwinter the enumerator arrived. Driving a large white Land Rover, he went from place to place in the countryside, trying to locate and enumerate the people in the rather out-of-the-way corner of the out-of-the-way province the Komachi lived in. Shortly after he arrived, he found that there were foreign anthropologists living in camp, and he sought us out before we found him. He was younger than we were, well educated, and urban. Like most urban Iranians we met, he did not particularly like living and working in a backwater, but he did not express the contempt for rural people and rural life we often heard from urbanites. So we spent a very pleasant evening talking to him, and agreed that we would work with him the next morning.

In our mind's eye, I think we had assumed that the enumerator would go from tent to tent, entering each household to gather information. What he did, however, was go to the tent of Shir Ali, our neighbor and the head of our camp. Many but not all of the men from our camp were there, and so was Agha Hossein, Shir Ali's cousin and the head of his own camp.

The entire process was fascinating, something between *Through the Looking Glass* and "Who's on First." The enumerator had special forms, carefully designed to collect information from tribal and/or nomadic peoples. For example, the forms provided space to orient the camps, showing the direction and relative distance from both the nearest towns and significant local geographical features. The forms also provided places to orient the group in genealogical space, asking for information on family, lineage, section, and tribe. People worked happily and successfully on the geographical orientation. There were some disagreements about just how far or in exactly what direction some towns lay, but by and large this portion of the survey showed what intimate and accurate knowledge of their environment the Komachi had. When the time came to orient the Komachi in genealogical space, things got curiouser and more confused. The form, clearly designed for larger tribes or confederations, presented terms for a large, ramifying genealogy. Since there were only about 550 Komachi all told, they hardly needed, and did not use, all the categories on the form. To make matters worse, the Komachi used the same word, *taife,* for "tribe" and for "patronymic group." Thus, when the enumerator asked them what tribe, *ashayer,* they were, initially they answered "Komachi." When he asked them what section, *taife,* they were, they promptly answered "Komachi." The enumerator clearly did not like the idea that they were "Komachi Komachi," but let it pass. He then asked what subsection, *tireh,* they were. The Komachi got blank looks on their faces. When he rejected the notion that they did not have *tireh* and repeated the question, the assembled Komachi engaged in a heated discussion among themselves, and gave him the names of the patronymic groups: Abrahimi, Mohammedi, and so on. Then he made the mistake of asking about families and was once again given the names Abrahimi, Mohammedi, and so on. The poor enumerator might have been willing to accept Komachi Komachi, or perhaps Komachi Mohammedi. He wasn't going to accept Komachi Komachi Mohammedi Mohammedi, but when he attempted to ask his questions again, he started getting worse answers. When he listened, which he did, he realized that the Komachi used *taife* for "tribe," and when he asked what *taife* they were, half the time he was told Komachi and half the time Mohammedi or Abrahimi. The terms just kept slipping away: truly, it was like watching Abbott and Costello. I must admit the enumerator was patient. Finally he and they worked out a system that included tribe, section, and family; it was somewhat fictitious but almost fitted the form. And this was only the easy part.

The enumerator now turned to collecting household composition and economic data. For our camp, Shir Ali answered all the questions.

Now, here I must point out several things about Shir Ali. First, he was literate; second, he was a shrewd businessman who could count and calculate very well; third, he was not a great believer in direct answers; fourth, although he would speak and argue forever about things that interested him, he had a very short attention span for things that did not; and finally, he had a puckish sense of humor. We had already found that these characteristics made him a somewhat difficult informant. If we asked him questions he found interesting, we got excellent information. Questions he did not like got very different answers. In our experience, he did not like questions about his economic affairs; such questions drew evasive answers. Questions about genealogy bored him. When I once asked him how many lambs he had, he said, "You tell me. You're the one who is counting them." And when Ann was collecting genealogies and asked Shir Ali his grandfather's name, he replied, "I don't know. He's dead."

Given this and the go-round on *taife*, we wondered how the enumerator would fare in the rest of his work.

Initially, Shir Ali worked down the list of the other tents in his camp, and things seemed to go rather smoothly. Shir Ali did a pretty decent job of telling the enumerator who lived in every tent; he was a little less accurate on people's ages, but for most people seemed close to what we thought. As he moved to economic information, we began hearing figures that were a bit surprising. We listened and noted them carefully. Finally Shir Ali came to his own household. Here things got really interesting. First, he dramatically underrepresented his holdings. He simply divided his flock among his sons, claiming that the animals his household controlled really belonged to three different individuals. When the census taker started asking where his sons lived, things became a bit complicated, but Shir Ali insisted, and it seemed the enumerator recorded the holdings as Shir Ali wished. Even so, the total for the three owners was so low, about half of what we knew of, that I found it hard to keep a straight face. But more was to come. The enumerator had to collect data on Shir Ali's family, particularly his animal-owning sons. That part of the interview went roughly like this.

"What is your name?"

"Shir Ali."

"How old are you?"

"About fifty."

"What is your wife's name?"

"Sekine."

"How old is she?"

"About twenty."

"How many children do you have?"

"Ten."

"What are their names?"

"Nur Ali, Sohrab, Nesrat, Esmat, Fatimeh, Dohrab, Bijan, Puran, Gilan, Gulan."

"How old are they?"

"Nur Ali is twenty-seven—"

"Wait a minute. Is your wife Nur Ali's mother?"

"Yes."

"You said that Nur Ali is twenty-seven?"

"Yes."

"You said your wife is twenty. You know she can't be twenty if your son is twenty-seven!"

"Okay. Write down that she's thirty."

I do not know what the census taker wrote down. I do know that all the data he got about our camp and Agha Hossein's were flawed. I think he knew it, too, but we did not have the heart to tell him just how awful we thought it was. We did not go with him on his rounds, but stories we heard from others convinced us he got the same kind of information wherever he went. After he left, we all spent the evening joking about the things he should have counted. Shir Ali, in particular, felt he should have counted the flies that swarmed about the camp.

Watching this census convinced us that we had been absolutely correct to hold off doing our own economic census until we knew people well. We became even more convinced of it as we conducted it late the following summer. By then, we really did know everyone and we knew a good deal about them. It helped. For example, one day we went to Qorban Ali's. We had been there several times before; his wife's brother was one of our closest neighbors; and Ann, in particular, had spent a long time talking with his wife about the very interesting way her marriage negotiations had unfolded. This time, we were sitting around the campfire, his wife was preparing tea, and we were going through our questionnaire, filling in answers on the establishment of the household and its economic history, discussing other things as they came up. Finally we came to the question "How many animals do you own?"

"One hundred twenty," said Qorban Ali, barely batting an eye.

Ann and I both looked at him.

"Come on," Ann said. "You've got more than a hundred and twenty lambs grazing in front of your tent." His wife, who was pouring tea, had started giggling at his first answer, and was barely able to control herself at Ann's comment. Laughing so hard that the teacup was shaking in its saucer, she turned to Qorban Ali and said, "Go on, tell them. It won't hurt you."

With that, Qorban Ali looked at us again and said, "Oh, you want the eye of the truth."

"Yes," we said. And just as quickly as before, Qorban Ali said, "Four hundred and thirty."

This time his wife nodded, and we all drank tea.

The problem of gaining relatively reliable information was not, of course, peculiar to us. Roughly 130 years before we attempted to get reasonably accurate information about the Komachi, Layard had claimed:

> During my journey from Hamadan I made careful notes of the country, taking
> bearings with my Kater's compass of the mountain ranges and peaks, and fixing
> by the same means, as well as I could, the course of streams and rivers, and the
> position of the towns and villages through which I passed or which I saw in the
> distance. I found great difficulty in obtaining the correct names of places.
> Whether from that inveterate habit of lying which appears to be innate in every

> Persian, or from suspicions of my motives in putting the question, the people
> whom I met on my way, and of whom I asked the name of a village, almost in-
> variably gave me the wrong one. . . . I had no little trouble in getting at the
> truth. (Layard 1841, 1:308)

Most rural Iranians have had excellent reasons for being very circumspect in their responses to authority. While in the 1970s the Pahlavi state drew the vast bulk of its revenues from oil, historically Iranian states were predatory, drawing what revenue they could from local peoples, often through such regressive means as tax farming. Under these conditions, underreporting one's holdings, hiding what one could, and generally avoiding the state and its representatives was an excellent strategy, one of those forms of quiet resistance that James Scott has described for other areas of the world (Scott 1986). Neither the kinds of answers given the census enumerator, nor Qorban Ali's response to our questions, nor the answers Layard received from the people he encountered are surprising.

The knowledge that most people are likely to dissemble does raise the question of how one gets relatively reliable data. The outline of an answer can be seen in the way the Komachi told and retold the story of how they fooled the census taker, and in Qorban Ali's—and, perhaps more important, his wife's—response to our own questions. The answer is also simple and old-fashioned: Regardless of the epistemological problems involved, the best way to get relatively reliable data is to be there long enough to know what's going on—long enough to know who did or didn't live in Shir Ali's tent; long enough to know what it meant to see a hundred kids and lambs in front of Qorban Ali's tent; long enough to know who Qorban Ali was and who his father was; long enough to know his wife and she us. While it is far from a perfect technique, spending a good long time with people, watching what they do, listening to what they say, understanding what is important to them, and constantly examining what one experiences living with them—in short, doing long-term fieldwork—remains the best way, and in my view probably the only way, to achieve some significant understanding of another culture.

Many of the events and circumstances that most powerfully force us—and I deliberately use the term *force*—to examine our expectations and to reflect on our understandings arise unexpectedly. Far from being planned, or plannable, they just happen. Many times these encounters are slightly uncomfortable. No one likes to feel slightly (or more than slightly) out of balance, foolish, confused, or just plain angry. But having been surprised enough times, one begins to get some idea where the surprises are coming from. At least in retrospect, then, one can examine a cumulative record of encounters as a means of seeing, or at least of illustrating, important aspects of another culture.

GETTING TO THE FIELD

Even the most cursory reading of the Western travel literature on Iran shows that no account is complete without its description of at least one spectacularly horrible, generally life-threatening trip.[1] At a minimum, the description of this horrible trip permits the author to reveal his/her incredible fortitude and the superiority of European (generally British) standards of courage and perseverance (roughly, "keeping a stiff upper lip"). It also permits the author to make invidious comparisons between the quality of British or European transportation systems and Iran's. In comparison to this genre, the sagas of our two most adventuresome trips—our drive from Tehran to Kerman, and spring migration—seem pale imitations.

TEHRAN AND LEAVING IT

We arrived in Tehran on the evening of December 4, 1973. All the Persian I had learned fled my mind. I was simply overcome by the hustle and bustle and intensity of deplaning and passing through customs. Our companions in customs were twenty or thirty men, of all sizes, with bull necks, broken noses, and cauliflower ears. Ann, who had never before seen cauliflower ears, later told me she wondered what endemic disease could have caused those ear deformities. I was just wondering where these guys had come from. (The next day, I read in the English-language newspaper that they were members of the Bulgarian national wrestling team.)

After customs, we were grabbed by a cab driver and whisked to the American Institute of Iranian Studies (AIIS). Although we had written ahead, all the rooms were booked; we spent our first night on the carpet of the director's living room. Jerry Clinton, the director, was, however, able to put us up for the next few days in the nearby flat of an American couple who were temporarily back in the States. There we slept on an unheated waterbed. No matter how many blankets we used, the mass of cold water sucked away whatever body heat we had. Those first nights were the coldest and most uncomfortable I spent in Iran, although the temperature was not much below 5°C.

Soon Jerry arranged a room for us at the British Institute of Persian Studies (BIPS), which was much larger and older than AIIS. Among other things, it had a truly excellent library of works on Iran, and Ann and I spent a good deal of time looking through them. What struck us most at BIPS was not, however, the library, or even the flatbread we had for breakfast, but the heater in our room. Neither Ann nor I had ever seen anything as quaint and odd as the somewhat smoky little stove sitting in the middle of our room. We were captivated by its cute name: Aladdin. We saw a lot of Aladdins in Iran, where kerosene was cheap and wood was scarce. They always smoked, they didn't give out much heat, and they were nowhere near as warm or efficient as the central heat we'd left behind. It was a marvelous irony to return to the States in 1975 to see the Aladdin featured in one of the mail catalogues as a great post-oil-crisis way to keep rooms warm.

Like most researchers en route to field sites elsewhere in Iran, we hoped that our stay in Tehran would be a short one. We planned to spend a few short weeks buying a four-wheel-drive vehicle, pulling together the last bits and pieces of our equipment, and getting our research and residence permits, but we were frightened by stories of the nine months it had taken another American to get permits. As it happened, we were able to leave Tehran on February 14, 1974. The following passage from Sir Henry Layard, written about an experience in 1840, could with small changes describe our experience:

> I was not without hope that at Isfahan I might find an opportunity of joining a caravan, or a party of travelers, going to Yezd, and that I might even perform the journey without attracting the attention of the Persian authorities. I determined, therefore, to separate from Mr. Mitford. . . . We accordingly asked for separate firmans [travel documents], which were promised to us. But we soon learnt the value of Persian promises. It was not until August 8, after having been detained nearly one month at Hamadan, that we obtained the documents we required and the permission of the Shah to continue our journey. We spent the greater part of our time in going backwards and forwards from the Prime Minister to the Minister for Foreign Affairs. We were always received with politeness, our remonstrances were listened to, and we were assured that on the

following morning, without fail, we should be in possession of all that was required to enable us to take our departure. The morning came, but not the fir-
mans. (Layard 1841, 1:267)

We did not deal with dignitaries as important as the prime minister or the minister of foreign affairs. We simply spent part of most days visiting the Ministry
of Culture and Higher Education, waiting, drinking the tea we were politely
served, and being told, "We are so sorry, you must come back again. Perhaps
tomorrow." One great difference was that we did not see our daily disappoint-
ment as negative evidence of the value of Persian promises. We were advised
that it was, and came to see it as, evidence of a culturally ordained politeness
that makes it difficult to deny someone's wish or to tell someone bad news.
Rather than say no, or that no one knew when the permits would be ready, we
were repeatedly let down softly.

Had we not been on a rather strict budget, I don't think we would have
minded our stay in Tehran. We took Persian lessons, studied materials readily
available in the BIPS and AIIS libraries, and talked with scholars staying at or
passing through both institutes. We learned a great deal and made valuable
friends. We also used the time to buy our jeep, which came to occupy a place
in our lives and our adventures almost as large as that of any living person.

Iran had strict import controls on automobiles, supporting an import substi-
tution policy. The most common locally made four-wheel-drive vehicle was a
jeep that was both too small for what we had to carry and—if new—was too
expensive for our budget. Land Rovers were so expensive as to be beyond
dreams, let alone serious consideration. We were forced to shop the second-
hand market. Even there, everything was expensive, and many of the cars
looked badly battered under their new coat of paint. We looked and looked.
What was in our price range seemed unattractive, and time in Tehran threatened to further diminish what money we had. Finally we found a car we
thought we could live with: an extended-body four-wheel-drive vehicle with
the simple, straight four-cylinder engine standard on early jeeps. The tag on the
chassis claimed it had been built by Willys-Overland, and the papers claimed
it had been manufactured in 1963. Later we decided that in fact it was something of a hybrid, a bit of bricolage pieced together from cannibalized cars.
Still, it ran, it was large enough, and a local mechanic, arranged through friends
at AIIS, thought it was the best we could do. We bought it.

After we got our jeep and had it serviced, we spent days getting ready to go.
We sorted through our belongings, and anything we couldn't carry we jammed
into a trunk to leave behind at the institute. We packed everything else—our
typewriter, notebooks, books, tent, sleeping bags, jackets, spare clothes, tape

recorder, blank tapes, camera, film, and medicine—into the vehicle. We also piled in all the tools and spare parts we had bought for the jeep. I didn't have any real confidence in my ability to fix the thing if anything went wrong with it, and since we knew we would be traveling with everything we needed for the next two years, we were scared. Friends had told us not to worry, that if we broke down, truck drivers would be helpful. Still, when we looked at the map and the long blank stretches on it, we worried. We didn't worry less when we discovered that the jeep was so heavily loaded that driving around a sharp curve made one of the front tires scrape against the wheel well. We hoped to avoid traffic by leaving Tehran early in the morning, and we planned to spend one night in Isfahan and drive on from there to Kerman on the second day. We said our goodbyes at night. Unimpressed, our fellow sojourners at the institute said goodbye and then added, "See you in the morning."

To our surprise, we made it out of Tehran by six-fifteen, leaving a leaking jerrican of water slowly draining in the institute's bathtub. The first part of the trip wasn't too bad. There was paved highway all the way from Tehran to Isfahan. The drive was long, noisy, and slow. The jeep handled more like a boat than a car, but we made Isfahan with little difficulty and congratulated ourselves on having really started. We stayed the night at a pleasant hotel and ate grilled lamb and rice at a restaurant called Sheherezade, a fittingly romantic setting for our mood. Next morning we headed off, aiming first for Yazd, and planning to push from there to Kerman.

The second day's trip was as rough as the first day's trip was smooth. Going over the mountains to the south of Isfahan, the car began to gasp and overheat. Worse, we noticed a rather strange burning smell, reminiscent of the childhood odor of caps shot off in a pistol. Stopping several times to let the engine cool down, we made it over the mountain pass. Once we had begun our descent to Yazd, we figured the die was cast. We coasted the whole way down the mountain to let the engine cool; going back over the pass would surely burn out the motor, so we had to go on. We told ourselves that if the car was really acting up when we got to Yazd, we could call a friend who was doing fieldwork there.

But getting to Yazd was harder than we expected. First we lost the road, or maybe the road lost us. The blacktop road from Isfahan continued until we reached the village of Nain. As Nain had but one main road running through it, we doubted we could get lost, and when we bought gas, we confirmed that we were on the road to Yazd. However, no sooner had we left the town than the road turned to a gravelly washboard. Bemused, we went on, found a sign for Yazd, and finally found a paved road. But it was in awful repair, filled with potholes, heaves, and buckles. After about two and a half hours bumping along on this strange road, we suddenly saw trucks and buses in the distance, running

along parallel to us at high speed. Periodically we passed tracks in the dirt leading from our road to the distant one. We debated driving to it, but decided to
wait until we reached the large village we could see in the distance. Finally we
entered the village and took a new strip of asphalt to the parallel road. It was
brand-new and beautiful. Rather grouchily, we wondered how we had missed
the new road at Nain, and finally decided that we hadn't, that the road did not
connect through. On the smooth-as-glass highway we made great time and told
each other we would be in Yazd before long. Alas, very soon the new road ran
out, and a man speaking perfect English told us we would have to ride on the
dirt service road. We did for a bit, and then, following the trucks and buses, returned to the good road until it definitively ended. At about two o'clock, we finally found Yazd.

The car was driving fairly well, and so we decided to just keep on going.
About sixty kilometers outside of Rafsanjan we noticed ominously that our
amp light was flickering. Since we were really out in the middle of nowhere,
we decided to go on, making the best speed we could. We did all right, though
the engine began to run more and more roughly. Then as sundown approached
and we turned on our lights, we made a horrible discovery: The lights did not
work well, and when we turned them on, the engine seemed to run worse. To
say we were scared is putting it mildly. We were afraid that if we stopped the
car, we wouldn't be able to get it going; we were also afraid that if it got too
dark, we would have to stop. We had some water and some food with us, but
we had no idea how we would get the car repaired if we did have to stop. So,
in the dark, in the rough, in fear, we just kept going, using a flashlight to show
oncoming traffic we were there. After a while a truck caught and passed us. It
went by before we thought to flag it down, but it solved one problem: I gunned
the jeep and followed the truck as closely as I could. It had headlights, and I
felt if I stayed close enough to it, we would at least know where the road was,
and we would be protected from oncoming traffic. So on and on we drove, our
lights dimmer and dimmer, our engine making funny noises. Finally we came
to another stretch of well-paved road, and we discovered we were on the way
into the small city of Rafsanjan.

Very soon we lost the truck; we also lost our lights, but at intervals there
were streetlights. We planned to find a place to stay and then collapse. However, the car collapsed first, and there we were with a dead car at the side of the
road, two young, frightened anthropologists on the way to "the field."

In the failing light, we got out of the jeep, raised the hood, and shone our
flashlight into the still, dark space. At this beginning stage of fieldwork, I was
still very much a novice mechanic. I didn't really know what I was looking for,
and certainly nothing caught my eye. As we stood forlornly in the growing

dark, a small crowd, mostly boys in early adolescence, began to gather. Two things very quickly became apparent. The first was that we were objects of great interest; the second was that our carefully studied Persian was not yet adequate for the situation.

Fortunately, the young men were able to deal with the situation for us. First they helped us push the jeep off the road to a space in front of a small store. Then things began to unfold in several fantastic ways. We entered the store, frankly confused. In our halting Persian we recounted news that the shopkeeper had doubtless received ten times over from the boys: We were driving to Kerman, our car had broken down. Now men as well as boys clustered around.

"Where do you come from?" they asked.

"America," we replied.

They asked if we had anything to do with the new copper mine under construction just outside Rafsanjan. We said we did not.

Meanwhile men and boys came and went. They looked at us, spoke to us, and, of course, spoke among themselves. We were objects of polite wonder.

We managed to ask about finding a place to service our car. There was a buzz of conversation. Much of it, I suspect, was an attempt among them to make certain they understood our question. After a time the reply came back that all the repair shops were closed. We would have to wait till morning.

What would we do? we wondered. Even if we could find a place to stay, what would we do with the car? What could we do to protect from theft all the things in the unlockable jeep with its canvas flap doors?

Our problem was shortly solved when several of the boys returned with a young man in tow. He introduced himself, speaking in English far better than our Persian, as Reza, a local schoolteacher. The boys, knowing we had a problem, had sent for him; what could he do? Starting again, this time in English, we explained who we were and where we were going. When we were done, he broke off and briefly spoke to several of the men gathered around. Turning back to us, he told us that nothing could be done for our car that night, but that if we didn't mind, we could stay the night at his house, and he would help us arrange to have the car fixed in the morning.

As we stood talking with Reza, the buzz of conversation among the men and boys intensified. They looked at me, they buzzed; they looked again and buzzed again. We could not catch their words. Finally one of the men motioned us over to the merchant's scale. One boy stood on it, and the storekeeper shifted the weights on the balance arm. An older man stood on it next, and the merchant weighed him. With a mix of words and signs, they asked how much I weighed. I told them I didn't know. During the previous summer in the States I had fattened up from my normal weight in the mid-190s. I suspected (I hoped) that I had lost some weight since coming to Iran, but I didn't really know. Anyway, I smiled and stepped up on the scale. Everyone crowded around while I weighed in. As the merchant moved the weights further and further out, there was an increasing commotion. Finally the weight bar balanced, and people clustered around in amazement. I weighed over 100 kilos. It seemed I was rather like a beached whale, the largest foreign object ever thrown up by the tides in Rafsanjan.

Now it was clear what one aspect of the conversation was whenever someone new came into the shop. It was that I weighed over "*sad* kilo."

The simple arrival of someone we could communicate with had cheered us tremendously; his invitation seemed a miracle. We readily accepted. With far more help than we needed, we pushed the car to the yard, locked it behind high iron gates, and set off with the teacher on his small Japanese motor bike. To our surprise, our first stop was not his house but the home of a local gendarme, who welcomed us, gave us tea, and checked our passports. Only much later did we realize what was going on: As was prudent in a police state, Reza was protecting himself (and us) by making our unexpected presence known to the proper authorities.

After more tea and politeness, we arrived at Reza's home. It was small, dark, and humble. We were introduced to his mother, ushered into a back room, and told to make ourselves comfortable. Although we had been in Iran for nearly three months, we had never before spent time with an Iranian who was not regularly working in direct contact with foreigners. We were tired and nervous, and we felt for the first time the discomfort that would become a nearly constant feature of much of our fieldwork: the discomfort of not quite knowing what was going on or what we were supposed to do. The evening was alternately surprising, scary (due to our own ignorance), boring, and pleasant. Reza's home was typically Iranian, with no chairs or tables; our evening meal was served on plates set on a cloth spread on the floor. After dinner we reclined against pillows placed against the wall. By the time we left Iran, sitting and eating on the floor had become second nature; that first night in Rafsanjan it was an oddity, and not an entirely comfortable one at that.

After we had eaten, two of Reza's friends dropped by. They brought a bottle of vodka and an opium pipe, and it became clear that part of the evening's plan was heavy drinking. It was also clear that this was something Reza's mother strongly objected to. We were uncomfortable. Our discomfort was not relieved when much of the discussion that followed centered about the Westerners our host knew at the copper mine, and we came to suspect that the drinking was doubly for our benefit. First, it was to provide us with something that Americans were known to like, booze; second, it was to show us that our host was

Westernized and therefore someone we could feel at ease with. Whatever the case, the alcohol simply made me more strung out and less able to follow the conversation, which, since our host spoke to us in English and translated every-thing we said into Persian for his friends, was cumbersome and hard to follow anyway. I think, in truth, that all we wanted was to go to bed, but since our presence and conversation were in some way our host's reward for the trouble and hospitality he extended us, we felt we had to be awake, alert, and good guests. The fact that Reza's mother sat on the edge of the room, visibly upset about his drinking and smoking opium, did nothing to relax us.

The evening's most uneasy and alarming moment came after we had been drinking and talking for several hours. Our host, probably conscious of the fact that we were fading, began urging us to make ourselves comfortable. We leaned back and assured him we were. He repeated his urgings several times, and then finally asked, "Don't you want to take your pants off?" "No, no, we're perfectly comfortable," we replied, whereupon our host jumped up and started to remove his pants. We were horrified.

We had, however, in our ignorance, done our host a disservice. That day we learned what Iranian men wear under their Western-style pants: long cotton pa-jamalike pants, called *shalvar,* wonderful for lounging around and sleeping. (In more rural areas, they are often worn as men's only pants.) In urging us to get comfortable, our host was simply asking us if we wanted to take off our tight outerwear so we could relax. In taking off his own pants, he was getting com-fortable, and the next day, Ann and I laughed long and hard at our foolishness.

Finally, after much drinking and talk, we prepared for bed, and our hosts' rolled-up bedding was the first Persian bedding we had seen. Next morning we rose, literally with the chickens, and after a brief breakfast of bread and tea cooked on an Aladdin, one of Reza's friends from the night before led us off into the dawn to find our car. To our immense relief, the car was exactly as we had left it. With help, we rolled it out to the road. There, in the sunlight, a young man wandered over; it turned out that he was the mechanic. He tried the ignition, heard the silence, opened the hood, and looked around. Then, jump-ing up and squatting on the fender, he pointed out our problem. There was a loose wire leading from, I believe, the voltage regulator to the generator. He quickly hot-wired the car, and we drove it to the little hole in the wall that was his shop. Two minutes' work with a screwdriver, and the wire was refastened. Then, to our unimaginable relief, I turned the key in the ignition and heard the engine come to life. Our mechanic, who could have charged us anything, vir-tually refused to accept payment. Reza's friend paid the mechanic the fifty ri-als (about seventy-five cents) he asked for, and he was even more adamant about not letting us pay; we were his guests, it was his pleasure. With more heartfelt thanks and happy goodbyes than I had imagined possible, we got in our jeep and set off for Kerman, arriving shortly after noon.

Losing the car lights and engine between Yazd and Rafsanjan was a frightening prospect. But what a hollow adventure compared with Bishop's trip from Kirmanshah to Tehran roughly eighty years before:

Hamilibad, Feb. 7.— The next morning opened cloudless with mercury at 18, which was hardly an excuse for tea and *chapatties* being quite cold. . . .

To write that we all survived the march that day is strange, when the same pitiless blast or "demon wind," blowing from the "roof of the world"—the Pamir desert, made corpses of five men who started with a caravan ahead of us that morning. We had to climb a long ascending plateau for 1500 feet, to surmount a pass. The snow was at times three feet deep, and the tracks even of a heavy caravan which crossed before us were effaced by the drift in a few minutes.

A sun without heat glared and scintillated like an electric light, white and unsympathetic, out of a pitiless sky without a cloud. As soon as we emerged from Sannah the "demon wind" seized on us—a steady, blighting, searching, merciless blast, no rise or fall, no lull, no hope. Steadily and strongly it swept at a temperature of 9 across the glittering ascent—swept mountain-sides bare; enveloped us at times in glittering swirls of powdery snow, which after biting and stinging careered over the slopes in twisted columns; screeched down gorges and whistled like the demon it was, as it drifted the light frozen snow in layers, in ripples, in waves, a cruel, benumbing, blinding, withering invisibility.

The six woollen layers of my mask, my three pairs of gloves, my sheepskin coat, my fur cloak, and mackintosh piled on over a swaddling mass of woollen clothing, were as nothing before that awful blast. It was not a question of comfort or discomfort, or of suffering more or less severe, but of life or death, as the corpses a few miles ahead of us show. I am certain that if it had lasted another half-hour I too should have perished. . . . My mask was frozen to my lips. The tears extorted from my eyes were frozen. I was so helpless, and in such torture, that I would gladly have lain down to die in the snow. The mercury fell to 4.

After fighting the elements for three hours and a half, we crossed the crest of the pass at an altitude of 7000 feet, to look down upon a snow world stretched out everywhere, pure, glistening; awful; mountains rolling in snowy ranges, valleys without a trace of man, a world of horror glittering under a mocking sun. . . .

We had been promised good accommodations there [Kangavar], and the town could evidently afford it, but Abbas Khan had chosen something very wretched, though it was upstairs and had an extensive snow view. Crumbling, difficult stairs at each end of a crumbling mud house led to rooms which barely afforded a shelter, with a ruinous barn between, where the servants, regardless of consequences, kept up a bonfire. . . . This imperfect shelter had a window frame, with three of its four wooden panes gone, and a cracked door, which could only ensure partial privacy. . . . The wall was full of cracks big enough for a finger, through which the night wind rioted in a temperature of 5 below zero.

Kangavar was full of mourning. The bodies of two men and a boy who had perished on the plain while we were struggling up the pass had been brought in. This boy of twelve was "the only son of his mother, and she was a widow." He had started from Kangavar in the morning with five asses laden with chopped straw to sell for her, and had miserably perished. The two men were married and had left families. (Bishop 1891, 1:127–31)

In truth, though nerve-wracking for us, our trip was easy compared with Bishop's or the travels of Sheil, Layard, or Wilson. It was far easier to reach Kerman by jeep than by horse or mule. Moreover, it was almost certainly safer as well. In a letter recounting a 1911 surveying trip, Wilson wrote:

I had an unpleasant encounter with tribesmen on my way to Nazar Ali Khan's camp. I had to pass through Chigini territory; this tribe, which owes no allegiance to him or to anyone else, has no recognized leaders. The headmen of two out of six sections were with me and, in return for my money, assured me that I should have no trouble on the way. Once across the Kashgan their courage failed them; they sought to delay me, to turn back, to camp—anything but go forward. I would not listen to them—I had heard such stories so often. Presently, as we emerged from a long gorge, we were suddenly set upon and surrounded by truculent tribesmen. They knocked my servants off their mules and cut the loading ropes; they struck at me with their sticks, bruising both my forearms and hands. . . . Not content with this one man put a loaded rifle to my ribs, his finger on the trigger threatening death if I did not hand over my rifle. Another struck me across the face with a stick and dragged me off my horse, declaring he would forthwith slit my infidel throat like a sacrificed bull and watch me drum my heels on the ground as the blood flowed. . . . One or two of the party seemed to disapprove of his language and the needless vigour of his onslaught, urging him to await the arrival of Kikha [Kadhkhada Ibrahim Beg]. A few minutes later he arrived, all smiles and apologies. His men had exceeded their instructions. "I told them to detain you with honour. I was not willing that you should pass this way without conferring distinction upon my poor abode. I said 'bring me a hat'—they have brought me a head." "Dirt be on your head— *Rid ba sar-at,*" he shouted angrily at my captor. . . . "What shameful act have you committed?" Then turning to me with a bow—"Be seated, I beg you—take your ease. My house is yours. My goods are yours. Recover here from the fatigue of your journey." I sat with my back to an oak and begged him to extend a like favour to my servants.

He turned again to his men: "Bring tea, bring coffee, bring a water-pipe [*galyan*]—Kill a kid, make *Kabat*—let the ease of our guests be our delight—

let us draw the pen of oblivion across the page of shame,"—with much more to the same effect. It was superb acting, for he had planned it all. . . .

There was no kid and no tea, no coffee, except in my servant's saddle-bag. He, also battered with cudgels, rose to the occasion nobly and suggested that he should act as the Khan's servant and serve us all with tea. The old bandit graciously accepted the offer. (Wilson 1941, 164–65)

Later, in a section phlegmatically entitled "Captured Once More," Wilson records another adventure:

When I neared Pul-i-Fasa, some nine miles from Shiraz, I saw ten armed men on horseback gathered on the bridge and assumed, not unnaturally, that they were the guard for whom I had asked. My own escort from Maharlu also saw them and, hastily bidding me God-speed, galloped off. I rode on, congratulating myself on the success of my arrangements. I was soon disillusioned. The leader of the guard bowed politely as I rode up, saluted me with compliments. This done, his party set upon me and my men, and beating me with a heavy stick, tore my watch and chain from my pocket, cut the bandolier of my rifle and snatched it away from me, as also my revolver. I was cudgelled heavily over the head and back and pulled off my horse. My servants fared as badly— stripped of their best clothes which they had donned in order to appear at their best when entering the city: they were dragged off their mounts and stripped of even their shoes. (Wilson 1941:189)

When our jeep broke down, we were afraid we might lose some of our things to pilferage. As it turned out, our belongings were perfectly safe. Similarly, the hospitality we were provided was real and genuine. Far from being taken advantage of, we were taken care of. Imagined dangers were mostly just that, and our fears and uncertainties generally exceeded the realities we encountered. Certainly one element present for us but apparently sometimes absent for earlier travelers was a warm welcome. Even if we occasionally felt that our welcome was calculated—part of an unfolding quid pro quo in which we, as foreigners, would be expected to provide some as yet unspecified return for our reception—we knew that was only fair. Why should we have been given anything? With that consideration, the treatment we received and the apparent real pleasure people in the countryside felt when they discovered that we had learned Persian made our lives easy. Wilson records with great irony the conventional phrases of hospitality offered him by Kadhkhada Ibrahim Beg. We experienced the hospitality.

Still, the anxieties that rose from our realization that we were in the *biabun,* truly out in nature, were not entirely imaginary. During our second spring migration with the Komachi we were nearly caught in a flash flood. The Komachi spring migration route rises from the plains of the Persian Gulf coast to mountains on the highland plateau. Most of the trip is gradual, but slightly before the halfway point the migration route leaves the lowlands and climbs to the high plateau through the course of a mile-long, narrow, steep canyon called the Tang Mordan, roughly "the defile of death." We approached the Tang Mordan in a downpour, but because the Komachi were afraid of a possible flood we camped at the foot of the pass instead of climbing it as planned.

Driving up the next day was an awesome experience. The roadbed was all sand, thick and deep, rarely more than thirty yards wide. Rising on each side were sheer, straight walls. For most of the climb there was little evidence of the previous day's weather. Then around a turn we found a dead donkey nearly buried by the sand; further on was a pickup truck. Having seen flash floods, we were delighted that our cautious companions had decided to spend the day at the foot of the pass rather than try to climb it. Given the pass's steep slope and its straight walls, the thought of a flood within its narrow confines was a nightmare. The following passage, from Sheil, suggests what one of these flash floods might be like.

> Our camp was near a deep ravine, in which ran a stream. One afternoon a storm came on, accompanied by such a deluge of rain as I never before had seen. In a few minutes the tent was filled with water, and the air became nearly dark. Suddenly a rumbling and very appalling sound was heard; it increased, it approached, it roared and shouts and yells went forth the whole length of the valley. We rushed in terror out of the tent into the drenching rain; I, at least, ignorant of the nature of the convulsion. Down it came, bellowing and pealing like the loudest thunder. The servants and villagers screamed "Syl Amed, Syl Amed," and cries and shouts preceded its course. It was a furious torrent which had broken loose. . . . Two members of the Mission had a narrow escape. Only that morning had they removed their tents from the dry bed of the stream, high up on the bank. . . . At dinner nobody could touch a particle of food, the gentlemen seeming to consider wine the best restorative for shock. In the morning I hastened to look into the ravine. It was terrible to behold, and inconceivable. Enormous rocks, six or eight feet in diameter, had been hurled down from the pass. The bridge had been carried away. . . . These torrents are common in Persia . . . the dry bed of a river is therefore not a safe place of encampment. (Sheil 1856, 171–73)

Not all passes were so dangerous. The Tang Mordan brought us through the mountains and onto the southern end of a plateau. At the northern end of the plateau, we crossed another pass before we headed to the true highlands in which the Komachi spent the summer. In March and April, a river ran at the foot of this pass. It was not a powerful, raging torrent, but a clear mountain

stream, forty or fifty feet wide, perhaps three feet deep—not an impassable ob-
stacle, but an impediment to passage. Kids and lambs had to be carefully shepherded across. The baby camel, born just days before, was tied to its mother,
and all the adult animals and people had to be driven or dragged across.

Grass, a movie by Merian Cooper, the creator of *King Kong,* is one of the
earliest films dealing with Iranian nomads. One of its key dramatic moments
records a group of Bakhtiyari crossing a fierce, rapidly flowing river during
their spring migration, people and animals all facing the very real danger of being swept away to their deaths. As the Komachi crossed their little stream, an
inconvenience rather than a danger, Ann and I shot *Grass II: The Komachi
Crossing,* a home movie never publicly screened. Comparison of the Komachi
crossing with *Grass* sharply represents the feel of our fieldwork with them.
Grass records the heroic struggle of the Bakhtiyari, including their challenge
by a river whose wicked current threatens disaster; our film is an ironic representation of the nonheroic lives of Komachi who were pastoralists, but seemed
far from being the descendants of Genghis Khan or the proud rulers of the Iran
of tribal dynasties. Living and traveling with them, we ultimately felt more secure in person and in possession than we had in New York City before we left.
From the events following the breakdown of our jeep on our first trip from
Tehran, to the Tang Mordan and beyond, we almost always felt we moved
within a layer of protective hospitality.

With this clear, I am compelled to note my impression that most narrative
ethnographies, from Turnbull's *The Forest People* to Chagnon's *Yanamamo*
and Shostak's *Nisa,* start with their bad trip in, though whether the danger and
discomfort they describe were more like mine or like Wilson's and Bishop's is
sometimes hard to tell. In reality, the difficult journey itself seems a subgenre
of both travel writing and narrative ethnography, some examples of which have
been collected in a pleasant anthology aptly titled *Bad Trips.* There, in one of
the most evocative demonstrations of a "stiff upper lip" I have encountered,
George Woodcock writes:

> My idea of a worst journey is conditioned by the fact that long ago, in my boy-
> hood, I read a book on Scott's Antarctic expedition, which came to a tragic end
> only a few days before I was born in 1912. The book was called *The Worst
> Journey in the World,* and even now, when I think of bad journeys, that title by
> Apsley Cherry-Garrard echoes in my mind. . . . We admire the fortitude with
> which such men endured their cumulative discomforts, and the kind of grim
> resignation projected in the last sentences of Scott's diary: "We shall stick it out
> to the end, but we are getting weaker, of course, and the end cannot be far. It
> seems a pity but I do not think I can write more." This was after Scott and his
> companions had learned that their efforts had been in vain. . . . Behind the

stiffest of upper lips, fear must have been there, and a growing sense of the futility of heroism.

Physically and mentally, in its progress and its results, Scott's was in an absolute sense a "worst" journey. For those of us who have survived our journeys, there are only worse journeys. (Woodcock 1991:10)

By contrast, the benign dangers and discomforts of our trip from Tehran characterized our stay in Iran. Far from being bad, worse, or worst, our trips were good ones, and it was generally the hospitality and help of the Iranian people that made it so.

Chapter

Chapter

4

SURVEYING WITH MR. ABUSAIDI

Shortly after we arrived in Kerman, we started on the path that would lead us to the Komachi. It began at the office of the governor of Kerman province. We had been told at the Ministry of Interior in Tehran that letters had been sent to Kerman, and we assumed that, if indeed they had been sent, they were the usual boilerplate, requesting we be shown courtesy, et cetera, et cetera. To affirm that we had arrived in Kerman, and to show proper courtesy to its officials, we went to the governor's palace. We expected little from this formality; we thought we would be served some tea while a clerk examined our research permits and confirmed that we were the people mentioned in the letters. Much to our surprise, we were told to return later in the week for an appointment with the governor. Even more to our surprise, when the day came, we were indeed ushered into the governor's office, where we spent an odd ten minutes gawking at the largest matched set of Kerman carpets ever seen, drinking tea, and trying to explain to the governor why we wished to see him—which we really hadn't quite—when we had nothing to request from him. I do not know what would have happened if we'd had a complicated request for him, but I do know that we were amazed to have any access at all to someone of his stature. We rather doubted that foreign graduate students in the United States would get appointments with most governors just because they requested it.

In any event, another note of introduction was written for us, this one from the governor to one of his aides, the man who was the tribal liaison officer for the province, Gholem Hossein Abusaidi. Actually, Mr. Abusaidi was much harder to contact than the governor had been. The governor worked in his office, but Mr. Abusaidi spent his time traveling about the province looking in on the various tribes. After several futile visits, we finally found him in his office. He seemed genuinely glad to meet us, and told us, among other things, how he had shown Ann Lambton, a renowned British Iranist, around the province many years before.

We made arrangements to go along with Mr. Abusaidi on his next trip—well, actually on the next trip after our jeep was repaired—and spent the following couple of weeks getting things ready to go. Finally, on March 4, three months after we had arrived in Iran, we set off with Mr. Abusaidi on our first trip to a tribe, heading out past Sirjan, south and west of Kerman, to the Luri and Qaroi tribes.

At this time of year, both the Luri and the Qaroi were in their winter quarters, which were in a not-terribly-warm portion of the plateau. In winter, these tribes lived in tents pitched over stone-walled pits three to four feet deep. The dugout space provided shelter from the winds, and it gave the nomads more protection than a tent alone would have. Dugouts were also used to protect animals, but they were roofed with earth rather than tent panels.

We spent several nights with the Luri and the Qaroi, sometimes with Mr. Abusaidi, sometimes traveling with the teenage son of the Luri chief. Up to that point, we had both wondered if we would ever really get into the field, if we would ever get started, so just being there was exciting. Everything was interesting and new: pitching our tent for the first time; waking in the morning to the sound of kids and lambs scrambling on our roof; being fed special meals as we visited people's tents; being relieved to discover that the meals, mostly chicken and potatoes, were not only edible but tasty; wondering how much of the chicken it was polite to eat, knowing that other members of the family would eat what we left; standing out in the chill early evening, looking at the sun going down in a vivid sunset, which made sharp silhouettes of the sheep and goats that stood and capered on the nearby hillsides; and waking in the morning wondering how and where one went to the "bathroom" when there wasn't a bathroom (or a tree or boulder to hide behind) for miles, then learning to walk off purposefully looking for a gully to squat in. We asked questions, mostly genealogical ones, but we also attempted to collect information on herd sizes, prices of pastoral products, and about where the groups migrated to and from.

Even in the adrenaline-spiked rush of our first contact with pastoralists, we experienced some difficulties. At sunrise on the first morning we spent with the Luri, we were given large, foaming glasses of warm goat's milk, and I faced the serious difficulty of swallowing something that activated my gag reflex. Here was the classic anthropologist's dilemma: The stuff tasted strange, but it was proffered as a treat. To say it was horrible would be boorish. What to do?

Of course one does the right thing—one swallows with a big gulp, wipes one's mustache, and, with a big smile, says, "That was wonderful." Naturally, since milk is plentiful and the guests have shown that they like it, the question of what they can be given if they drop in when it isn't mealtime is answered: goat's milk. The first glass of milk tasted strange, the second was worse, the third horrid, and after that the very thought of warm goat's milk, the anticipated possibility of it, made me gag. But every glass I drank, every smile I smiled, brought the prospect of more. "Oh what tangled webs we weave . . ." Ann, after the first glass, just smiled demurely and passed me her cup in a touching act of wifely deference.

Our difficulty with sheep's and goat's milk was not a small problem, and it was not limited to our stay with the Luri. Kerman's pastoralists do not generally drink their animals' milk; they convert it to yogurt, *roghan* (clarified butter), and dried buttermilk, which, when mixed with water, a bit of butter, and some herbs and sopped up with bread, formed the bulk of the pastoralists' diet. To eat their food was therefore to taste that taste. It turned out that I could stomach the taste of the milk far better than Ann. If from the first I found it difficult to swallow, she found it repellent. If, later on, I found it semipalatable, she found it consistently awful. If, ultimately, there were specific dishes in which I came to find its taste appropriate, perhaps even pleasant, she found her aversion growing. My weight ultimately stabilized; Ann's did not.

But even for me the taste remained alien. Late in the winter we spent with the Komachi, more than a year after our first encounter with goat's milk among the Luri, I traveled with Shir Ali, my Komachi neighbor, to another Komachi camp. The people were poor, and the meal they fed us was a humble one to give guests: rice with some raisins in it. Shir Ali ate it slowly, picked at it. I found it delicious and wolfed it down. When we returned to our own camp, we went to Shir Ali's tent. His wife, Sekine, grilled us about the day, asking, among other things, the question that was always posed: What had we been given to eat? "Nothing much," said Shir Ali. "Some rice with raisins. But it was awful. They made it with vegetable shortening instead of clarified butter, and it had no taste." And with those words, I knew why I had liked the rice.

In truth, our dilemma with the milk was somewhat exacerbated by our travels with Mr. Abusaidi. While we found it unpalatable, he found it delicious—which he proclaimed in heavily accented English. The first time we visited his home in Kerman, before we set off with him, we were given a breakfast of tea, bread, quince jam, and a huge plate of clarified butter. As we were served it he called it to our particular attention and told us how much he liked it, how much better than commercial butter it was, and how delicious it was. Mr. Abusaidi really did love the taste of sheep's milk and *roghan*. One of the perquisites of his job was that, traveling among the region's pastoralists, not only did he get to eat fresh dairy products while he was among them, but also the nomads gave him gifts of clarified butter to take back to the city. Since they all knew that he loved butter and sheep's milk, when we traveled with him we were sure to get it. And, of course, whenever we got it, he would comment on how wonderful it was, and would ask us if we did not find it tasty, too. To be polite, we said, "Of course we do. It is delicious." And he would respond, "Yes, delicious." To this day, we when we get dairy products that taste heavy, almost a little off, we are instantly reminded of that clarified butter. It made a profound impact on us.

Our reaction to the pastoralists' dairy products (which we know barely count on the lists of strange food eaten by anthropologists in the field) taught us just how powerfully our culture shapes something we might think of as natural, namely our sense of taste. What we found most interesting about eating new food was not that it tasted strange (and hence unpleasant) to us, or even how strange it tasted, but the way it revealed how completely and totally our taste might be shaped. Oddly enough, the vehicle for our discovery of the pervasiveness of culturally determined taste was not something bizarre, like a sheep's eye, but commercially baked cookies. Minoo brand cookies were available everywhere in Iran. They were commercially produced, neatly packaged, easy to carry, and a excellent quick snack. Many of the standard Minoo cookies were Iranian-made versions of familiar cookies and biscuits, but they all tasted a bit strange. Fairly quickly Ann, who is much better at picking out tastes than I am, recognized the difference. The cookies all tasted of rosewater, some strongly, some betraying just a hint. Once we became sensitized to rosewater, we tasted it everywhere: ice cream, cakes, traditional desserts. At first it was odd and cloying; then, as we came to expect it, we almost forgot it was there. Thinking it over, we realized that rosewater functioned in Iranian sweets the way vanilla does in ours. It is the taste put in to bind the other tastes together, the background against which they play. All our lives we had eaten cookies, cakes, ice cream, and other sweets laced with vanilla flavor. We'd never tasted it. Like the air we breathe or the water fish swim in, that taste is just there, a part of culture we live in without realizing it. Only the shock of its absence, its replacement by another element, let us see that it was there and that it could be replaced.

Chapter

5

DEFERENCE

After visiting the Qaroi and Luri with Mr. Abusaidi, we accompanied him on a second trip to the south and east of Kerman. This was much a longer trip than the first one. For a number of reasons it was also a more interesting one. Several camps we visited on this trip undertook the long migrations I was, at that time, interested in studying. Thus we felt we were meeting people we might actually work with. We also crossed into the *garmsir,* or winter quarters, on this trip, and so entered a vastly different region of Iran, one filled with date palms and citrus trees. Finally, our headquarters for this trip was Mr. Abusaidi's own house in the village of Esfandagheh. Traveling with him in his home region, we got to see things that we never saw living among the Komachi.

From the very beginning, the trip had charm. After several hours on the road, about halfway to Mr. Abusaidi's home, we stopped in the village of Qaleh Asghar. On the surrounding hillsides, we could see watchtowers that formerly had been filled with brush. In earlier times, when marauding tribes passed through the area the brush had been fired; the burning chain of towers alerted the people and, in theory, the army in Kerman, Baft, or Sirjan. Even more remarkable than Qaleh Asghar's towers was our lunch there. The meal was served on long plastic floor cloths, with elaborate trompe l'oeil *chelow kebab* pictured on them.[1] What was most striking was that our hosts provided several cans of cold, sliced pineapple for dessert. It wasn't Dole or Del Monte, but other than the label, it was just the same. The slices looked and tasted exactly like every slice of canned pineapple we had ever eaten. That was what made it so wonderful: There, after a long, hot car ride, in a village that seemed very exotic, after a meal that was served in an unusual and new way, we were presented with nothing less than a slice of home, totally familiar and welcome. It was wonderful.

From Qaleh Asghar we drove on to Esfandagheh. The road followed the bottom of a dry stream bed, led us across the stream I described in the last chapter, and took us over mountain passes on a narrow, winding, and often rough dirt track that we later learned was part of the Komachi migration route. We saw and learned many things on this trip, but among the first was how to drive where there is no road.

American television is filled with ads for four-wheel-drive vehicles that go storming up mountains, scramble over rocks at high speed, and take on the world in an arrogant and aggressive fashion. My view of desert driving was probably first conditioned by *Rat Patrol,* a television show in which a multinational commando force careened about the North African desert in souped-up jeeps, spewing sand and leaping dunes as they drove at breakneck speed. That was aggressive driving.

I know of few places where drivers are more arrogant and aggressive than Iran. Ann and I had left Tehran at dawn to avoid its traffic. We weren't concerned with the crush of rush hour; I had been driving in New York City for years. We just didn't want to drive in a traffic flow in which everyone attempted to constantly assert their right to the right-of-way, whether they deserved it or not. We had seen people drive on highways, and they drove fast. Having thus been primed by Tehran traffic and *Rat Patrol,* I fully expected to be hard pressed to keep up with Mr. Abusaidi's Land Rover. I was surprised to find that it proceeded at a sedate, even leisurely pace. My primary problem was not keeping up but having to constantly shift back and forth between first and second gear, because our jeep had only three speeds while the Land Rover had four. As we crawled along, it slowly dawned on me that there was method to this madness. People didn't drive looking far ahead to sort out upcoming traffic patterns, searching for openings that would let them keep up their speed. People drove peering intently through the windshield at a point roughly ten feet in front of the car, picking out the track that would get them through without dropping a tire in a bottomless hole or catching the underside of the car on a jagged rock cresting out from the middle of the alleged roadbed. In the middle of nowhere, where having a breakdown did not mean just calling for the tow truck or waiting for the AAA, Iranians drove very defensively. They were not worried about people in other cars; they were worried about tearing their own car apart. We learned to worry about that, too. Unfortunately, we also learned that no matter how careful we were and how slowly we drove, this kind of driving ultimately so battered our car that we could not avoid breakdowns. With some luck and careful driving, however, we managed to avoid having them in the worst places.

Having learned to drive slowly and carefully, we figured out something else as well. In Persian, the word *dur* means both "far" and "long." On first learning Persian we found that odd, and in a rather arrogant way felt it to be a semantic deficiency. Eighteen months of slowly grinding along in first gear, moving at a speed little faster than one can walk, changed our view. Walking, riding, or driving over rough paths, there is no difference between long and far; there is only a difference between long and longer, far and farther still. Modern transportation and communication may have severed the link between time and distance elsewhere in the world, but in Kerman it was intact.

Esfandagheh was Mr. Abusaidi's home territory. His house was a good-sized, fairly modern structure, standing near a relatively new garden and orchard. With one exception, both the house and grounds were comfortable but undistinguished. The exception was the plane tree, standing near the mouth of an underground water channel, called a *qanat,* about thirty feet from the house. It was not the tallest tree we saw in our two years in Iran, but it was by far the largest. At least fifteen feet in circumference, it cast a huge and wonderful shade over the cool running water. The tree was visible for miles. It was a wonder in a land where trees do not often occur in nature. For natives of temperate climes (and even more so, I imagine, for inhabitants of tropical areas) the desert reverses the relations of nature and culture. In the desert, verdant landscapes are almost always a sign of human effort and cultivation. That is what makes Persian gardens so wonderful.

Mr. Abusaidi was an important man in the area around Esfandagheh, not because of his position in the regional government, but because for several generations his family had been major landowners in the area. He was, therefore, treated differently there than in the area southwest of Sirjan. In the southwest, to be sure, he had been treated politely; he was served elaborate meals wherever we stopped, and people gathered to hear what he had to say. But near Esfandagheh, as soon as he alighted from his Land Rover, men came running. Approaching him, they grabbed his hand. The resulting scene was something to see: The men, holding his hand, would bend over and attempt to draw his hand to their mouth so that they could kiss the back of his hand. He would try to draw his hand away to force them to shake his hand, and if he knew them well, he would try to kiss them on both cheeks. Neither succeeded perfectly, but the attempted demonstration of deference, successful or not, spoke volumes.

Deference was conveyed in other ways was well. Twice Mr. Abusaidi's approach to a nomad camp was marked by the ritual slaughter of animals. Men from the camp stood in two lines as Mr. Abusaidi's Land Rover (and our jeep) approached. As the car drew near and entered the crowd, men stepped forward on either side, dragging large goats; their throats were slit in front of our cars, blood staining the ground before us. At both these places, Mr. Abusaidi's greeting encounter was long and elaborate, and there were many attempts to kiss his hand, some successful and some not.

Although to us they seemed spectacular displays of acknowledging status, the greetings Mr. Abusaidi received were rather diminished examples of the traditional display put on for "superiors." Sheil's description of the welcome she and her husband received on their entry to Iran indicates some of the scale possible.

> Our entrance to Marand was distinguished by a most disagreeable ceremony, which was attempted to be repeated at every village at which we halted, not only on this but on every succeeding journey during our residence in Persia. On approaching the town, I observed an unfortunate cow in the midst of the crowd, close to the roadside, held down by the head and feet; when we came within a yard or so of the miserable animal, a man brandished a large knife, with which he instantly, before there was time for interference, severed its head from its body. He then ran across our road with the head, allowing the blood to flow on our path in torrents, and we passed on to encounter a repetition of the same cruel rites performed on various sheep. This ceremony was called Korban, or sacrifice. . . . So intent are the Persians on the observance of this mark of reverence to power and station, that the most rigid prohibition could hardly prevent its fulfillment. (Sheil 1856, 82)

Perhaps the struggle of those welcoming Abusaidi to kiss his hand as he attempted to shake theirs can be taken as evidence of the continued importance of marking "reverence to power and station"; that and the slaughter of sheep certainly seemed to us a striking display of deference.

Slaughtering an animal was just the beginning of hospitality. After it was dead, the animal was carefully skinned and prepared for eating. Generally, the heart, liver, lungs, kidneys, and intestines were cut into bite-sized pieces and fried on a griddle in the fat taken from around the viscera. The animal's flesh was reserved, to be served later in a kind of stew. Since no visit was complete until both kinds of meat had been eaten, a visit to a camp in Mr. Abusaidi's company always took a long time. We did not mind, for it always gave us plenty of time to walk around, ask questions, listen to conversation, and just see and sense what was going on. It became uncomfortable only once. On that occasion we drove into a camp with Mr. Abusaidi, he in his Land Rover and we in our jeep. An animal was slaughtered and food preparation begun. Then, to the clear chagrin of the nomads, Mr. Abusaidi jumped up and announced that he had to travel on. We were left as hostage guests. We were treated splendidly and fed well, and all our questions were politely answered. But we could not answer *their* questions—we could not tell them about wheat prices, government subsidies, or government plans. We felt that we had somehow cheated them out of their animal and were counterfeit participants in their feast.

Traveling with Mr. Abusaidi, we could not help but see the deference shown

him by the tribespeople. We were made even more aware of the subtle grada-
tions in deference when our usual party—us, Mr. Abusaidi, his driver, his
teenage son, and his gun bearer/hunting companion (a wonderful-looking man
with hooded blue eyes strikingly set in a lean, hawklike face, who always carried Mr. Abusaidi's shotgun)—was joined one day by a very high official in the
regional Justice Department, the man's wife, his young children, and his aged
and rather infirm father-in-law.

We now traveled in three cars, and visited several villages rather than nomad
camps. At each stop there was a momentary rush for Mr. Abusaidi, then a
falling back as people realized there was a much more august personage in the
party. Invited inside, we always sat down to several rounds of tea. On our earlier trips, the tea always went to Mr. Abusaidi. Now, when the tea bearer entered, everyone flashed an instant's glance at the minister of justice, and he was
brought tea first. But he never drank the tea. Instead, he took it and passed it to
his father-in-law. Although it was served to the minister with formality, proffered or presented with suitable humility and ceremony, his transfer to his
father-in-law was perfunctory. He would simply pass the saucer and glass.
Generally his father-in-law then just drank his tea, after which the minister
would accept his cup, and then others down the line would be served. It was an
impressive display of absolute and relative ranking of status. In the public
sphere, the minister outranked everyone, so he had to be served first. His father-
in-law, though old and less powerful, had a superior internal family rank, and
consequently the minister deferred to him. True, the minister's deference, a
kind of noblesse oblige, was different from the deference that led to his being
served first by the villagers, but it was still deference and was accepted as such.

Later, when we lived among the Komachi and I traveled with Shir Ali, I
found myself caught in this game of deference, but with a twist. I was twenty-
eight or twenty-nine; Shir Ali was old enough to be my father. In camp, I deferred to him, to his age, knowledge, and position. When we traveled outside
the tribe, however, and particularly if we encountered urban or "more sophisticated" Iranians, of whatever rank, I was the distinguished guest, I sat at the
head of the room, and I was served tea (or food) first. But because in other contexts I deferred to Shir Ali, I continued to do so on the road. It got strange; people would fall all over me but barely acknowledge Shir Ali's existence; a servant would bring tea, and I would be served with a flourish, after which I
would then pass the tea to Shir Ali—no noblesse oblige, just the deference he
deserved. At least once he deferentially passed the tea to our host, who did not
seem amused. Deference could get very complicated.

6

MEETING THE KOMACHI

I should at this point note why we were going on survey with Mr. Abusaidi. Until we arrived in Kerman, no one had undertaken any long-term study of pastoralists in the region. Actually, we planned to work in Kerman because we had heard from two anthropologists we had come to know—Bill Beeman, who had passed through the Kerman area, and Bob Dillon, who had worked on the economics and history of carpet production in a village near Kerman city—that they had both seen lots of pastoralists. A search of the literature had failed to turn up anything substantial about them. It seemed, in short, an opportunity to study new groups in an unstudied area. Nothing we learned in Tehran altered our view of that situation. There were a few pieces in Persian on carpet weaving among the tribes, and there were some census and survey data. When we got to Kerman, however, we found that much of that material was incomplete. Traveling with Mr. Abusaidi, we were able to visit many groups. This permitted us to get some feel for the nature of pastoralism in the province. We hoped we would be able to use this knowledge to help us pick a group to work with.

Our survey work with Mr. Abusaidi was fascinating, arduous, and frustrating. For each week or so we spent with him out in the field, the car spent a week in the shop. We replaced burned-out pistons when we arrived in Kerman; we had the generator repaired (for the first time) while we were in Esfandagheh; at the end of another trip, we had just gotten back on the paved road to Kerman when the main bearings burned out. Invariably, once the car went into the shop, Mr. Abusaidi set out on another trip, and we would then have the further delay of waiting for his return.

Although the survey process was frustrating, it seemed worthwhile. We visited roughly ten tribes and began a process of elimination. Some groups seemed too small and marginal to work with. Some spoke a Turkic dialect as their primary language; we did not think that we were ready to work through layers of both Turkish and Persian. Some groups had such short migration routes that I felt I wouldn't be able to carry out my proposed research project on decision making during migration. Some situations just seemed uncomfortable—we really did not like the *khan* of one group, and felt that working with and around him would be difficult.

On the other hand, some groups seemed very interesting and attractive. We visited several Sulemani camps and thought they seemed an ideal group to work with. They had a reasonably long migration; they spoke Persian; at least one camp made their winter quarters around a deep-bore well. In several of the Sulemani camps we met people whom we found friendly and easy to talk to. We had the same experience with the Guderi, a tribe smaller the Sulemani. So we resolved that we would try to stay with one of these groups for a longer time.

By now it was March, and groups like the Sulemani and Guderi had started their migration; we were getting worried that extending the survey would make us miss a whole migration season, a real problem given my intention to study it. We met with Mr. Abusaidi and explained what we would like to do. He told us that would be fine, and suggested that we come with him again to his home in Esfandagheh. Since we already knew that many of the pastoralists in the southern part of the province passed through Esfandagheh on their migration, this seemed an ideal plan. We would not have to spend our time tracking people down; they would come to us, and then we would still be able to travel with them for about half of their migration.

Off we set. We had been to Esfandagheh before, and for the first time we were traveling a road that was familiar. We recognized some of the places we passed, and we even began to feel that we were getting to know the road. Moreover, the area was full of migrating pastoralists. Seeing members of many different groups pass by, we began to get a real feeling that the people we were going to study were not the last practitioners of some dying tradition but part of an ongoing, vibrant way of life.

Only one thing disturbed us—Mr. Abusaidi. We stopped at various camps and he hailed groups as they went by. As he did, he began to suggest to us that it might not be possible to find the Sulemani or Guderi. This seemed peculiar to us, for they could be in only one of two places: south and east of Esfandagheh, in which case they would pass through the town, or north and west of it. In the latter case, they would either be in their summer quarters, where we should easily be able to find them, or they would be on the road, where it seemed inevitable that we should meet them. Still, as we traveled on, Mr. Abusaidi became more and more discouraging, and as he became more discouraging, he began to suggest that we consider working with some other groups, none of whom we had met. He specifically mentioned one group with what sounded to us like the improbable name "Comanche."

We were resistant to this suggestion. We had met the Sulemani and the Guderi; we had seen their camps; we liked the people; we wanted to work with them. The repeated conversation began to take on a comic air. Mr. Abusaidi would introduce us to a group and ask if we wanted to work with them.

"No, we want to work with the Sulemani or the Guderi."

He would say, "I don't know if we can find them. They are almost finished with their migration. This group is better."

We would say, "Let's see if we can find the Sulemani or Guderi," and so it would go.

Needless to say, Ann and I began to feel uncomfortable. We could not understand what was going on. It did not seem to us that it could be that difficult to find one of the groups in question (and in retrospect, it still doesn't). More and more we got the feeling that Mr. Abusaidi did not want us to work with the Sulemani or Guderi, but that he would not or could not just say so. So on we went, ultimately arriving at Esfandagheh without having met the people we were looking for.

Disgruntled and discouraged, we ate a late dinner at Mr. Abusaidi's. Later still he invited us into a small room for tea. Sitting there on the floor was a middle-aged man in a very dusty and battered Western-style jacket.

"This is Meshedi Shir Ali Abrahimi of the Komachi [though it still sounded like *Comanche* to us] tribe," Mr. Abusaidi said. "He has told me that the Sulemani and the Guderi have all completed their migration. You will not be able to travel with them now. He says that you can migrate with his camp. Is that good?"

I sat there stunned. Whatever my feelings, and whatever the truth, it seemed to me that we were beaten. To demand that we press on to find the Guderi and Sulemani would be tantamount to accusing him of lying. So, seething inside, I agreed that we would meet with the Komachi the next morning, and Ann and I retreated back to Mr. Abusaidi's large and formal living room, which was where we were staying. Trying to fall asleep on the beautiful, extremely large, but not extremely soft Kerman carpet, Ann and I talked the situation over well into the night. We were angry at the outcome, upset, feeling that we had been tricked. No matter how we looked at it, it seemed there was nothing to do but go with Shir Ali and the Komachi. The only alternative involved direct confrontation with and insult of Mr. Abusaidi, which we didn't want. So we decided to play Mr. Abusaidi's game. We would go with the Komachi, finish the migration with them, and then move on to one of the Sulemani or Guderi camps we felt we would prefer.

The next morning we breakfasted with Mr. Abusaidi, and he gave us a rough overview of the Komachi. Essentially, this boiled down to three things. First, the Komachi had the longest migration of any group in the province. We were never able to determine whether this was absolutely true or not; however, the Komachi summer and winter quarters were very far apart, and quite likely their migration route was one of the longest, if not the longest. Second, Mr. Abusaidi told us that the Komachi were among the wealthiest pastoralists in the province, that they tended to have more animals per camp and per household than most others. This too ultimately seemed correct. Finally, he told us that because the Komachi were wealthy, they did not bother weaving the carpets and kilims that other groups wove. Instead, he said, the Komachi just sold their wool and animals, and lived on that.

I must admit that none of this information made me any happier. First, at the time, I doubted that it was true, and second, I was so angry that I didn't much care. Still, we had decided to play along, so I tried to be pleasant. We set off in our jeep, following Mr. Abusaidi's Land Rover to Shir Ali's camp. When we got there, Mr. Abusaidi reintroduced us to Shir Ali. In effect, he said, "This is Mr. Daniel Bradburd and Mrs. Ann Sheedy, who are anthropologists from the United States. They are studying pastoralists in Kerman. They will be staying with you for a while." Another way of putting it is that if we felt we were being sloughed off to the Komachi, to the Komachi it was clear that we were being dumped onto them by an official of the government that they could not afford to challenge. We felt put upon; they were imposed upon.

Our feelings weren't helped by the state of the Komachi camp. As we later learned, when they—or indeed other pastoralists in the region—camped during migration, they generally did not pitch their tents. Instead, barring inclement weather or a stay of several days in one location, they put up only a single tent panel. As a result, the camp looked small and very poor, more like some gypsy camps we had seen than like the substantial, attractive camps of the Guderi and Sulemani we had visited in winter quarters. So there we were, still feeling tricked and angry, stuck with a group that seemed to live in poverty in the smallest, scrappiest tents we had seen thus far. We were depressed and all the more determined to stick out the migration and move on.

Eighteen months later we left the Komachi, having never gone on to study other groups. We were not compelled to stay by Mr. Abusaidi, nor did we stay simply through inertia. By the time we had been with them for a while, snippets of information about their marriage patterns and social organization had begun to pique our curiosity. We also were attracted by the quiet beauty of their summer quarters, in the high valleys between the peaks of Kuh Hazar and Kuh Lalehzar. The longer we stayed, the more interesting things we found, until when we left we were certain that we had been lucky to live with such a fascinating group of people. To this day, I do not know if the Komachi were particularly interesting, whether the singular play of kinship and class we found there was peculiarly matched to our interests, or whether, as I suspect is the case, all peoples everywhere are equally interesting, and we would have found something just as engaging among any group that we had chosen or that had been chosen for us.

It is also worth noting that, although we did not realize it at the time, we arrived among the Komachi just a day after Nesrat, the oldest daughter of Shir Ali and Sekine, had a miscarriage. She rode with us in our jeep for the remaining half of the migration. We knew at the time that regardless of how welcome we were, our jeep was certainly welcome. Later, knowing about Nesrat, the reason for that welcome became far more clear. We never did find out whether that was a consideration in Mr. Abusaidi's placing us with the Komachi.

Chapter
7

RUZ AQRAB

Our first migration with the Komachi was over, and our camp was established outside the village of Shirinak. The high mountain valley we lived in was breathtakingly beautiful. To the east stood Kuh Hazar, a fifteen-thousand-foot snow-capped peak. A small, clear stream ran along the valley floor, bordered on one side by a meadow kept vividly green by the numerous springs that watered it and on the other by freshly planted fields. The contrast between the green irrigated fields and the rough brown hillsides jumped out in the incredibly clean mountain air. We were busy getting to know the Komachi, watching them with fascination as, for the first time, we saw them do things that became commonplace to us later on. We had abandoned all thoughts of moving on.

I cannot overemphasize how new and fresh everything seemed. We had to learn people's names and what they did. "The man in the green shirt," as he appeared in my notes, soon acquired a name: Ali. Later he became Ali the former shepherd, Sablu's husband, a man with a wry sense of humor, and many other things. We also had no idea what to expect in terms of daily life, how long we would stay around Shirinak, or where the camp would move if it moved, and when and why. These last two questions were one of the primary things I had come to Iran to study, and so, in and about the thousands of other things we were trying to learn, I kept listening for discussions of moving; every once in a while I would ask about it. I learned that we would spend the entire summer around Shirinak; I learned that we would move two or three more times; and I learned very little about when and why we would move.

After about a month, I began to hear talk of moving. We would, I was told, be moving nearer to the village.

"Why?" I asked.

"To be closer to the village; because the campsite here is unfresh and dirty." In short, it was to be a move only for better housekeeping. Still, I was interested, and I imagine I was also annoying. I wanted to know when we would move.

"Soon," I was told.

"When is soon?" I wanted to know.

"When Tavakoli comes." Consternation on our part. Who or what was Tavakoli? More asking, and an easy answer.

"Tavakoli is our eldest son," Sekine said. And that was that.

Eventually they told me, "We will move tomorrow." Ann and I awoke early on moving day and poked our heads out of the tent, looking around for signs of unusual activity. There were none. Well, we thought, perhaps because it was such a short move, it would be done later in the day. It wasn't. Finally, when it became clear that we would not be moving, Ann and I began asking why we hadn't moved.

Shir Ali, whose decision it was, was not around, so we asked his son-in-law Qoli, Nesrat's husband.

"We could not move today because it was *ruz aqrab,*" he said.

"*Ruz aqrab,*" we repeated, and ran for the dictionary. And there it was: *aqrab,* "scorpion." We weren't moving because it was the day of the scorpion.

As was often the case, we felt as though we had moved one step forward and two steps back. We had an answer, but we hadn't the faintest idea what it meant. We were pretty certain it didn't have anything to do with real scorpions, because we hadn't seen any. We were also pretty certain that we hadn't heard any mention of them. So back we trudged to Qoli's tent, and we started asking more questions. Slowly it became clear. The scorpion was not a real, living one; it was the constellation Scorpio, which Qoli later pointed out to us on the horizon.

We had never seen Scorpio before. But then, we had never before seen a night sky like the one in Shirinak. Summer nights there were crystal clear: no clouds in the sky, day or night. At nearly nine thousand feet, the desert air was so clear that distant objects looked sharp and detailed. At night that clarity translated into a sky filled with more stars than we had ever seen. To us, raised around New York City, the Milky Way was a memory from a textbook, if not just a candy bar. In Shirinak, the sky looked paved with stars. We would often sit outside our tent at night, staring at the sky, using the guide to astronomy we had brought along to pick out constellations, stars, and features that were invisible at home.

The clarity of the air and the near-total absence of ambient light made amateur astronomy both easier and more rewarding than it had ever been. As a result, we had little problem spotting Scorpio. But since Scorpio seemed likely to be up every night, we had a little more difficulty understanding what *ruz aqrab* might be. We gathered it had to do with Scorpio; it also seemed to have something to do with the moon. All else seemed unclear. Finally—in desperation, I think—Qoli scratched a picture on the ground. *Ruz aqrab* was a day on which the rising moon looked as though it were caught in the constellation's outstretched claws. Retreating to our tent, and reviewing all we had learned, we discerned that the move had not taken place because it was bad luck to undertake a new activity on those days when it appeared that Scorpio would catch the rising moon.

We checked back with Qoli and with Shir Ali. We were right, we had figured it out. Unfortunately, what we had figured out made no sense. I do not mean that it made no sense to believe that certain days or times were not propitious; superstitions are superstitions. What did not make sense was using the configuration of the night sky—a configuration that was quite predictable—as the reason for canceling the plan to move that had been made the day before, when the heavenly conjunction would have been perfectly apparent.

Mulling it over again, Ann and I decided that *ruz aqrab* was an excuse. It was a reasonable reason for not doing something, but it wasn't the reason for not moving. And the real reason? We never knew. In fact, over the course of the time we spent with the Komachi it gradually became more and more clear that trying to discern the reason events did or did not happen on a given day—discovering why the camp would or would not move today instead of tomorrow, for example—was a nearly impossible task.

I had written my research proposal and planned my research around the assumption that I was looking for positive criteria. The choice to move was, in my initial perception, an active one. I therefore assumed it would be predicated on a triggering event: if *x*, then *y*. Over time I came to realize that I had it totally backward. As I got to know the Komachi better, and they got to know me, their answers to my pestering questions of "When are you going to do this or that?" began to take on a different cast.

To each question, they would patiently answer, "*Ma'alum mishe*" (it will become apparent). At first I thought that this was another kind of excuse, a brush-off, the "we'll see" answer one gets from a parent who hasn't the energy for the hassle of saying no. As time went on, however, we began to see that "*ma'alum*

mishe" was not an excuse; it was the answer. This crystallized for us at the beginning of the following spring as we sat in winter quarters waiting to start out
on our migration north. We were anxious to go, and so was everyone else. The
pasture was drying out; we had been in our current campsite for weeks, and the
constant presence of the sheep and goats that were being milked and their
young had filled the site with dung. The site really was dirty. But the decision
to move depended on the weather; on finishing local business; on people getting paid for goods they had sold in the surrounding area; on each of the leaders of the three camps that would move together getting all of their affairs together; on rumors about the grass ahead, en route, and in the summer quarters.
In short, the decision to move depended on many things.

The Komachi put off moving not so much for a specific reason as because
they still had to do one thing or another; because the weather was still uncertain; because there might be more grass here than there was ahead; because one
didn't know whether it was better to go by way of Sarras or take another route.
And since in these circumstances, which involved grass, weather, or people
other than the Komachi, the Komachi could not control the situation, they did
not make their decisions by planning that they would move here or there when
x or *y* occurred. Rather, the Komachi planned to sit tight, to wait, to watch, and
not to move until, as possible choices fell by the wayside and obstacles either
disappeared or grew so large as to become insurmountable, the only possible
time or way emerged. Ultimately, there would be so little fodder in the winter
quarters that whatever was ahead would have to be better. Ultimately, it would
be clear if the Lurrak were or were not going to be at Deh Pain. In fact, what to
do would become *ma'alum,* and then the Komachi would do it. Until then, they
would wait and watch, and tell the anthropologist who was pestering them that
"*ma'alum mishe.*"

Looking back at my response to Komachi decision making, I realize that my
confusion was largely generated by my own expectations. My research proposal was based on Barth's famous study of migration and decision making
among the Basseri and other tribes in Fars province, to the west of Kerman.
The vision of nomads that Barth projected, in common with most other views
of pastoralists in Fars, was of heroic peoples—the figurative, if not literal, descendants of Genghis Khan and other nomad conquerors—boldly dealing with
the world, actively engaged in shaping their future. By contrast, the Komachi
were not heroic. The active decision making I expected was replaced by a very
conservative process. Rather than taking maximal advantage of their opportunities, the Komachi decision-making process was an attempt to minimize the
risks they had to take. Far from being bold nomads, the Komachi made deci-

sions like classic risk-aversive peasants, which indeed they were. Before we left the field, Ann and I finally came to the realization that the Komachi, and most nomads in the region around them, were "pastoral peasants." But in the field, trapped in the pastoral literature, though I knew what their decision-making process was not, I did not quite see it for what it was.

Kuchek Ali, one of the wealthiest men among the Komachi. His hair is cut high in the front and back in a traditional style.

Hajji Biveh wearing the traditional head covering.

Komachi men dressed in modern style. Ma'adi Yarbok, who bought my motorcycle, is second from the left.

Sekine standing in front of her tent.

Amon Ali standing before a tent wall. He is wearing the fedora and sport jacket favored by men of his age and status.

Shir Ali wrestling goods onto a camel during spring migration.

Ali, a retired shepherd, is dressed in traditional clothing.

A camp scene in Shirinak. Ali, the retired shepherd, is spinning goat hair. Behind him, a girl brings in a load of fire "wood."

Taqi Arbab; his driver is seated behind him. The test of strength reflects the use of power.

A partially pitched tent, used for shelter at night during migration.

Pack bags exposed as the tent comes down during spring migration.

Taj Ali standing among a household's goods during spring migration.

Our small tent pitched in Shir Ali's yard on the outskirts of Shirinak.

Our belongings piled up for packing.

Our new tent and our jeep in winter quarters.

Pitching a tent.

A close-up of our small tent. Note how much is stored outside.

Ann, wearing modified Komachi women's clothing, and a friend.

The view from our tent early one morning.

Malike bringing a tray with a sugar cone and apple to present as a gift at a celebration.

Young women dressed up for a celebration. Maraste, who went crazy for love, is second from the left.

Mohammed Katkhoda driving his jeep that has been decorated for a celebration. Note the apples on twigs. Shir Ali is the older man to the left of the jeep.

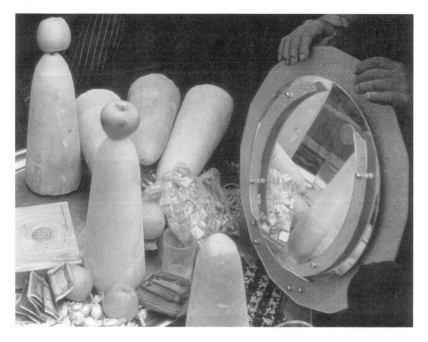

Celebratory tray at a wedding. Note the cones of sugar, the candy and cookies, and the Koran.

The scene at a wedding celebration in Shirinak. In color, it looks like a painting by Breughal.

Camels leaving Baft toward the end of spring migration.

The ruined fortress of a local chief in winter quarters. The palm leaf houses are summer dwellings that are cooled by dowsing them with water.

Threshing wheat the old-fashioned way. The diminutive cattle pulling the sled are the source of whatever beef is eaten.

Constructing a reed tent wall in summer quarters.

Dan Bradburd conveying Hossein Fezallah during his wedding celebration.
Motorcycles had replaced the horses formerly used for these occasions.

Chapter

8

IS THERE WHEAT IN AMERICA?

Practitioners of a discipline that claims to represent one culture to another ought have some feeling for the problem of successful representation or translation. I suspect most of us do, and that we take seriously the task of making sure what we write or say conveys a "good likeness" of what we "observed," both to our professional colleagues and to our students. Occasional comments arising in the peer review process for books and journal articles and some of what I read in student papers point to certain difficulties in this process. One of the nice things about fieldwork was that it brought into sharp focus the difficulties inherent in making apparently easy translations, showing why it is sometimes difficult to securely reach common understandings even on what seem simple, descriptive points.

One day, driving to Kerman with some Komachi and some peasants from the village of Shirinak, Ann and I were drawn into a conversation about the similarities and differences between Iran and the United States. This was a favorite topic for many Iranians (including the Komachi) when they first met us, and once we learned some of the rules (for example, never, ever say anything about Baha'is), it was a very useful conversational tool and research gambit. As we were passing near Baghin, an agricultural village outside Kerman surrounded by large stands of wheat, the question came up of whether or not we grew wheat in the United States.

"Do you grow wheat in America?" we were asked.

"Yes," we replied, "there's lots of wheat in America."

"Is it planted the way it is here?" one of the Iranians asked.

"No," we answered, "there are many differences." This was indeed the case.

First, in the high valleys around the Komachi summer quarters, wheat was still threshed by clearing a hard, flat place on the ground on which cattle pulling a threshing sled were driven round and round over the grain. Later it was taken up on wooden forks and thrown into the wind to separate the wheat from the chaff—a process as biblical-looking as it sounds. There were therefore plenty of differences in technique to discuss. Second, the fields in the high mountain valleys south of Kerman were small even by Iranian standards. They were planted only where they could be watered from irrigation ditches running from either small horizontal wells or small mountain streams, and many fields were no larger than a big room.

"Ah," they said when we explained that American wheat fields were usually larger. "So in America you have wheat fields like these here in Baghin?" And there the simple question seemed to get out of hand.

Baghin was a much larger village than those in the narrow mountain valleys of the Komachi summer quarters. Because it was near but not in the mountains, it had a good water supply. Because it sat right off the main highway linking Kerman to northern Iran, Baghin was fairly well developed. And indeed, compared with villages in the mountains and perhaps even other villages on the plains around Kerman, Baghin did have large wheat fields. I am not sure how large they were. We always drove by Baghin, not into it, but surrounding the village were fields of perhaps a hundred or two hundred acres, which in turn were surrounded by desert, with the next set of fields miles away.

Sensing a problem, Ann and I began to try to describe wheat fields in America.

"Yes, in America we have wheat fields like Baghin's," we said. "But we also have places where there are bigger wheat fields. There are places in America with lots and lots of wheat." And then we tried to describe Kansas. "There are wheat fields in America that are so big that you can drive all day and still see only wheat, where the wheat fields look like the desert here."

"Correct," someone said; someone else made the peculiar, nasal "hunh" sound the Komachi used to show they were following a conversation. But the topic quickly shifted and we knew that though they had heard our words, we had not successfully represented our vision of the Great Plains wheat fields. We were so certain of our failure that in our next letters home we asked friends and family to send pictures of the United States, including fields of wheat and corn, so that they would know what we meant by "lots of wheat." We never got them.

While the question "What is a big wheat field?" seemed a straightforward one, I later came to realize that it was not. I think that to a substantial degree our friends' inability to grasp the notion of wheat fields as far as the eye can see was not simply based on the differences between dry and irrigated agriculture or the use of mechanical versus human and animal power for plowing or harvesting. What really underlay the gap in our communication was not that the Komachi had never seen vast, continuous stands of wheat; rather, they had never seen vast, continuous stands of *any* vegetation. The game of expectations worked the other way as well. Before we migrated to the lowland winter quarters for the first time, we asked people about it. Over and over, people told us how green it would be, about the trees we would see. Kokojon, a member of our camp, would hold his hands out in front of him, showing a diameter of twelve or fourteen inches, and say, "In the winter quarters, they have trees *this* thick." Indeed they did. But the trees were some distance from each other, and to someone raised in the northeast United States, what the Komachi called *jangal* did not look like a heavily wooded area. To the Komachi, though, it was almost forest.

The depth of different expectations about how, why, and where things grow is perhaps best encapsulated in a story we heard in Bandar Abbas from some American expatriates working there. One couple had befriended a young Iranian boy from around Bandar Abbas, a notoriously dry area on the Persian Gulf coast, and took him with them to the United States when they returned for a visit. The story we heard, more than once, was of the boy's wonder, not at the buildings, roads, cars, or signs of "civilization" that he saw, but at the grass he saw everywhere—on people's lawns, at the side of the road, in uncultivated fields. "Whose grass is it? How does it grow there?" he apparently asked again and again. And when his hosts explained to him that it wasn't anyone's, that it was just there, it just grew, the boy couldn't fully grasp it.

Note that the problem the boy faced was not just understanding whom the grass belonged to, it was how it got there. It is this latter question that is, I think, the main issue. In much of the United States and most of Europe, we expect things to grow. When we contrast "nature" and "culture," nature is unkempt, uncontrolled, filled with a riotous profusion of growing things. Culture, cultivation, for us entails the control and restriction of nature, the limiting of species and of growth. And even if we don't consciously think of this as we garden, it is still our model, revealed, for example, when we learn—and teach—in our anthropology classes about the ways in which a swidden patch mimics nature in the diversity of species cultivated there. By contrast, in Iran, and perhaps elsewhere in the arid Middle East, the relationship of our "nature" and "culture" are reversed. Nature is the *biabun,* the place without water—brown, sere, and largely bare. It is culture that is green and verdant, filled with plants and flowers. A Persian garden is not walled to keep out the unwanted species growing just outside its borders; its border marks the limit of growth, and its walls keep out the drifting sands of the emptiness around it.

So the question of wheat fields was not one that ultimately could be answered by pictures or by descriptions of their size. Rather, it involved expectations of how, why, and where things grow, about the essence of nature and culture and the distinction between them. No wonder we had trouble with that conversation; it was about far more than we thought.

Chapter 9

RELIGION IN THE BACKLANDS

Just as we were curious about the Komachi, they were curious about us and about our view of the world. Different people had different kinds of questions, but one question arose again and again, both from the Komachi and from settled people in the vicinity of their summer quarters. We would be sitting in someone's tent or house, and our host, or a guest of his, would ask, "What do you do with dead people in America?"

Initially Ann and I were puzzled by the question. It seemed so strange. One aspect of the strangeness lay in the fact that the answer we always gave seemed so ordinary. Asked the question, we would respond, "We bury dead people in holes in the ground."

People would nod and say, "Oh, so you bury people just like we do?"

"Yes," we would answer. And when we did, people seemed satisfied far beyond the simplicity of the answer. We were curious about the question, wondering why it was asked. It wasn't long before the answer became apparent. The Komachi and all their immediate neighbors were Shi'ite Muslims (as are the majority of Iranians). In Kerman city, however, there were some minority populations. A dwindling number of merchants in the fabric bazaar were Jewish; there was a small Christian community in town, largely associated with the Anglican church that was a holdover from the days of the British Consulate and its associated school. Kerman was also home to one of Iran's remnant Zoroastrian populations. Traditionally, Zoroastrians believed that interring a body polluted the earth. To avoid this, the dead were first set out in *doxme,* "towers of silence," high, walled structures built on the tops of hillsides well outside the city. Bodies left there would eventually be reduced to bones, which were later placed in an ossuary. In 1975 one could still see the *doxme* outside Kerman, though they were no longer in use. The question of what we did with our dead was therefore a theological question, comparing us to the only strikingly different group the Komachi knew of. What exactly would have happened had we answered "We leave the bones out to be cleaned, and then put them in an ossuary" is an interesting question.

One of the things that makes the question of Komachi religious relativism interesting is that I do not think religion was relative for them. Religious relativism was so deeply inculcated in me as a child in Fair Lawn, New Jersey, that I vividly remember the one time notions of that relativism were violated. I must have been four or five, and one of my playmates was attending catechism classes. At one point during a day of play, whether in response to an expletive or just as a means of sharing superior knowledge, he solemnly told me, "Every time you say 'Jesus Christ,' you have to bow your head," slowly lowering his head as he told me this. Later that day I told my mother, "Mom, Paulie says we have to bow our heads every time we say 'Jesus Christ.'" My mother told me that while Paulie was Catholic and might have to bow his head every time he said 'Jesus Christ,' I was Jewish and did not have to; indeed, I should not. Paulie blew it by generalizing his knowledge beyond the bounds of his community, but that is the only time in my childhood I can remember when someone accidentally addressed issues of differing religious practice in an inappropriate way. Moreover, even then my mother did not have to tell me that people had different religious beliefs and practices: My friends and I had already explored the differences between Chanukah and Christmas, and I also knew by age five that no matter what I or anyone else felt about the relative merit or sense of our religion or anyone else's, one never expressed those thoughts in mixed company.[1]

No Komachi were inculcated into this kind of relativism. All Komachi were Twelver Shi'ite Muslims. Virtually everyone they knew, and certainly everyone with whom they had regular contact, were also Shi'ite Muslims; the Komachi lived in a totally and absolutely Shi'ite world. In part, this arose from Komachi understandings of formal theology. They believed, indeed they knew as a commonsense truth, that Mohammed is the seal of the prophets, the conveyer of the perfectly correct, final revelation. More important, the Komachi world was governed by an imminent deity and centered on a sacred history of Shi'ite Islam that was manifest in almost every aspect of daily life. The views and understandings of Shi'ite Islam, at least as they filtered down to the local level, were all-encompassing and unquestioned. The nobility and perfection of Ali, Hossein, and the Twelve Imams were givens, as was the worthiness of emulating them. This was made strikingly apparent in the names given men.[2] Of the sixty-one adult men who lived in the main body of the Komachi tribe, thirty-three had names of obvious and direct religious significance. Of these, seventeen were Ali or compounds of Ali. An additional ten were either Mohammed, Hossein, or the combination Ma'assein (Mohammed-Hossein). In our home camp, when we first moved in, the men's names were Shir (Lion of) Ali, Taj (Throne of) Ali, Mard (Man of) Ali, Ali, Irej (called Qoli), and Kokojon. Only the latter two had no religious significance that I could determine. Other members of camp, shepherds living there or unmarried men living with their mothers, were named Hossein, Mohammed, and Ain-allah (Eye of Allah). Thus our first months among the Komachi were spent in a small community of men who almost all had religiously powerful names. The ordinary discourse of daily life, not to mention more marked practice, constantly brought to the fore the encompassing reality of a Shi'ite worldview. In this context, relativism had little meaning.

Earlier travelers in Iran had noticed the absence of relativism that I have described. But what we saw as a feature of Komachi life was for those travelers a *problem* of Iranian religiosity. That they saw the nature of Iranian religious belief as a problem is, I think, well indicated by the recurrence of the terms *fanatical* and *fanaticism* in their works.

Layard, describing his initial dealings with Iranians while traveling in a caravan with them from Baghdad to Iran, claims: "The seyyids, the hajjis, and the Kerbelayis kept aloof from us, for as Christians we were unclean and not fit company for such holy persons. The Persian Shi'as are much more *fanatical* in this respect than the Turks, who are Sunnis" (Layard 1841, 1:211, emphasis added). Sheil, his near contemporary, writes: "The Persians are a curious combination of bigotry and tolerance, or perhaps indifferentism; but in the towns where Europeans reside, *fanaticism* is obviously fast decaying" (Sheil 1856, 140, emphasis added). Roughly fifty years later, Bishop still claimed that "in some respects the Shiahs are more *fanatical* than the Sunnis" (Bishop 1891, 1:103, emphasis added).

In reading these authors, two reasons for characterizing Iranians as fanatics seem to emerge. The following passage from Layard suggests that one reason, certainly, was a fear of violence.

> In those days the fanatical Persians were apt to deal very summarily with any
> one who might have used words which could be construed into an insult to their
> religion, or as blaspheming their Prophet. A Christian thus offending would
> have caused a public tumult, and might even have been torn to pieces. (Layard
> 1841, 1:334)

Something akin to injured pride seems close to being the second reason for identifying Iranians as religious fanatics. Shi'ite Iranians had the temerity to believe that they were religiously superior to the English and to act on that assumption. Over and over again, Layard, Bishop, and others show their chagrin and discomfort at being thought of as unclean, impure, or less worthy than the people among whom they traveled. Layard notes of "Persian Shi'as":

> They will not allow a Christian to eat out of the same dish with them, nor to drink out of the same vessel, nor to smoke the same pipe. The more bigoted will not even permit a Christian to touch their clothes or their hands, and will perform an ablution immediately after such contact. (Layard 1841, 1:211–12)

Often Layard's comments register his surprise and dismay at being treated, even politely, as one who is less than fully clean or equal. In the writings of Bishop, too, one can sense the dismay she feels in recognizing that to others her faith is a mark of inferior rather than superior status. On the one hand, she may almost lightly comment, "Even the touch of a Christian is regarded as polluting, and I nearly got into trouble by handling a 'flap-jack,' mistaking it for a piece of felt" (Bishop 1891, 1:103). But elsewhere she, in effect, writes off Iranian Muslims:

> Of God as a moral being I think they have little conception, and less of the Creator as an object of love. Of holiness as an attribute of God they have no idea. Their ejaculation, "God is good," has really no meaning. Charity, under the term "goodness," they attribute to God. But they have no notion of moral requirements on the part of the Creator, or of sin as the breaking of any laws which He has laid down. They concern themselves about the requirements of religion in this life and about the future of the soul as little as possible, and they narrow salvation within the limits of the Shiah sect.
>
>   After Mohammed and Ali, they speak of Moses, Abraham, and Jesus, as "Prophets," but of Moses as a law giver, and of Jesus as aught else but a healer they seem quite ignorant. . . . If I have interpreted their views correctly, they must be among the most ignorant of the races bound by the faith of Islam. (Bishop 1891, 2:101–3)

One might write off the Komachi in much the same way. Komachi understanding of formal theology was limited. They knew that Mohammed's was the last, perfect revelation. They knew, vaguely, that there was a relation between the earlier prophets' revelations and Mohammed's, and they knew that the Baha'is were to be scorned—"They have no book; they have no proof." But the Komachi were not terrifically observant: In our camp of seven tents, two men prayed regularly. On visits elsewhere, I saw a similar degree of observance. Relatively few fasted throughout Ramadan. I am not certain that they reflected on the world in a manner Bishop would have liked. Still, they were among the most devout people I have ever known.

It is interesting to note that it is Sheil who finds the Iranians least "fanatical," and indeed, as we have seen, she saw them as possessed of "tolerance" or "indifferentism." One wonders whether Sheil's moderate view arises from her rather exalted position as wife of the English ambassador to Iran, which clearly sheltered her from the threatening or discomfiting situations experienced by more vulnerable travelers such as Layard and Bishop, or whether her own, deliberately noted, Anglo-Catholicism had fostered in her a notion of religious relativism greater than what her compatriots possessed.

This concern with the source of Sheil's relative religious relativism may seem to have brought us far from the Komachi, but I think it has not. Throughout the nineteenth century, travelers commented on the degree to which Iranian Shi'ites inhabited an absolutely Shi'ite world. By the mid-1970s, more than a hundred years of contact with the West had transformed some aspects of that absolutism—no one we knew or met seemed much concerned about us ritually polluting them or their things. But the lack of relativism, the totally Shi'ite-centered worldview, remained.

I have suggested that one sign of the Komachi commonsense appropriation of the Shi'ite world can be found in their use of names significant in Shi'ite sacred history. I shall shortly discuss the Komachi familiarity with that history. Here I wish to record that it was also manifest in their use of oaths and the invocation of the religiously powerful, an aspect of Iranian life that had been noted but misinterpreted by earlier travelers there.

As in almost any community, the Komachi were faced with the problem of making some utterances seem more factually correct, more binding, more true than other discourse. Among the Komachi these emphatic utterances were made by swearing, and so a serious discussion would be punctuated with statements of asserted truth, supported by an interjection such as *be Koran* (by the Koran), *be Peighambar* (by the Prophet), *be Khoda* (by God), or others. In fact, we soon realized that there were fashions in oaths. For weeks in camp, all one would hear was *be Koran,* then suddenly we would hear *be Peighambar.* Later still the new declaration would be *be Amir-almolmenin* ("by the Commander of the Faithful"—in Shi'ite dogma, Ali). By becoming attuned to the oaths, not only did we begin to be aware of the importance of Shi'ite sacred history in Komachi daily life, we became aware of what figures and elements were salient. *Be Koran* was easy. *Be Peighambar* sent us to the dictionary. *Be Amir-almolmenin* required a good dictionary, and the questions of just who were Abol-Fazl and Hezrat Abbas inevitably broadened our understanding of Shi'ite sacred history.[3]

This discussion of oaths changing like a fashion might seem to suggest that they were only words, imbued with little power. This certainly seems to have been the attitude of earlier travelers when they encountered similar patterns among other Iranians. Sheil, who often provides quite sympathetic and perceptive views of Iranians and Iranian religion, still wrote:

> A Persian is perpetually swearing, either by the Almighty or the Prophet, or Ali, or Hoossein, or his beard, or his or your life or death. The women are as profane and emphatic in their discourse as the other sex. A favourite and amusing mode of asseveration among the syeds, especially in testifying to an untruth, is "Beh ser e jeddam" (by the head of my grandfather), meaning Mahammed; indeed it is a common adage that the greatest swearers are the greatest liars. (Sheil 1856, 105–6)

Bishop, whose eye toward Iranian religion seems far more jaundiced than Sheil's, noted:

> The light and profane use of the divine name is universal. The dervishes curse, but every one uses the name *Allah* where ever they can bring it in. The *Ya Allah,* as an expression of fatigue, or discontent, or interest, or nothing is heard all day, and the boy who drives a cow, or a team, or a mule in a caravan, cries *Ya Allah* incessantly as an equivalent of "go along," and the gardener pushing his spade into the ground, the chopper with every blow of the axe, the labourer throwing up bricks ejaculates the same. *Mashallah, Inshallah,* interlard all conversation. (Bishop 1891, 1:238)

But our experience with the Komachi suggests that these views, and particularly Bishop's ironic one, miss the point. For the Komachi, the use of oaths and sacred names seemed a means of constant contact with an imminent sacred world. The claim *be Koran* or *be Khoda* might be bandied about in casual daily discourse, but just beyond them were oaths with real bite. We saw a spectacular instance of this involving Mard Ali, an elderly man who still had a son and a daughter to marry off. During the course of complicated marriage negotiations involving three families, it appeared that other people's interests might undermine Mard Ali's effort to marry his daughter to his brother's son. Mard Ali, who was old and recuperating from an operation, sat in the door of his tent shouting out curses to those who he felt were interfering with his wishes.

"May *Amir-almolmenin* strike them down. May the Prophet burn their houses," he yelled out.

Mard Ali's curses were yelled into an already tense situation. People had been hollering at each other for nearly an hour. But while other people's shouting brought retorts and returns, Mard Ali's curses generated a totally different response. People poured out of every house and tent and ran toward Mard Ali. His eldest son grabbed him by the face and attempted to force his mouth shut, shouting, "Stop it, old man, stop it!" No one matched Mard Ali's anger or cursed him back. Either people seemed struck silent or they begged Mard Ali to be quiet, even as his son struggled to literally shut him up. And when Mard Ali's rage was finally spent, people stood around in small clusters, visibly upset and concerned.

Mard Ali's curses were not taken lightly; they were not just ephemeral words shouted out. What he said was taken to have real power, and to retract his words, two goats were sacrificed. In less dramatic situations, people who had taken an oath to do this or that but broke their word also sacrificed a sheep or goat. Since the Komachi did not kill animals lightly (we once saw Shir Ali nurse an animal for weeks before it finally died), a sacrifice seemed a significant manifestation of the sacred brought into daily life.

Behind the generally low-key and mundane Komachi use of the figures of sacred history lay a far more emotional relationship with them, revealed in Komachi responses to recitals of the martyrdom of Imam Hossein, at which they wept bitterly and were racked by deep sobs.

The Komachi response was not uniquely theirs, nor is it even uniquely Iranian. It is *the* Shi'ite response to the central, sacred tragedy of their history, the martyrdom of Imam Hossein. The story, as in this recounting by Sheil, is simple, yet, as she notes, it has tremendous emotional power.

> The month of December chanced this year to be one of woe and wailing externally, but really of relaxation and amusement to all classes of Persians. It was the month of Moharrem, which among Sheahs is solemnized in commemoration of the slaughter of Imam Hoossein and his family in the desert of Kerbella. The story is affecting. The Persians have converted it into a theatrical representation, somewhat resembling the Mysteries produced on the stage in old times in England and elsewhere. Hoossein, the son of Fatima, daughter of Mahammed, is marching through the desert with his wives and family of young children and attendants, chiefly his near relations, numbering 70 persons. They are attacked by the troops of Yazeed, commanded by his general Obeid Oollah, the monarch of Damascus, and the second sovereign of the Benee Ommeya dynasty. Hoossein defends himself valiantly during several days; till at length he is cut off from the Euphrates, and his family perish, some from thirst, some fighting. Hoossein is finally killed and his head is cut off by Shimr. It requires to be seen to conceive the emotion of the Persians at this performance. On every side, and from all ranks, sighs, groans, and weeping without restraint, are heard, mixed with imprecations against the perpetrators of the cruelties suffered by the prophet's grandson and his family. . . . The representation lasts ten days, and several hours each day. I confess with some shame, that my patience and curiosity were insufficient to carry me through a complete performance of the entire drama; nevertheless, I have been to several representations. . . . It is a

sight in no small degree curious to witness an assemblage of several thousand persons plunged in deep sorrow, giving vent to their grief in the style of schoolboys and girls. The Persians have a peculiar manner of weeping. Various extraordinary and ludicrous noises accompany their demonstrations, which one is sometimes inclined to mistake for laughter. When one begins the contagion spreads to all. I too felt myself forced, would I or not, to join my tears to those of the Persian women around me, which appeared to give considerable satisfaction to them. The events are indeed affecting, and many of the parts are acted with great spirit and judgment. (Sheil 1856, 125–29)

We witnessed similar emotional outpourings of tears, sighs, and sobs at each *roze,* or ritualized recounting of the martyrdom at Kerbala of Imam Hossein and his entourage, that the Komachi sponsored each fall.

In searching for a way to describe a Komachi *roze,* the phrase that comes to mind is "camp meeting"—a kind of multiple pun, apt partly because the primary congregation for a Komachi *roze* was the residential group that camped together; partly because the *roze* invariably took place at night, in a tent lit by lanterns and fires and opened to provide room for all the people attending, calling up images of old-fashioned tent revivals; partly because the *roze* was indeed a kind of revival, in which the Komachi, hearing the story of Hossein, would be powerfully moved; and partly because, like a camp meeting, a Komachi *roze* was led by an itinerant preacher who traveled from camp to camp, staying a night or two, leading the service, giving a brief sermon, and then passing on to the next camp. Each service centered about the telling of a portion of Hossein's martyrdom. The account of the martyrdom was preceded by brief prayers led by the preacher and was followed by more prayers and a simple sermon. Following the performance, its sponsors provided a large meal of meat stew for the congregation.

Each year, several men sponsored *roze,* and the preacher was passed on from camp to camp to lead them. He was available and willing to travel to the countryside to lead the *roze,* but the Komachi met him more than halfway, transporting him from camp to camp, men going out on their motorcycles to bring him to their camp for their *roze.*

We became aware of this proprietary view of *roze* during our second fall with the Komachi. The first year we attended a *roze* hosted by Shir Ali, head of our camp, and another performance just down the road. The second year we attended many more. We were spending a lot of time riding up and down the valley, visiting people to check on marriage negotiations, and we were frequently urged, even pressed, to attend their *roze.* Indeed, one day we were flagged down as we passed a camp, the women calling us over saying, "Tonight, come here for our *roze.*" For some reason, we knew we could not make it back to that camp, so we stopped on the road and made our apologies in advance. While other women talked with us, one went off and came back with a piece of meat that was clearly to have been part of the stew served to all those at the *roze*. We tried to decline the gift, thanking her profusely, but she would not be refused, and pressed it on us, saying, "Take it, take it, it is the Imam Hossein's meat."

The raw display of deep emotion showed the power of Shi'ite sacred history for the Komachi, though I think that Ann and I were then too young to understand how the drama of Hossein was cathected onto personal loss and tragedy to create that emotional intensity. But the fullness of their devotion was also revealed in unspectacular events. The constant use of *ensha'allah,* "if God wills," nearly as we would use the conditional tense, suggests the degree to which Komachi understandings of their world were grounded in the notion that there is one God, that Mohammed is his prophet, and that the lives of Ali, Hossein, and the Twelve Imams are the paradigmatic events in human history. The Komachi truly lived in a Shi'ite world.

Ann and I were not prepared for the totality with which the Komachi were embedded into the Shi'ite world. Barth's *Nomads of South Persia,* which when we left for the field was the primary ethnographic source on southern Iranian pastoralists, claimed that the Basseri were essentially irreligious and placed its discussion of Basseri ritual in an appendix. If the Basseri had any religious contact with the larger Shi'ite world, Barth did not report it. By contrast, the completeness of Komachi habitation in a Shi'ite world was marked not only by their use of sacred names and sacred themes, but also by surprisingly direct links with formal religious practice.

For instance, one day during spring migration, we were camped by the side of a trail, deep in the countryside and far away from even the smallest village. We were sitting in Shir Ali's half-pitched tent, drinking tea, when down the trail we heard the bleating of animals and the whistling of a shepherd. When the animals got near enough to see, I discovered that there were two men with the flock: the shepherd and, on muleback, a man dressed in the brown robes and turban of a cleric. He stopped at Shir Ali's and was offered tea. That didn't surprise me at all. The conversation that took place did. It quickly became clear that he knew Shir Ali and that Shir Ali knew and expected him. The *shaikh,* as Shir Ali called him, was collecting *khoms* and *zekat,* tithe and tax. Here we were on the migration route in the middle of nowhere, and a brown-cloaked cleric had come riding up on a mule to meet Shir Ali and collect the sheep and goats that composed part of his formal charitable contributions for the year. Still, bemused by Barth, my record of events like this was kept more as a list of interesting exceptions to a rule than as the basis of a study of Komachi religion. In spite of clues, religion remained far from a research focus. To the degree that I observed the importance of religion in Komachi life and recorded it in my notes, I "saw" it as an external, overarching system that so completely and naturally answered (universal) existential questions that the divisiveness and fractiousness of Komachi social process never threatened their fundamental sense of world order.

Hindsight being what it is, in the aftermath of the Iranian revolution—which was itself in good part promoted through a discourse centered about the martyrdom, sacrifice, and resistance to tyranny exemplified by Hossein—I began to see the very deep, absolute religious conviction of the Komachi as a far more powerful force than it had seemed in 1975. I have tried to give some feel for this in the text above. Perhaps in evaluating the power of religion in Iranian society we all would have done well to think more seriously about the words of Bishop:

> The traders [in Qum] accept it as a forgone conclusion that Russia will occupy Persia as far as Isfahan on the death of the present Shah, and regard such a destiny as "fate." If only their religion is not interfered with it matters little, they say, whether they pay their taxes to the Shah or the Czar. To judge from their speech, Islam is everything to them, and their country very little, and the strong bond of the faith which rules life and thought from the Pillars of Hercules to the Chinese frontier far outweighs the paltry considerations of patriotism. (Bishop 1891, 1:170–71)

While the intervening hundred years of Iranian concern with and response to foreign domination and national integrity have, I think, shown that Bishop's analysis was not entirely accurate, her recognition of the central importance of Islam seems almost prescient.

Comparing the significance that the travelers' accounts gave to religion with the place assigned religion in the work of many Western anthropologists working in prerevolutionary Iran points powerfully to how much historical context shapes what we see and write. As I hope the preceding account shows, Ann and I saw religious practice everywhere; we just did not see how important it was.

Chapter

10

BATHING

One of the mysteries of entering a new culture is figuring out how to accomplish life's simple, ordinary tasks: providing ourselves with food and water, learning how and where to go to the bathroom when there is no bathroom, and keeping clean. Obviously, some of these problems are more immediate than others. Within twenty-four hours of our arrival in the field, we knew that going to the bathroom meant walking off a bit from camp, if possible into a small gully, and hoping no one would suddenly appear. It also meant doing this as inconspicuously as possible; ideally, it meant choosing a time of day when people were not likely to be about. Of course, people were still more apt to be going to the gully (if there was one) at some times of day than at others. Gullies have no doors, and I did not feel I had much privacy squatting with my pants down. But there were ways around this, too. Since everyone knew where the "bath gully" was, people approached it noisily. People in the gully, hearing the noise of another person's approach, coughed loudly. The approaching person could then either turn away completely, pretending that he or she was off for a walk for an entirely different purpose, or, if the gully was large and winding, wander down a few twists and turns to an empty place.

When they were out of camp, men would urinate without going to a gully. If they were with a group, they would wander some distance away, squat, pull down the elasticized front of their pajama-bottom-like *shalvar,* and urinate squatting. This is not as easy as it sounds, and—as far as I can tell—it absolutely cannot be done in Western-style pants with a fly front. I say this from personal experience and from traveling with young, "sophisticated" members of the tribe who would wander off, and then, confronted by both a zipper fly and *shalvar* with an elasticized waistband, would totter most uncomfortably before they gave up and stood up. I must add that I found it extraordinarily odd to see men squatting to urinate. Everything about it seemed all wrong—men stand, women squat—and I fruitlessly wondered more than a bit about what it meant to work in a culture of men who piss squatting like women.

Using a gully took some getting used to, but it was far better than using "bathroom" facilities in many places we visited, for they were often filthy, while the gully was always clean. Indeed, it was extraordinarily clean: Most of the time someone coming upon the gully would have virtually no clue about how humans used it. This cleanliness, remarkable to us, was not a product of human endeavor. Within seconds of a stool being deposited, dung beetles arrived. Looking like tiny vehicles encased in some cheap black plastic armor, and sounding like a small plane in flight, they flew in, took hold of feces, human or animal, and worked it into spherical balls, which they then rolled away to only the entomologist knows where. Ann and I wondered if the beetles constructed vast subterranean cities, fecal palaces. (We weren't to know for many years, but apparently that is what happens.) The result was a constantly cleaned surface. Between the beetles and the dry heat of the desert, the gully was a far better place than it might have been.

Though we recognized that our fantasies of dung cities were probably part of our adaptation to our new kind of "bathroom" facilities, Ann and I felt a bit foolish about our foolishness. We were thus greatly amused to discover that we were not alone in our wonder at dung beetles, and that the usually most proper and straitlaced Bishop had noted them, too.

> Ever since leaving Kum all the dry and hard parts of the road have been covered with the industrious "road beetle," which works, like the ant, in concert, and carries on its activities at all seasons, removing from the road to its nest all the excreta of animals. . . . These beetles hover over the road on the wing and on alighting proceed to roll the ball towards the nest, four or five of them standing on their hind-legs and working it forwards, or else rolling it with their heads close to the ground. Their instinct is wonderful, and they attract the attention of all travellers. (Bishop 1891, 1:242)

Clearly, traveling Europeans and Americans of all eras have had similar reactions to adapting to some aspects of life in the Iranian countryside.

Over time, going in a gully no longer seemed strange; in fact, it became too natural. Once in the middle of the night, I woke up with fairly intense stomach cramps. I needed little reflection to realize that I had picked up another of the intestinal upsets we more than occasionally suffered. I staggered out of the tent and, like the fellow in the doggerel verse of my childhood, "The Midnight Ride of Diarrhea," began the "fifty-yard dash to the outhouse seat," which was in this case a gully. Fate was against me, and I made only about thirty yards. It was awful and I did not feel any better, and I certainly did not feel any smarter when, after she had helped me with the worst of the mess, Ann asked, "What did you think you were doing?"

"I had diarrhea, so I was running for the gully," I answered.

"You were running for the gully," she echoed. "It was three o'clock in the morning, you had five hundred thousand square miles of desert to take a shit in, and you shit in your pants because you had to go in the gully. What makes the gully different from the rest of the world?"

I was speechless. What could I say—"the gully is my bathroom"? Culture is a powerful thing, especially at three o'clock in the morning.

If figuring out how to go to the bathroom was an urgent problem, developing a strategy for keeping clean was a chronic one. When we were out on survey with Mr. Abusaidi, having done miles and miles of driving in the desert, we would often come back to Kerman city covered with dust. Once, staying in a hotel where the bath water was a bit salty and having soap but no shampoo, we made the mistake of washing our hair anyway. The combination of salt, soap, and dust turned our hair into an incredible goopy mass. It was as though we'd poured glue in it. It was so bad that Ann insisted on photographing it.

As luck would have it, that happened on a Friday, when most of the stores were closed. It took me most of the day to find a store where I could buy shampoo so we could clear the muck off our heads. After that experience, we were never without shampoo, but we still needed a place to use it.

We first met up with the Komachi during their spring migration, and we traveled with them toward their summer quarters. All we knew about their summer quarters was what they told us. One of the things we heard about was *ab garm,* literally "warm water," which was described as a wonderful hot spring. It was, we were told, a great place for bathing, both to get clean and for the curative powers of the water. As I have already noted, the valley that the Komachi lived in during the summer was magically beautiful. Having seen that, we set off for *ab garm* with great expectations a few days after we arrived in summer quarters. I did not quite expect tiled Roman baths, but I pictured something like a small, deep pool in a mountain stream, clear water running over rocks, differing from other mountain streams only in that steam would be rising from its bath-temperature surface. That was not *ab garm.* What we found was a pool of rather oily, slimy, and dirty-looking water that, while not as cold as the water in the stream or *qanat,* was little more than tepid. We bathed, but we did not feel clean, and the prospect of using this as our regular bathing site was depressing.

Fortunately, Shirinak had a *hammum,* a public bath. It was housed in a small fired-brick building that had been built a few years before as a state-sponsored public works project. There was a tank on the building's roof that the bath-keeper filled with a hand pump. Water was heated with a brush-wood fire. The *hammum* was open only one day a week: mornings for women, when the bath-keeper's wife presided, and afternoons for men. Having experienced the *ab garm,* we determined to try the *hammum* as soon as we learned of its existence. So, on the first day we heard it was open, we trekked off to it. Almost certainly to the scandal of everyone around, Ann and I went together. The bathkeeper pumped water up to the tank, and inside we were able to scrub and scrape, shampoo, shave, and take a long, hot shower. I must admit, we did not bathe Iranian style, scrubbing, scraping, and soaping first, then rinsing off in the shower. We stood, one after the other, in the running water and washed. We were particularly long at it, and we could hear the bathkeeper pumping more water into the tank. We had no real idea what to pay the bathkeeper, and when we asked, he said, "Whatever you want." We gave him about fifteen tomans, roughly two dollars, and felt we were getting a bargain. In fact, the feeling of coming squeaky clean out of the humid *hammum* into the dry, clear air was al-ways exhilarating; it would have been worth a lot more.

Once every week, then, Ann and I would go off to the bath. The bathkeeper and his wife always seemed happy to see us, and ultimately we got to know where they lived, so that we could try to stir up a bath if they were not at the *hammum,* assuming they were in town, which, since they were also peasants, working fields around the village, was not always the case. As the summer wore on and fall approached, the villagers, including the bathkeeper, began harvesting their crops. These included wheat, chickpeas, lentils, and potatoes. Then something strange happened. One time when we saw the bathkeeper's wife, she pressed some potatoes on us. At first we protested; she insisted, so we accepted them and thanked her profusely. We thought nothing of it. The next week, in the evening, after we had taken our baths and paid the bathkeeper, his wife came to our door. We invited her in, but she said she could stay only a brief while, and had come to give us something. At that, she presented us with a small sack filled with large, beautiful potatoes. She then retreated and left us with our gift. Shortly afterward, the Komachi and we left for their winter quar-ters. It was only very late the next summer, well after we had returned to Shiri-nak, that we tumbled to what might have been going on. One day Ann was talk-ing with Sekine, and somehow the subject of the public bath came up. In the course of the discussion, Ann asked Sekine what people paid. "Oh, one or two tomans," Sekine said. And then she quickly asked, "How much do you give?"

"Oh, a little more than that," we lied. Given other experiences, I am quite certain that Sekine knew exactly how much we paid. She also probably thought it was an outrageous amount. Most likely the bathkeeper thought it was an extraordinarily generous sum, and the potatoes were his way of saying thanks. We appreciated them greatly. I should note too that while we were using the *hammum* no one else would or could use it. We felt that as we were possibly depriving the bathkeeper of trade, we should pay for our privacy.

Once we had found the *hammum,* bathing in summer quarters was a pleasure. The move to winter quarters brought its own problems and pleasures. In winter quarters, the Komachi camped well away from the local villages, and Shir Ali's campsites were always so far from Jaghin that bathing there would have entailed a long drive. Fortunately, there was a solution closer at hand. Most fields in the area were irrigated from deep-bore wells equipped with large, diesel-driven pumps. These brought a forceful stream of water up through four- or six-inch pipe, and in most places the water first entered a concrete tank about four feet high. So as long as people were irrigating fields, bathing wasn't too difficult. Again, Ann and I would head off together, and while one of us kept a lookout the other would bathe. Although it came right from the pipe, the water was never terribly cold, and the turbulence where the jet of water entered the tank was rather like a giant Jacuzzi. It wasn't quite as comfortable as our *hammum,* but it beat *ab garm.*

Moreover, since nearly half of our migration route passed through territory irrigated by these pumps, we were able to bathe even then. Once we stopped at a pump near a field of millet that a woman from a winter quarters village was guarding. She was fascinating to us, as she was dressed in clothing quite different from what the Komachi wore. She stood on a platform at the edge of the field, protecting her crops with a sling and a pile of stones. We, I am sure, looked far stranger to her: two light-haired, light-eyed, obvious foreigners, driving up to her field in the absolute middle of nowhere. We chatted with her a bit, and asked her if we could bathe in the irrigation tank. She said, "Of course," and politely turned her back. After we had bathed, we talked a bit more. Then we watched in fascination as she bent, picked up a rock, put it in her sling, swung it around her head four or five times, and launched the stone like a rocket at a donkey that had entered the field. The stone hit the donkey in the ribs with a thud that was clearly audible even though we were a good thirty or forty yards away. If that was how David popped Goliath, it's no wonder he won.

We bathed in one more irrigation tank on migration. We were approaching the point at which we would leave the lowland winter quarters. The nomads had pitched camp for the day, and we drove over to a pump we had heard in the distance. All the pumps had a deep, pulsing throb, but as we drew near, this one was louder than any we had heard before. When we got to it, it was also larger than any we had seen. Standing in the middle of a vast field, with no village and no one nearby, the pipe from the pump, which looked to be at least eight inches in diameter, rose from the ground like a great inverted J and pumped down a powerful stream of water. After looking about carefully and finding no one, Ann and I took . . . well, I guess one would have to call it a shower rather than a bath. We hadn't been able to bathe since we'd left the woman with the sling, and washing off the dust and dirt that had accumulated on our trip was a pleasure. After we had bathed, we climbed on the jeep to look around. We were curious, for the pump was by far the largest and fanciest that we had encountered; the fields around it were enormous, stretching off in all directions, and they had a finished look, unlike most fields we had seen. They were much more like cornfields in Iowa than most fields in Kerman. Moreover, though we couldn't be sure, we thought that in the far distance we saw other, similar pumps. When we returned to camp, we described what we had seen.

"Yes," our friends said, "the pumps are huge and the fields are impressive." They also said, "You did not see it, but there is an airfield there."

"An airfield?" we said.

"Yes, this all belongs to Asadallah Alam. Do you know who he is?"

We did. He was the minister of court, and was reputedly the shah's oldest and perhaps only friend. He was also alleged to be rich beyond most people's wildest dreams. Everything became as clear as the water we had bathed in.

Chapter

II

PEGGING IT DOWN

Our first tent was small. It was made of high-quality, lightweight, neon orange rip-stop nylon and had a fly that served as a sunshade. It was totally inadequate for life with the Komachi. It was compact enough for backpacking, but the Komachi migrated only short distances every few weeks. During the vast stretches of time that they did not migrate, our tent's size limited us greatly. Because it was small, we could not invite guests in. If it rained, we could not cook in it. Even though it had a fly, in the heat of the summer it became an oven. Because it was only slightly larger than a queen-sized bed, when we were both in it we couldn't move without bumping into each other. Nothing we could do made the tent more comfortable. The longer we were with the Komachi, the more we accumulated things that did not fit in it. It might have been, it probably was, a great tent for camping. It was a horrible tent to live in. I came to hate that tent.

One of the things that annoyed us about the tent was that it frequently blew over. Once we realized that the desert soil was light and that the tent pegs had to be very carefully placed and hammered in, it blew down less often, but it was still vulnerable to whirlwinds.

Neither Ann nor I had ever seen a tornado. My only experience of cyclonic activity was dust devils, small columns of dust or leaves scooting down a street or across a playing field, fun to jump into or through when I was a child at play. In summer quarters we were introduced to whirlwinds. Kerman's whirlwinds were not tornados, but neither were they just dust devils. Ten to fifteen feet across and forty to fifty feet high, whirlwinds were common in the late afternoon; they moved rapidly across the valley or down an open field. They were not large enough to injure a person, but they could make a great mess: blowing around anything light enough to be moved, driving dust into anything open, playing havoc with cooking fires, scattering anything set out to dry. And they played with our tent.

Our tent was triply susceptible to the whirlwinds. Because it was small and light, it would blow down if a whirlwind passed near. When that happened, anything in the tent that wasn't packed got tossed about. It made a mess. Even if the tent didn't get knocked down, the blowing dust filled it with a fine grit that penetrated everywhere. Finally, since we couldn't really fit all our things in the small tent, whirlwinds scattered our plates, dishes, and the other things we left outside.

There wasn't much we could do about the last two problems. We tried to keep the tent tidy and we tried to store as much as we could inside, but there were limits. Having the tent knocked down, however, was a problem we thought we could fix.

Whirlwinds rarely knocked down Komachi tents. These were made of rectangular panels, each roughly six feet wide by thirty feet long, woven from coarse black goat hair. Each panel was draped over its own ridgepole, which was a long plank held up by a stout tent pole. Long pins were used to loosely fasten to each other the panels making up a tent. Each panel was held in place by stout ropes that joined it to even stouter pegs. When a whirlwind hit a row of tents, the tent panels would generally rise a bit, strain at their ropes, or even slip a little on their poles, but we didn't see them come flapping down. When a whirlwind hit our tent, by contrast, our tent would fully catch the wind. The pegs pulled free from the ground, the fly took off, and the tent, fly, and poles formed a tangled pile on the ground.

Finally we decided we had had enough. We had been with the Komachi several months, long enough to diagnose the problem: the tent pegs. Our tent was staked with smooth yellow plastic pegs, about eight inches long, and one or two iron pegs, no thicker than a ten-penny nail, that we had bought to replace broken plastic ones. Komachi tents were held down by real tent pegs—wrought-iron monsters made of three-eighths-inch square stock twisted and tapered down to a point. As we talked about it, it became clearer and clearer that we should replace our camper-style pegs with some sturdy iron spikes. Their spikes, the Komachi told us, came from gypsies who passed through the area in the fall. We felt we couldn't wait that long, and the Komachi assured us that would be no problem; for a bit more money we could get them from the ironmonger in the bazaar. And that is just what we did. On our next trip into Kerman, we bought a set of lovely, long, heavy black wrought-iron spikes, and I went around the tent happily banging them in. When we had replaced the pegs, we were confident that no whirlwind would be able to blow our tent down.

We had to wait only a few days before the test came. We were walking in a field with some Komachi and were about fifty yards from the tents when we saw the whirlwind touch down. From the moment it hit, it was apparent that we were going to have a real trial; it touched down a little before the last tent in the line and swept along it, hitting each one in turn. It kicked up a huge cloud of dust, ash, and litter, and it was making a terrific mess. Finally it reached our tent. Standing there enthralled, we watched as the whirlwind hit our tent. First the swirling dust buffeted it, blowing and pulling at the tent and fly. Nothing moved, and I nearly cheered. Then the whirlwind itself hit the tent. I can still see it. The spiraling winds slammed against the nylon, the ropes strained and tightened, and the vacuum from the whirlwind made the tent and fly puff out as though they were being inflated from some huge tank of compressed gas. Larger and larger they puffed, and the cords stretched tighter and tighter and tighter, and the pegs—the pegs didn't give an inch! Then there was an audible pop, and the tent and fly settled gently to earth. We ran to the scene, and there, still firmly held by tent pegs that had barely budged, were our tent and fly, both burst like overinflated balloons. The rip-stop nylon had ripped.

I spent the rest of that day and part of the next sewing, patching, and sealing the tent back together. It was hard work forcing the needle through folded layers of rip-stop nylon, and my fingers were sore for days. But from then on, whatever else befell us, we knew that our tent pegs would hold.

We always assumed that the problems with our tent resulted from our inability to buy the "right" one with our limited resources. Given that feeling, I felt a somewhat perverse pleasure when, reading Western travelers' tales, I discovered that even those far better equipped than we had had problems with their tents.

In 1914 Arnold Wilson was seconded to the Turco-Persian Boundary Commission, a body consisting of commissioners from Turkey, Iran, Britain, and Russia, assigned the task of negotiating and marking the then-disputed boundary between Iran and Ottoman Turkey along its length from the Persian Gulf to near Mount Ararat. The difference in their budget and ours is perhaps best marked by noting that Wilson, who was in effect quartermaster in charge of supplies for the party, disbursed £5,000 a month, and in 1914 a pound was a pound! With that budget, Wilson provided the Boundary Commission with tents to construct a camp modeled on "the Royal Camp at Rawal Pindi . . . when King George V as Prince of Wales visited India" (Wilson 1941, 272). Nonetheless, on May 18 Wilson noted:

> Yesterday a sudden rain-storm came down and loosened the pegs—before we
> had time to hammer them in . . . a veritable hurricane struck us, snapping the
> poles, uprooting the tents, and in a couple of minutes half the camp was laid
> flat. This is really a blessing in disguise, for had the tents not fallen they would
> have been ripped up. (Wilson 1941, 285)

As we learned to our sorrow, Wilson was right.

Of course, in the long run our real problem was not the quality of our tent
(the problems encountered by better-outfitted Western travelers showed that);
the true problem was having the wrong kind of tent. We ultimately learned this
in a way far less spectacular than having our tent burst.

Our first tent had shown its inadequacies long before it exploded in the
whirlwind. So before we left the mountains at the end of our first summer we
arranged for a new tent to be sent from home. Poring over a Sears catalogue
that had once belonged to a Peace Corps worker, we found one that seemed
ideal. It was canvas instead of nylon; it had an external frame that looked more
substantial than the poles and lines of our current tent. It was ten feet by thir-
teen, large enough to walk around in and high enough to stand in. And, like all
tents made in the USA, it had double doors and windows, canvas to pull down
or zip closed for privacy, and screening to keep the insects away. It looked like
a piece of paradise. Our only problem was how to ship it to Iran and get it
through customs without both tremendous delay and great cost. Fortunately,
my father worked for a corporation that had a substantial presence in Iran; they
had direct mailbag service from the United States. In good Iranian fashion, we
played *parti* and prevailed upon my father to request a favor from his connections. And so the unit arrived in Tehran.

Though there were some complications, we got the tent just in time for the
move to winter quarters, and we were ready to live in comfort and style. Alas,
when we arrived we found that although fall had truly been upon us in the
mountains, it was still summer in the lowlands. The first week or so after we
arrived was the hottest and most uncomfortable time we spent in Iran. It was-
n't only us—the Komachi too did only a minimal amount of work and spent
most of the day sitting or lying in the deep shade around their tents, moving
with the sun so as to stay in the tents' shadow. In reality, no tent would have
been comfortable, so we put up with what we had.

Still, we had our tent. It was large; we could stand up in it; we could cook in
it (violating all rules of safety, we set up our stove in our tent); we could eat in
it. It was not quite like the picture in the catalogue, but our new home seemed
wonderful. We took photos of it. There were, we discovered, only two problems with it: the way it shrank and the flies that flew in it.

Problems with the cap and rear door of our jeep had already taught us that canvas items tended to shrink. We were sure that Sears would have prewashed the canvas so that the tent wouldn't shrink. We either placed too much faith in Sears or we underestimated the *garmsir* weather. Winter in the *garmsir* was never truly cold; there was no snow and no frost. This was ideal for the Komachi, since they did not have to fear losing animals to the chill. But there was rain, then gray, then some bright sun, then rain, and gray, and *nem,* something between a fog and a mist, and more sun and more gray. As a result, the tent got wet, and then it dried; and it got wet, and then it dried; and it got wet, and then it dried, over and over again. As it dried, it shrank a little. Just a bit, not too much, but enough to make it harder and harder to zip the J-shaped door. Ultimately the zipper failed, but we patched the door with the legs of a pair of jeans and some Velcro that my mother sent me. The doors wouldn't have been a great problem but for the flies.

During February the year before, Mr. Abusaidi had taken us to the camps of other tribes in their lowland winter quarters. At several of them we had been repelled by the swarms of flies that hovered around the tents, the people, and the food they served us. We had joined the Komachi midway on their migration and till now all the time we'd spent with them had been in the highland summer quarters. There were some insects at eighty-five hundred feet, but not many, and we had forgotten the flies. Now we learned that we had avoided the flies not because the Komachi were clean or because they had good campsites. Rather, we discovered that timing was everything, for when the flies swarmed, they swarmed on the Komachi as well as other tribes.

And did those flies swarm! They filled people's tents; they buzzed around everywhere, settling on faces and food, hovering around our eyes and mouths, covering babies' faces if they weren't draped with cloth. One sat automatically waving a hand back and forth, trying to keep the flies away, but it was useless, and they were disgusting. Only at night, as the desert temperature plunged, did the flies settle down. Before fieldwork, when I had seen pictures of pharaohs and other potentates surrounded by slaves with palm or feather fans, I had always assumed that the fans were there to cool the ruler with their breeze. Now I was certain I knew the real reason for the fans—they were an attempt to keep the flies off the ruler and his dinner.

Before continuing on to the main point of this discussion—how our encounter with flies confirmed both the superiority of Komachi tents and the power of cultural expectations—I want to digress briefly to consider another question: Western concerns with insect life. As I began going back through travelers' accounts, I was struck by the frequency with which accounts took note of insects. Occasionally the comments have the relative good humor and interesting, ironic tone of this passage from Sheil.

The house we resided in was rather distant from the wells, and we found a ride through the long ill-paved town twice a-day disagreeable. Having seen at the other side of the town near the well, a neat new-looking dwelling, we resolved to take possession of it. The Lareejanees advised us not, saying we should regret the change. This counsel we attributed to more Persian plotting and intrigue, and in spite of admonition we went. In the night we found ourselves attacked by legions of bugs; for that night, rest was out of the question. Next day we thought we had hit on an expedient for baffling these our mortal foes, and we pitched a small tent in the open court of the house, and calmly retired to rest. Judge the horror we felt when on awakening, we perceived they were in ten times greater numbers than on the night before! The whole nation of the invaders had, as it were, been let loose against us, and we were on the point of being devoured; the marvel was where they had come from. . . . We decamped at daybreak, too happy to regain our old abode. I should exceedingly like to know on what these bloodsuckers subsisted before the night of our arrival, and how they have gained a livelihood since that memorable epoch. (Sheil 1856, 263–64)

More commonly, insects appear in travelers' accounts in a faint but noticeable refrain devoid of humor or irony. In Layard's writings, "vermin" seem part of the ratification of his claim that his travels were hard. Bishop seems less concerned to use insects to prove her hardiness; her constant comment on encountering insects seems more an attempt to use their presence as a sign of some moral failing in the human inhabitants of the insects' abodes. Assuming that encounters in fieldwork reveal "our" culture as well as "theirs" and that comments of travelers can be equally revelatory, one element of our culture appears to be an obsessive concern over contact with insects.

Why we are all so disturbed by bugs is a question I cannot answer, so I will return to the issue of tents and flies. Flies were everywhere, and nothing had any impact. Shir Ali, in an effort at fly control, bought some horrendous poison. The color alone, a virulent yellow-green, looked lethal. He spread the poison on plates and trays in his tent, and it did indeed kill flies; it killed them by the hundreds, the thousands, for all I know by the millions. Plate after plate and tray after tray became filled with buzzing, kicking flies that had been attracted to their deaths. He, and we, would watch them land, feel the effect of the poison, roll over, spin round and round and round, and then die. It was a hecatomb of flies, and it was all in vain. Every fly that Shir Ali killed was replaced by at least one more. No matter how full his plates were, his tents were no less full of living, buzzing, annoying flies than anyone else's.

We tried a different tack. Our tent had screens. We therefore attempted to keep it clear of flies. We would stand outside the screen, waving and flapping to discourage the flies, then unzip the door as fast as we could, jump in—flapping all the while—and try to zip the door shut before any flies entered. We failed. No matter how quickly we tried to move, no matter how we flapped and flailed, flies came in. And, of course, we couldn't always keep the door closed. People came by to chat, to visit, to ask for things, to tell us what was going on. We opened the screen to talk, and flies came in. Worse, if we went away, neighbors entered our tent to borrow this and that. More used to flies than we, or perhaps more resigned to them, they did not take our elaborate precautions. They might leave the door open, and the tent would fill with flies. One time, we left for an overnight stay at another camp. We returned to discover that our kerosene lamp had been borrowed while we were gone, and that the borrowers had not rezipped the door. Our tent was jammed with flies.

Like Shir Ali, we also had a secret weapon: Piff-Paff, a lethal spray packaged in an aerosol can. If the tent got too crowded with flies, we could lower the flaps over the screens and, holding our breath in the closed tent, fill it with Piff-Paff and run out. If there were enough flies in there, we could hear the buzz of them dying as we waited outside. We would then go in and sweep the floor of flies. We could not always get Piff-Paff, and it was expensive, so sometimes we abandoned our support of the Iranian petrochemical industry and resorted to brute force. As the air cooled in the early evening, the flies settled on the walls of the tent; armed with flyswatters, we began the counterattack. At first we killed flies in droves. The more we killed, of course, the more we had to labor at killing the flies that remained. But we worked hard at it, and Ann, who I think hated the flies even more than I did, often obsessively struggled to get the last one. The day after our tent door was left open overnight, she even counted the bodies, losing interest at 254, with dozens of other uncounted dead still scattered on the floor.

As our epic struggle with the flies continued and took on a nearly ritualized dimension, we slowly came to realize that our plight was not quite the same as our neighbors'. During the day their tents, which were wide open, filled with flies. But as evening fell and the air cooled, the flies disappeared from their tents. If they did not disappear, they settled on the black panels and slept, bothering no one. As a result, in the early morning and in the evening, the Komachi tents were flyless and comfortable. Ours, alas, was different. With its screen door and windows, our tent was a veritable Roach Motel for flies: The flies could come in, but they couldn't get out. The very screens that were supposed to keep us free from flies trapped us with them in a cycle of struggle that our neighbors could avoid. If we did not kill flies at night, the very first light of morning coming through the yellow fabric of our tent's roof would wake our buzzing guests, and we would arise with the flies. We could, with work, keep our tent clear of flies for periods of time; our neighbors couldn't. But, with their tents open, our neighbors were guaranteed peace in the morning and evening, key times of day, while we, our screens keeping flies in rather than out, were doomed to fight them all the time.

Culture is powerful. Every day for nearly two months, our screened tent filled with flies trapped inside by our screens. But because cutting the screens out would let in the flies, we never even thought to do it.

Still, we never labored under the delusion that our tent was better than the Komachi black tents. We knew that though there were many days when the heat made our tent uninhabitable, there were few days that Komachi tents were equally uncomfortable. Moreover, there were no days on which their tents were less comfortable than ours. The black goat hair cast a deep, full shadow that was comfortable, if not cool, most of the summer. On the hottest days, their tent panels were propped higher to let in any breeze; on cooler days, the panels were draped over the reed "wall" of the tent, and with a fire the tents were far from cold. The black goat hair shed rain well, and the tents were heavy enough to stay up during whirlwinds. They were also flexible. Kermani tribes whose winter quarters were further north and much colder than those of the Komachi pitched their tents over rock-walled dugouts three to four feet deep. We stayed with them in February, and their tents were far more comfortable than our own.

Given the apparent superiority of the tribal tents, it is surprising to read comments like those of Bishop, claiming that local habitations

> consisted of stones rudely laid to a height of two feet at the back, over which there is a canopy with an open front and sides, of woven goat's-hair supported on poles. Such tents are barely a shelter from wind and rain, but in them generations of Ilyats are born and die, despising those of their race who settle in villages. (Bishop 1891, 1:315)

The oddity is double. First, I have seen the pictures in Cooper's *Grass* and I know that the Bakhtiyari tents are, essentially, the same as those of the Komachi. Even allowing for a harsher environment, it is hard to see how they could be construed as providing "barely a shelter," unless Bishop, like us on our first encounter with the Komachi, confused the small shelters set up during migration with a fully pitched camp. Second, virtually all travelers unfortunate to possess a European tent constantly noted the problems they had with them, of which the most serious—as we found, too—was their ovenlike heat. I can only assume that the same kind of cultural blindness that prevented us from removing our window screens prevented Bishop from seeing the superiority of tribal tents.

Chapter

12

A TEST OF STRENGTH OR A TEST OF POWER?

One evening in late July of our first summer among the Komachi, Kokojon, commonly called Kawki, dropped by, urgently inviting me to have dinner at his tent. I was reluctant to go. Well into his forties and married for many years, Kawki had no children. The year before we arrived, Kawki and Senne, his wife, had sold most of their flock. They kept the pastoralists' equivalent of a kitchen garden to provide themselves with yogurt, dried whey, and clarified butter, and they raised the cash they needed by partaking in small entrepreneurial ventures. Senne also wove tent panels, bags, and bread cloths for other households. Since they had so few animals, they had a great deal of spare time, and we were a kind of blessing for them. From the day of our arrival in camp, they had gone out of their way—virtually tracked us down—in an attempt to have us as their constant guests.

At first we were flattered and amused. But spending a great deal of time with Kawki and Senne—whose household was clearly atypical—meant we had less time to spend with others. And for all the time we spent with them, Kawki never seemed to catch on to what we were doing. As a result, we often felt that time spent with them was hard time.

But the real reason I did not want to go to Kawki's tent that evening was that Taqi was there.

Taqi lived in the town of Qaryeitalarab, over the mountain pass on the way toward Kerman. Kawki called him both Taqi Maqi, his name and patronymic, and Taqi Arbab, which, roughly translated, meant "landlord Taqi." Taqi did own some land around Qaryeitalarab and some land in the high valleys around Shirinak and Giborj, but he was best known to the Komachi as a *taraf,* someone who bought (and to a lesser extent sold) goods from the Komachi on credit. Once when we asked a Komachi what a *taraf* was, we were told, "A *taraf* is someone you are indebted to." In short, a *taraf* was the Iranian version of those agents of the expanding capitalist world market system who bind peasants to the market through debt. In the valleys around Shirinak, Taqi Arbab was the gross embodiment of this process.

And he was indeed gross. He was large and fat; he always looked unkempt; he was a rude boor, a loudmouth, a braggart, a blowhard, and a bully.

Because he and Kawki were partners in minor business deals, Taqi often stopped at Kawki's tent when he was in the valley. Ann and I had been paraded before him early in our stay, and hadn't liked him much when we first met him. His conversation consisted mostly of a leering commentary on the licentious wonders of Western society, all of which Taqi seemed to crave. Taqi may have been the only person we met among the Komachi who, for us, had no redeeming merit. Ann nicknamed him "Arbab Piggy-Fat," and to this day the name seems appropriate.

So that evening, when I saw Taqi's blue Chevrolet Apache pickup truck near Kawki's tent, my heart sank. But Kawki pressed us to come, and in spite of my misgivings we went. I do not remember just why our attendance was so urgently required. My notes record that the major topics of conversation, selected and dominated by Taqi, were Jacqueline Kennedy Onassis, the likely final damnation of Gougoush (at that time Iran's most popular female singer), and Taqi's accounts of what he had heard was going on in the "coed dorm rooms" at the University of Tehran. Parenthetically, when we heard Taqi's rumors about the University of Tehran, we dismissed them as nonsensical babble. In retrospect, those rumors of sexual impropriety and deviance associated with a very Westernized icon of popular culture and with the university appear as attacks on modernization, and hence as early engagements in the struggle over Iran's future that culminated in the Islamic revolution. If one imagines that Taqi was not unique, the constant iteration of rumors of this kind would not have been an insignificant force in shaping public views.

Anyway, our presence may have been requested for a reason as prosaic as wanting to borrow some paper or our tape recorder to listen to a tape, but I suspect Taqi simply wanted a larger audience to brag to. After dinner, the conversation became desultory, and Taqi turned to other amusements. He challenged his driver to a form of arm wrestling. After much discussion of his prowess and power and his numerous victories—all of which was seconded by a sycophantic Kawki—Taqi intertwined his pudgy fingers with the driver's; then, twisting his hand and wrist until the driver's hand was bent back in a painful-looking position, he happily decreed that he had won. Next he challenged Kawki, who looked terrified and scurried about the tent, throwing up a flood of excuses and suggestions for alternative opponents. Taqi got the same response from Emir, Kawki's wife's brother, a very solidly build young man. Ultimately Kawki proposed, "Why don't you wrestle with Daniel?" Taqi thought that was a great idea; I was dubious, but, cajoled, challenged, and teased on all sides, I finally relented. In light of the preceding events, I did not know what to expect, and so when I locked grips with Taqi I was surprised to discover that I was able to turn his wrist with little more difficulty than one would turn a slightly stiff doorknob. Taqi sulked and left shortly thereafter, claiming that he was tired from smoking too much opium. Meanwhile Kawki could do nothing but prattle on about my amazing conquest.

It had been bad enough to hear Kawki describe and redescribe this epic battle in front of Taqi, although the fact that it clearly discomfited Taqi made the prattle less bothersome. But Kawki's newfound respect for me knew no bounds: He told and retold the story in camp and in neighboring camps, and he always told it the same way. There was a long buildup about Taqi's awesome power, about the number of people whose wrists he had twisted, and then Kawki would break into a fairly accurate description of how, without apparent effort, I had twisted Taqi's wrist while Taqi grimaced but could do nothing against my extraordinary power. Kawki would then launch into a panegyric about how powerful I was, generally repeating over and over again, "*Che gardan koloft,*" literally "What a thick neck," as a kind of descriptive exclamation over my strength.

I was mystified. People clearly thought that Taqi was stronger than they were, and since I was stronger than Taqi, they assumed that I must be that much stronger than they. Much to my embarrassment, people even acted on this assumption. When things got stuck or something heavy needed a lift, people came to me. But I knew what they were assuming wasn't true. At about six feet tall and weighing roughly 190 pounds, I was larger than almost any of the Komachi. I had wrestled and played lacrosse in school, so there had been a time that I was in fine shape. But it had been years since I had seriously competed at anything, years since I had put any real effort into staying in shape; and since I attended the Graduate Center of the City University of New York, which is on Forty-second Street between Fifth and Sixth Avenues, I hadn't even had the opportunity to play the kind of pickup games that one gets at a university with a real gym or field house or playing fields.

Having spent over a year with the Komachi, having lived with them, worked with them, and helped them move on migration, I had no illusions about my physical condition vis-à-vis theirs. I had seen small men throw around heavy bags of wheat and barley in ways that I could not. I had seen shepherds spend a full day chasing sheep and goats up and down mountainsides, and I knew that I could not run and climb like that. I knew that immensely pregnant women would walk miles to attend a wedding. I had watched men shear sheep for hours, clipping animal after animal by hand. I had seen men and women in their seventies haltingly set off during migration for a fifteen-mile walk over a ten-thousand-foot-high mountain pass. At first I was certain that they would collapse on the way, but I saw them finish their marches day after day, through-out the whole 150-mile migration. I knew that young girls carried goatskin bags filled with more than half their weight in water miles back from a spring. I had observed women weaving tent panels, packing the warp down hour after hour with a heavy wood-and-metal tool. I knew that even if the Komachi were not in the same league as South American Indians who ran through the forest shouldering huge logs, or Maasai warriors who ran all day, they nonetheless were in a totally different kind of physical condition from almost anyone—in-cluding the college athletes—I knew back home. Given what I had seen, given my certainty that they were far stronger than I, I did not understand how they could believe that Taqi was stronger than they were.

I got my reality check several months later. Among the Komachi, there was a tendency for wealth and size to be correlated. While not all wealthy people were heavy, the heaviest people were all from wealthy and important families, and all poor people were rail thin. The biggest people that anyone knew, peo-ple renowned for their size up and down the valley, were several members of the Taiori tribe, neighbors to and affines of the Komachi, whose territory the Komachi's abutted at the extreme eastern end of the valley system. Several Taiori were large, but the largest by far was the current "big man" in the tribe, Hossein Taiori. We had visited Hossein several times and had always enjoyed ourselves. He was intelligent, cynical, and somewhat suspicious of us, but in many ways open and direct. Hossein was also very large. He was at least six feet three inches tall, and I am sure he weighed well over 250 pounds. Some of that was fat; he had had an operation for a kidney stone and, like Lyndon John-son, wasn't embarrassed to show his scar, which traversed a round and well-padded belly. But Hossein was big-boned, with huge hands and wrists, broad shoulders, a true *gardan koloft,* and a massive head.

Either because of my reputation or perhaps from politeness, no Komachi ever challenged me to an arm-wrestling match. But in the fall of 1974, Hossein and all his enormous relatives came down the valley to attend a celebration in Shirinak. As they had come a good distance, and as the celebration lasted sev-eral days, Hossein and his family had plenty of time to spend in Shirinak. Since they were at best very peripheral kin to those throwing the celebration, and since they were somewhat honored guests, they were frequently left alone in tents or rooms prepared for guests. For our part, when there was nothing much going on during the celebration, Ann and I took the opportunity to drop in on the guests. The Taioris seemed genuinely happy to see us, as we helped pass the time, and we were happy for the opportunity to learn more about a neighboring tribe and to see how they interacted with the Komachi.

One afternoon things were quite quiet. Ann was off with the women, most men were sleeping, and I dropped into the guest room. No one was there but Hossein and his younger, much smaller brother. We began to chat, and then Hossein's brother said, "I heard you beat Taqi at wrestling." I said that was right, I had.

"Do you think you can beat me?" Hossein asked. I was quite certain that I could not, so I sort of shrugged, looked down, and murmured, "I don't know." Hossein instantly held up his hands, and with some trepidation I took up the challenge.

The match was quick and interesting. Hossein held his hands not in a relaxed posture but in a position that ensured him the advantage when we started. But he could have started with his hands in any position, for trying to twist his wrist was like grabbing hold of a mountain with one hand and trying to turn it upside down. And attempting to resist his twist, particularly from a disadvantage, was no easier than trying to prevent the wheel of a car from turning by holding the hub with my fingertips.

After I capitulated and sat down, Hossein turned to me and said, "I guess I'm stronger than Taqi." I agreed wholeheartedly. I suspected that the same was true of many, many of the Komachi, though even after they knew that Hossein had beaten me, I received no further challenges.

Other than my lack of surprise that Hossein was far stronger than I, one thing stood out about our contest: that as we had joined our hands to begin to wrestle, Hossein made sure that my hand was in a position that forced me to start at a disadvantage. I noticed it at the moment because it annoyed me; I thought about it later because it seemed part of a pattern I had already noticed.

Early in our time in Kerman, Ann and I did a brief survey of tribes to the south and west of Kerman City. Each of these tribes had a *khan,* and we were their guests. While at their camps, we often played a card game, *hok,* that we had been taught by friends in Tehran. We later played *hok* with some Komachi. *Hok* is rather like a simplified form of bridge; there is no bidding, and the contract is just seven tricks, but there are trumps, though they cannot be drawn. Since there is no bidding, trumps are declared by the dealer, who is the winner of the previous hand. The connection between *hok* and my arm-wrestling match with Hossein is that the dealer's ability to declare an undrawable trump gives him an enormous advantage. Unlike bridge, which starts evenly at each deal, in *hok* the deck is virtually stacked to the dealer's advantage. To a substantial degree, the way Hossein arm-wrestled and the rules of *hok* reflected a fundamental reality of prerevolutionary Iranian society: Those with advantage used it to maintain and sustain their position, and to some degree that use of advantage was a recognized part of the rules. There was not a great deal of noblesse oblige in prerevolutionary Iran, and while that was revealed to us in many ways, it was brought home sharply as we participated in the games and contests people played.

Chapter

13

CELEBRATIONS

Throughout most of our first summer with the Komachi, people told us about the *eizh* that were to take place in the fall. An *eizh* was the celebration given by a groom's family for their son's wedding or hosted by the parents of boys who were being circumcised (a circumcision *eizh* was also called a *sirun*). People's descriptions of these events were rich and detailed, and the tellers were filled with anticipatory excitement. We learned that the time after all the herds had been sent to winter quarters and all the harvesting had been done was a time *bi-kar,* "without work." In this lull in the annual calendar, all the members of the tribe would gather in the host's camp. People described the meals that would be served, the music, the giving of gifts. Their descriptions had a nearly physical immediacy, as if they were seeing or perhaps reliving the events they recounted. No one hearing the excitement in their voices and seeing the expressions on their faces could doubt that the Komachi considered their *eizh* to be great events.

All the Komachi *eizh* took place in early autumn, and they took place one right after another. Thus, from the end of August on, life took on a hectic pace and at the same time the period was almost liminal. People hosting *eizh* went to Kerman city to buy printed invitations, clothing (or the fabric to make it), candy, blankets, tea, sugar—everything for the feast. Men and women cleaned wheat and sent it to the mill. All the while, tension grew as marriage negotiations progressed and some families inevitably suffered disappointments.

Ann and I began to be almost as excited as the Komachi. There were many reasons for this. First and foremost, the excitement was catching. Second, despite all the description, we were still puzzled about many aspects of the *eizh,* and we had become nearly overwhelmed by curiosity itself. We wanted to see what had been described. We ran hither and yon: accompanying people to the city to see what they bought, from whom, and how; following negotiations; driving people here and there as they moved goods or tried to find musicians. Everyone's energies, all the hustle and bustle, were centered on festive events. It seemed like time out of time. And for us, even the weather, with beautiful cool, clear, sunny days and crisp nights, made the days seem to take on an edge and focus that was sharper than real life.

On September 13, I drove to Rabor to pick up the musicians who would play at the celebrations. On the morning of September 14, preparations began for Asghar's *eizh,* which would take place the following day. Accompanied by hired musicians, men and boys went off and cut a poplar tree, which they stripped of most of its branches and carried back to the host's camp. There sacred names— Hossein, Ali, Mohammed—and designs were painted on the trunk, while fruit, flags, and mirrors were tied to the remaining branches and the tree was erected.

Knowing that the *eizh* were celebrations for either circumcisions or weddings, Ann and I were immediately struck by the wonderful phallic imagery of the tree. Indeed, later the imagery would be sealed almost beyond our wildest dreams when, at the end of the circumcision celebration, men from the tribe gathered about the tree and proceeded to shoot the fruit off the top, their shotgun blasts stripping off leaves and branches as well. For two young anthropologists, it was like stumbling into symbolic anthropology heaven. And so, of course, we asked people what they were doing, why, and what it meant. We got the answer that we heard over and over again throughout the *eizh,* the wonderful answer that both did and did not answer our questions, that told us everything and nothing.

"*Rasm-e mah,*" we were told. At this point, *rasm* was not a word we knew, and after hearing it, we could hardly wait to find out its meaning. Alas, *rasm* turned out to be "custom," and *rasm-e mah* to be "it is our custom."

"*Rasm-e mah*" was not the answer to every question. People could explain very cogently why in the giving of the *fazl* (cash gifts ceremoniously presented to the boy being circumcised or the groom) they gave ten tomans, fifty tomans, or five hundred tomans. People easily explained that closest kin gave the first gifts and the largest ones. But when we noticed, and how could we fail to notice it, that these gifts were delivered on trays decorated with large cones of white sugar, fifteen to eighteen inches tall and topped with apples, all we were told by way of explanation was "*Rasm-e mah.*"

Still, we could not be disappointed at the *eizh.* Some of the events were striking in themselves, such as the stylized stick fights. While the musicians played and most of the rest of the guests watched, two of the younger, high-status men in the tribe would dance around in a circle. Then, suddenly, one would rush at the other with his stick, striking at his feet, while the other blocked the attack with his own stick. They would engage furiously for a few seconds, then retreat, dance, and start again. Although there were several bouts of stick fighting during each *eizh,* the best ones invariably took place at night. Then, with the dancers circling a huge bonfire and the flickering flames only partially illuminating the faces of the people standing around, the dance took on a truly extraordinary quality. Standing there, watching people, we saw on their faces the same look we had seen when they first described the events. They were living a magical event and might have been the audience at a great performance. And, of course, so were we. For us, everything was new, wonderful, and exciting. It was extraordinary to see guests arrive in a tent and sit according to rank. We had read about it, but there it was: ethnography come to life. It was extraordinary to see men and boys taken out of camp, stripped of their old clothes, bathed, redressed from head to toe in new garments, and then returned to camp, riding in state on a motorcycle, feet never touching the ground. We had read van Gennep's description of the ritual rebirth of celebrants, but now, seeing those abstract rites become concrete, we were overtaken both by the intellectual excitement of seeing something that we'd only read about become real and by the excitement of the event itself.

And of all the exciting things at all the different *eizh,* nothing was as mind-blowing for me as the stick fighting at Janallah's *sirun,* the feast celebrating the circumcision of his sons. Janallah's celebration, which took place on September 14, was the first *eizh* we saw among the Komachi. As I noted earlier, we started that day watching and very tentatively helping in the ritualized preparations for the *sirun* at Asghar's, and when things quieted down there, we returned to our camp, thinking we had experienced the high point of our day. Much to our surprise, at about four in the afternoon Tavakoli, Shir Ali's eldest son, came over to us and asked if we wanted to go to Giborj, the next village up the valley. We said we certainly did, and the three of us rode off on his motorcycle.

When we arrived at Giborj, we were greeted by ululating women carrying plates of wild rue being burned as incense. Much to our surprise, we realized that we were attending our first *eizh,* a *sirun* hosted by Janallah Mohammedi. Ann and I sat in the guest tent trying to keep track of who was there, occasionally wandering out to see what was going on and watching our first round of stick fighting. Around this entertainment, we were served numerous cups of tea and had our first official taste of the ritual meal served at all Komachi *eizh:* a meat stew, rice liberally seasoned with clarified butter, and bread.

After the meal, as the night grew darker, the musicians began to play and people began to filter out of the guest tents and gather round the fire to watch the stick fighting. Looking about, I began to get intimations of a pattern that I later found held true at all celebrations. I noticed that while only young men from prominent families actually danced in the stick fight, the audience consisted largely of women, children, and poorer, less important men. Powerful and wealthy men stayed in the guest tents and conducted "business"; not for them the frivolity of music and games. I was torn between watching and listening, but finally decided to watch the dance, which I found exciting and colorful.

The circle formed, and young men began to dance. I watched, enjoying the music, engaged by the young men's verve and skill. Then, suddenly, while two young men flailed at each other, a piercing whistle cut the air; a third and then a fourth figure dashed into the circle, attacking the other two. The crowd roared with laughter, and I stared, amazed. The new dancers, intent on disrupting the dance, were dressed as no Komachi I had yet seen, but it was clear from their headdresses and their clothing that they were women. But they were stick-fighting; they were also attacking the first two dancers in a fashion that could only be considered sexual, grabbing at their genitals and thrusting themselves at them. Next to me, almost beside himself with laughter and excitement, Moqtar, Janallah's brother, grabbed my arm and pointed.[1]

"Look, look," he said, "it's Qoli and Isau." And as I looked again, I saw that Moqtar was right: One of the dancers was my neighbor Qoli, Janallah's wife's youngest brother. The other "woman" was Isau, who was Janallah's father's brother's son and was also married to Janallah's sister. My head reeled—men dressed as women drawing gusts of laughter from an audience of women and children as they broke up the serious business of men engaged in stick fighting. Judging from their reactions, the Komachi derived great pleasure and excitement from watching the dance, but I am sure that I was more excited. Here, in a society in which men like those dancing did little while women worked hard, where men clearly dominated the public sphere, the crowning entertainment at the most public of public events saw men dressed as women enacting naked antagonism between the sexes. I watched, transfixed, while at the same time I longed to grab Moqtar and have him tell me what was going on. In the end, I just watched until the "women" disappeared.

As soon as we could, we sought Qoli out. We had many questions: What was the costume he wore? Why did they dress that way? Predictably, the last question, which was for us the most important and interesting one, elicited the least interesting answer: "We dance that way for fun."

Our other inquiries drew more response. Qoli's outfit was more of a costume than we realized. He and Isau had been wearing their sisters' wedding dresses; the rich red knee-length tunics and dark pajamalike pants were in the style of what women had worn before the advent of their current costume of garishly colored synthetic dresses similar to those worn by settled women in the region. His sisters had saved their wedding dresses, and now they were worn at these special occasions.

The next night, at Asghar's *eizh,* there was again stick fighting but no transvestite dancing; the same was true at the celebration of Hossein's marriage to Shir Ali's daughter. Then, at the fourth celebration, the transvestite dancing returned, with even wilder mock hostility. When we asked, Qoli had no trouble explaining why he and Isau had danced in women's garb at Janallah's *eizh* but not at Asghar's or Hossein's, and the answer was simple. Shir Ali, who was Asghar's brother-in-law and business partner and Hossein's new father-in-law (and rich uncle), was religious—as Qoli put it, "He says prayers." Being religious, Shir Ali did not care for that type of dancing; he thought it scandalous. Naturally, therefore, it would not be done at his daughter's wedding. Asghar was not as religious as Shir Ali, and he did not mind that kind of dancing. But he was very close to Shir Ali, so out of respect for him, he chose not to have people dance that way at his sons' *sirun.*

Our experience with the transvestite stick fighting suggested to us that custom is often customized, as it were, by personal predilection. Our inability to gain any deeper explanation of the apparent symbolism of rituals beyond "it is our custom" powerfully raised the point that people like the Komachi, living within a large and complex cultural system, may have no more meaningful explanation than this for why they do what they do or what those actions mean.[2]

A chance encounter at Janallah's *eizh* also helped alert us to a very important feature of Komachi life: the difference between their relations among themselves and their relations with people in the outside world. It also helped us see our place.

We had spent a full summer with the Komachi by the time we attended the celebration that Janallah hosted to mark his sons' circumcision. During that time, we had visited other camps as frequently as we could, collected and organized genealogies, and made a determined effort to begin to know who was who. That there were two of us, with different kinds of mental skills, seemed to enhance our work. It turned out that I was good at faces, able to recall where and when in the blur of travels and introductions I had met someone; Ann was extraordinary at both piecing together and remembering genealogies. If I could recognize a face and put a name to it, she could put the name in a genealogical web. This placement by kin seemed to be at least one way the Komachi organized their social universe, and for us it ultimately became a very effective way of knowing who someone was and where they were likely to stand in the tribe.

The first round of celebrations we attended in the fall of 1974 stretched to the breaking point our abilities to place people. Virtually all members of the tribe, as well as some members of neighboring tribes, some peasants from the area, and some local notables, were invited, and many showed up at one time or another. We were constantly checking with each other, and on occasion with Komachi we knew, in order to determine who someone was or whether they were who we thought they were.

Tavakoli, who took us to Janallah's *eizh,* was one person that we knew well. Tavakoli had been finishing up a tour in the army when we first arrived among the Komachi, so he had spent time outside the tribe. As we got to know him, we found a young man a bit at loose ends and under some pressure to get on with the next stage of his life: getting married.

As I noted earlier, on our arrival at Janallah's camp, we were greeted with wild-rue incense, and then we were shepherded to a guest tent. We knew some people there; others were strangers to us, including a young man pouring tea for the guests. Although it was fall, the day was warm and soft, and the panels of the guest tent had been raised to let the light breeze in. One could, as a result, look over the reed wall of the tent and see people outside the tent and those approaching at a distance. Tavakoli was sitting with us, and the young man with the tea was serving guests across the tent, perhaps ten or fifteen feet away. Wondering who he was, Ann asked Tavakoli, "Who is that?" tilting her head in the general direction of the tea server.

Tavakoli followed Ann's glance, but he looked puzzled. He rose and stared out under the tent flap into the distance. He seemed even more puzzled. "Who?" he asked.

"That man over there," Ann replied, "the one pouring tea," and she began to describe him.

Suddenly Tavakoli understood. "Him?" he said. "That's Hossein Kuchek." Then Tavakoli called Hossein over and introduced him. Hossein (who was in fact Tavakoli's father's father's brother's son) was someone we later got to know quite well, but at the time he was just one more face and name nailed down.

Tavakoli's first, puzzled response to our question passed in an instant. But the nature of his puzzlement—his initial inability to conceive of how anyone in a Komachi tent would not know another member of the tribe—was something we remembered throughout our stay, and ultimately it stood as a crystallized representation of what seemed to us a fundamental aspect of Komachi life: All the 550 members of the tribe knew each other. Moreover, all of them knew each other in a way that we could never duplicate. In a community of 550 people, who lived most of their lives in tents, who were forced to publicly pack and unpack their belongings for spring and fall migration, who had as their primary source of wealth animals that were herded up to the family tent to be milked, who negotiated marriages and other dealings almost exclusively within the community, there were few secrets, and everyone knew most everything there was to know about one another.

But while everyone knew everyone, not all relations were equal. Some people were friends, and others were enemies. Friendships were based on commonalities of interests and experiences that generally went back to earliest childhood and extended throughout people's lives; enmities seemed less total, if only because the small community seemed unable to contain polarizing rivalries. As I have written elsewhere, the Komachi claim "We are all one, we are all kin, there are no strangers here" was not entirely true, but there were very few strangers, and the rest were very well known to everyone else.

Where, then, did Ann and I fit in? As some of the following chapters will show, in dealing with the outside world, the Komachi talked of *ashna,* literally "acquaintances," and *rafiq,* "comrades" or "friends." In practice, the Komachi did not seem to distinguish greatly between the two categories. Both connoted non-Komachi whom they trusted and with whom they had built mutually valuable, sometimes close to symbiotic, relationships. Some relations with *ashna* and *rafiq* were long-standing, but the Komachi also worked assiduously at cultivating new relations, creating ties through business deals, invitations to weddings and circumcisions, and the provision of hospitality. Ann and I fell into these categories; we fit a slot in the Komachi framework for dealing with the outside world. We also fit into the additional category of *mehmun,* "guest." To say that we were *ashna* or *rafiq* is to say that our relationship seemed good. It did, I think, pass the test that Evans-Pritchard raised in *Social Anthropology:* "An anthropologist has failed unless, when he says goodbye to the natives, there is on both sides the sorrow of parting" (Evans-Pritchard 1962, 79). On the other hand, I do not think that a stranger asking Tavakoli who we were would have elicited the puzzled response brought forth by our asking who Hossein was. Not for one instant of one day did we feel that we knew the Komachi as they knew themselves or that we were friends with them as they were among themselves. In this text, I sometimes call the Komachi friends, sometimes neighbors, sometimes hosts. When I call them friends, it is in this sense of *ashna* and *rafiq:* accepted by, useful to, even welcomed by, but always distanced from the Komachi.

Chapter

14

EATING AT AMON ALI'S

Early on in our travels with Mr. Abu-
saidi, it had become apparent to us that meat made a meal. At every stop we
made with him, sheep or goats were slaughtered; if we traveled with a lesser
escort, we were fed chicken. Honor dictated that guests of any significance be
fed meat.

Living among the Komachi let us experience the practical implications of
this rule. Early in our stay, it meant that virtually every household we visited
either served us meat or apologized profusely for not doing so. Our arrival, I
think, placed a terrible burden on the collective chicken flock of the Komachi.
This was not a trivial thing. Throughout our stay Ann and I found it difficult to
visit poorer households in other camps. We had to time our visits carefully, arriving in the early morning, when we could assure our hosts that we had eaten
breakfast, that we did not want or need lunch, and that consuming no more
than tea was fine with us. There was a similar window of opportunity in the
middle of the afternoon. I should note that for the truly poor, and there were
truly poor among the Komachi, even extending hospitality of tea and sugar was
a financial burden. It made us uncomfortable.

The social requirement had impact in other ways as well. Whenever Shir Ali
and Sekine prepared a meat meal—and with a flock of over eight hundred
sheep and goats, that was not infrequent—we were invited over. Indeed, we
could mark our increased acceptance in camp by the declining formality of
what we were served. When we could be invited in for a meal of bread and
whey and rice, we had moved from guests to neighbors. The same was true in

other camps. Early on, before people knew us and accepted us as casual visitors, they felt obliged to serve us meat. As a result, for a while we would be mysteriously invited to one camp or another, to one tent or another, to meet with people and eat meat with them. I say mysteriously, because at the time we had little idea what was going on. One of our younger acquaintances, usually Qoli or Reza, both of whom had motorcycles and were very mobile, would come and say, "Would you like to visit so-and-so's camp?"

Since, early on, we were unlikely to know either the person or the location of his camp, we would jump at the opportunity. Once there, we would sit in the tent belonging to the head of the camp, drinking tea and talking. Over the course of our visit most of the men of the camp, and often men from camps close by, would trickle in for conversation and tea, staying awhile and then leaving. Finally, we would be served meat—in these cases, mutton or goat. In retrospect, the timing of our invitations became quite clear. No one wanted to kill a sheep or goat to host us, and rightly so. On the other hand, early on no one felt that they could *not* serve us meat on our first visit. So in those first days, when for whatever other reason an animal was slaughtered and meat was available, we got an invitation.

As with most things, it was the unfolding of later events that made things clearer. One day Kuchek's son, Hossein, literally tracked us through the valley, flagging us down on the road. "We are killing a sacrifice," he said, "and my father told me to find you to invite you to eat meat with us."

Another time we were pressed to stay at Naght Ali's. By then we knew Naght Ali and his wife, Gohar, quite well. We had visited them often, and we had reached a point in our relations with them where we could drop in casually, have several cups of tea, talk—usually, since they had a son and three grown daughters, about marriage rumors down at our end of the valley—and leave. But since one of the peasants who sharecropped for them had killed a cow and given them some meat, on this visit they were insistent that we stay and share a proper meal. The beef was memorable. Gohar used a pressure cooker in which the meat stewed away for hours. Even after that, though Gohar was a fine cook and the resulting dish tasted delicious, the meat was as tough as old shoes. Of course, when we saw the local cattle—scrawny, small things, little larger than a good-sized calf, pulling plows and threshing sleds—we knew why their meat, though very lean, was so very tough.

Indeed, the image of that memorable meal came powerfully to mind when, doing my detailed research on the economy of nineteenth-century Iran, I came across documents noting that while people loved lamb, mutton, and goat, they avoided beef. Henry Layard noted of the Bakhtiyari:

> Cows, bullocks, and oxen are chiefly used by the Iliyat [pastoralists] for the
> plough and as beasts of burden during migrations. The animals, and even their
> calves, are very seldom killed, and I never saw their flesh during my presence
> in this part of Persia. (Layard 1841, 207b)

James Morier, infamous as the author of *The Adventures of Hajji Baba of Is-
pahan,* noted that Mervdesht, a large, well-watered plain outside the city of
Shiraz that serves as a kind of crossroads for pastoralists in Fars province,

> is a favourite of the Iliots or wandering tribes. . . . The Iliots of Fars are numer-
> ous but not rich. . . . Their revenues consist in the sales of milk, mast, doug [the
> liquid left over after butter has been churned from yogurt], &c. which their
> flocks afford them, as well as in the sale of the cattle themselves, which consist
> entirely in that of lamb and mutton, the flesh of oxen being despised as coarse,
> and only fitted to the vulgar, unbelieving stomachs of Jews. (Morier 1811, 17)

Having eaten at Gohar's, I thought it most likely that if people eschewed beef,
it was because they couldn't chew it.

The requirement to serve a meat meal was so important that Komachi wedding invitations clearly stipulated the meals that would be served. The event
called for the guest to present a gift and for the host to serve meals worthy of
the gift. Indeed, what made the meals festive was not that they involved special
foods; store-bought cookies, baked with chickpea flour, were the only extraordinary food served at celebrations. Rather, what made the meals at celebrations
out of the ordinary was their sheer magnitude. At a celebration everyone, man,
woman, and child, was fed lots and lots of meat. Since the Komachi celebrations immediately preceded the fall migration, one of the few times that all Komachi were well fed was the time just before they returned to winter quarters
to begin the period of peak productive activity.

Meat was also served in abundance in the middle of spring migration, perhaps the period of greatest fatigue for all Komachi, as many households sacrificed an animal when passing a nearby shrine and distributed the meat among
neighbors and kin camping nearby.

The existence of a cultural rule enjoining hospitality and making meat its
embodiment did not, of course, mean that people were always happy to bear
the cost of killing an animal. I am sure that the Luri who killed a sheep for Mr.
Abusaidi and were left with only us to feed must have felt little pleasure. Similarly, once when Shir Ali and one of his shepherds were engaged in a bitter
dispute over renewing the shepherd's annual contract, Assadallah, the leading
man of the tribe to which the shepherd belonged, stopped by our camp. Shir
Ali was not there, but his wife, Sekine, acting as the host, killed and prepared

a chicken for Assadallah. Round and round the conversation went as Sekine attempted to gain assurances that he would put pressure on the shepherd, ensuring that he would work for Shir Ali. As Ahmad Sanjeri, one of the other disputants and another important Komachi, was much closer to Assadallah than Shir Ali was, Assadallah remained quite noncommittal. Later in the evening, as we all sat around her fire drinking tea, Sekine gave her pithy view of providing hospitality when she bitterly commented, "Well, that was the waste of a good chicken."

But people did not always react that way. When people came to visit Akbar seeking the hand of his sister, he killed the only animal he had on hand, a young female, to serve them the requisite meal. Later, when one of his neighbors, realizing what Akbar had done, protested that he would have provided a male animal instead, Akbar simply replied that it was unfortunate, but it was okay; one had to do what was right. And, clearly, it was a matter of doing what was right.

Although we were slow to catch on, we finally realized why the one question people—including us—were inevitably asked when they returned from visiting another camp was "What did they feed you?" When we were asked that question, the answer seemed especially important if the people were not close kin or close friends of Shir Ali or Sekine. That was certainly the case with Amon Ali, a relatively wealthy head of camp who was not a member of one of the tribe's central lineages and who, even more significantly, had close kin who worked as shepherds. As a sort of bridge between wealthy and poor Komachi, he occupied a vital but particularly ambiguous place in the Komachi social order. For reasons we never fully understood, Shir Ali seemed not to like him and often referred to him as "that Amon Ali." So it was not that surprising that after one visit to Amon Ali, when we told Shir Ali that we had been fed *ab gusht,* meat stew, Shir Ali slowly nodded and muttered, *"Adami shod"*— roughly, "He has become human."

Appropriate hospitality was important. Knowing exactly how to receive it was often tricky, and Ann and I did not always find it easy to understand its nuances. I stress that the nuances I am referring to were almost always those of receiving hospitality rather than giving it. Our few attempts to act as hosts were failures. Early in our stay with the Komachi, we served several people tea. The pained though polite expressions on their faces strongly suggested that we didn't quite have it right. Thereafter, if we invited people to have tea, we were almost dragged out of our tent and ushered to theirs. It is most embarrassing to be thought incapable of even preparing tea. But then, as I noted above, if we were friends and acquaintances, we were also guests, and we could never fully dislodge that status, even when we tried to be just like them.

For example, one of the most important parts of every *eizh* was the *fazl*, the presentation of gifts to the groom or the boys being circumcised. The young man or boys sat on a "throne" of bedding as other members of the tribe came forward to present them with gifts of cash. Each gift was announced, and the amount was recorded so that the recipient could later make the appropriate counterprestation.

We attended everyone's *eizh*, whether the host was a wealthy employer or a poor shepherd; having noticed that everyone who attended an *eizh* gave a gift, Ann and I always gave a present. We had debated between ourselves what the appropriate amount would be and decided to give every recipient, except for people we knew very well, the same gift.

Our decision elicited only one negative comment. Sekine, knowing that we would not be there to give our own *eizh* in the future, said, "Why are you giving gifts? You won't get anything in return."

However, since we attended, since we ate the food, we thought that giving a gift was the least we could do. Other than Sekine's one comment emphasizing the balance of the reciprocity, no one else expressed a concern until the end of our second year among the Komachi, when Hossein Fezallah got married.

We became involved in Hossein's marriage in a variety of ways. Fezallah, his father, was roughly seventy; he had worked as a shepherd for many years, and Hossein and his brothers worked as shepherds, too. Unlike most shepherds, Fezallah had lived long enough to see all his sons grow up, and since his sons had worked all that time, Fezallah and his sons were the wealthiest Komachi currently working as shepherds. And while Agha Hossein had probably been exaggerating a bit in winter quarters when he complained, "Fezallah has more lambs and kids than I do, and they can't help us with the milking" (the uncompensated labor that the wives and children of hired shepherds provided to the employers was an important but hidden economic contribution, and in this case Fezallah and his sons owned so many animals that the women in their tent had no time to help Agha Hossein's wife), Fezallah and his sons did own more animals than many Komachi who did not work as shepherds.

During the time we lived with the Komachi, several of Fezallah's sons had worked for our friend Agha Hossein, and indeed, Fezallah himself had, years and years ago, been one of Agha Hossein's father's shepherds. Agha Hossein's relationship with Fezallah was not just economic; he was his patron as well. Therefore Agha Hossein was deeply involved in the preparations for the wedding. In some ways, both economically and socially, he was the wedding's sponsor. He arranged for the musicians; he helped with the purchase of goods; he helped serve food at the celebration, and his wife and children assisted with the food preparation. Agha Hossein helped even though Fezallah was relatively rich. As an employer, as a truly wealthy Komachi, Agha Hossein had connections and access to credit that Fezallah could not match. To have a really good *eizh,* Fezallah needed Agha Hossein's assistance. Conversely, putting on a good *eizh* for his shepherd bolstered Agha Hossein's prestige and was likely to give him an edge against other employers when he needed to hire a shepherd.

Because Agha Hossein was involved, we became involved. Not deeply, but when Hossein was borne off to the sound of music to be bathed, shaved, re-clothed, and carried back to camp to receive his *fazl,* the transport used was my motorcycle, and I was one very nervous anthropologist as I attempted to drive slowly enough to let the musicians keep up but fast enough to make sure the motorcycle stayed up, so that Hossein's feet would not touch the ground.

Obviously, then, we attended Hossein's *eizh,* and we gave him a gift. Shortly after the three-day period of seclusion for Hossein and his bride was over, Ann and I began to hear rumors that Hossein felt he had to come visit us, that he was concerned because we had given him a gift. Shortly thereafter, Hossein showed up at our tent. Looking extraordinarily uncomfortable, he said that he thanked us for his gift, but that he was upset because he would not be able to give us a gift in return. At first, as I talked to him, I tried to take the tack that it did not matter: "We know that we will not have an *eizh* here," I said, "but that doesn't matter. We attended your *eizh,* we ate your food, we gave you a gift. It is what we wanted to do."

But Hossein still felt uncomfortable. I tried a different approach. "Don't worry," I said. "We may return someday with our children, and maybe we will have an *eizh.* Then you can give us a gift." That did not work either. We talked round and round. Finally, after much discussion, Hossein asked, "I know you sometimes take eggs when you give people a needle. What if I gave you a chicken? Would that be all right?"

Since all I cared about was letting him stop worrying, I told Hossein it was fine with me. Smiling and looking much happier, he took his leave.

A day or two later, Hossein returned, carrying with him a good-sized, very angry-looking rooster. We thanked him profusely, telling him again and again that he needn't have taken the trouble. He responded with all the appropriate conventions about how we had taken the trouble to give him a gift. He then departed, and we were left with the rooster.

Here Ann and I made a mistake. If we had been smart, we would have taken the rooster over to Sekine and said, "Here's a chicken. Why don't you cook it up when it is convenient, and we'll come over and join you for supper?" However, we were worried about insulting Hossein by seeming to slight his gift; we also thought that since this was our only chicken, we had an opportunity to prepare a chicken our way and eat a festive meal. So we asked Shir Ali to kill the rooster correctly. He did so, and we wound up with a dead rooster. We consulted a cookbook that had a section on preparing chickens, and, following directions, we first quickly scalded the bird so that we could pluck its feathers, and then set about cutting and cleaning it.

We had by then eaten a fair amount of chicken among the Komachi and other nomads, and certain things had become apparent to us. First, although I am sure there are vast differences between Frank Perdue's battery-raised birds and the rather expensive free-range chickens one can get at gourmet food stores, I suspect that there is just as large a difference between those birds and the chicken we got among the nomads. Komachi chickens were truly free-range, living on the grasshoppers, grubs, worms, scorpions, stale bread, and whatever else they could find around the nomads' tents. The birds were scavengers.

Early on, Ann and I also wondered why when we visited someone, we got the leg and thigh portion of a bird rather than the breast. Further examination revealed the answer. A life running around and scratching rather than sitting in an artificially lit cage apparently leads to a distribution of body weight rather different from what we were used to. Far from having large, meaty breasts, these semiferal birds had small, relatively meatless breasts. The meat was on the hind quarters. And though the chickens were generally tasty and always lean, they were also tough enough that ads for free-range chickens do not set my mouth to watering.

Given that, we thought the chicken might take a while to cook, so we put the meat in a pot to cook as soup. Alas, as the soup cooked, the smell that rose from the pot was not that of a delicious, delicate broth. It had a sharper, more acrid odor. We sniffed, told ourselves it was our imagination, and cooked on. As the smell continued, we became more concerned. We examined the rooster's entrails and determined that we had cleaned it properly; we had not spoiled the meat by getting bile or gall on it. Moreover, we had washed the bird several times before we cooked it. The horrible truth was that the meat itself smelled, and cooking did not reduce the taste. The broth, so eagerly anticipated, was awful. The meat was more than unpalatable—it was inedible.

Worried about how we could dispose of the chicken qua albatross, we decided to feed it to the village dog that had befriended us when it discovered that we would not throw stones at it and that we would occasionally feed it leftovers. Late at night, we stealthily passed the plate of meat out of our tent. To our horror, there was no joyful slurping or crunching of bones. The beast sniffed the bird, licked it once or twice, and turned away. We had truly cooked up the world's worst chicken.

To this day, I do not know quite what the problem was, whether the animal was awash in a surge of hormones pouring forth in anger and fear, or whether, as careful as we thought we were, we had done something wrong in cleaning it. All I know is that, thank goodness, in the small hours of the morning the village cats and other small creatures came and finally ate, or at least carried away, the chicken that Hossein had given us.

Though the bird itself came to an ignominious end, Hossein's gift of the chicken was intended to make certain that our gift to him was appropriately paid back, because as guests—as non-Komachi—the balance of reciprocity could not be tipped in our favor. Because we were guests (and probably also because they genuinely disliked our food), people politely rejected virtually every kind of food we might prepare. At best, they would take a small bite, perhaps mutter politely that it was a bit strange, and eat no more. Indeed, we had only three successes trying to provide food for others: popcorn, canned tuna fish, and fresh fruit.

One of the treats the Komachi prepared for themselves were fresh chickpeas. Peas in the pod were thrown into a shallow pan with a handful of salt and quickly roasted over an open flame. The peas were warm, salty, and very good. Of course, fresh chickpeas were available only for the briefest period in early summer, so most of the year there was no equivalent salty snack. Having had the peas ourselves and seen everyone else gobble them, we suspected that our neighbors would appreciate popcorn, and they did. Like the chickpeas, it was warm, salty, and had a good chewing texture. We could not, of course, serve it with melted butter (and did not have the stomach to try serving it with *roghan,* though the Komachi probably would have loved it), but that did not seem to bother people. They thought popcorn was wonderful, so whenever we could get some popping corn, we did.

There was also a government cannery in Bandar Abbas and at irregular intervals we were able to buy canned tuna in either Bandar Abbas or Kerman city. Often we could buy only limited amounts, but sometimes we were able to pick up more than a few cans. Most people's meals most of the time were either bread and fresh yogurt or bread and reconstituted dried whey. Supplemented with large numbers of calories from the sugar in their tea, this was the basic Komachi diet. On migration, even wealthier Komachi who often ate a more varied diet consumed lots of tea, bread, *kashk* (dried buttermilk), and yogurt. One day during migration, Ann and I, Qoli, Nesrat, and Agha Hossein had traveled a bit ahead of the loaded camels. Our friends pulled up some dried brush and began preparing tea. They also brought out some *tiri,* an unleavened bread that is, I am sure, the original version of matzah, and sat down to wait and eat. The bread, although it was fresh, chewy, and delicious, was nonetheless very plain, and since we had been able to get some cans of tuna in Bandar Abbas just before migration, I unpacked a few and asked if people would like some. I have never seen cans of tuna disappear so quickly. We all gobbled bits of the fish wrapped in bread, and we used the bread to sop up the oil from the cans. Those were the plainest tuna fish sandwiches that I have ever eaten, but in some ways they were among the best. Unfortunately, we ran out of tuna long before the migration was over.

It was at one of these stops during migration that we were given a most natural and very naked explanation of hospitality. It was a brutally hot day, and the road was hard. When we stopped for a rest and food, I was exhausted. What I really wanted was a shower and something cold to drink, nothing else. Our friends, however, brewed tea. I was sitting with my back against a small tree, getting as much shade as I could, when Qoli asked, "Tea, Daniel?"

The thought of the hot, sweet liquid practically made me sweat, so I answered no. But that was not the end of it. Qoli offered the tea again and again. And, since I did not want the tea, I refused again and again. As hot and tired as I was, I was slow on the uptake, but eventually I began to notice that he was upset.

"What is the matter?" I asked.

"You are refusing our tea," he said.

"Yes, I don't want any."

"You are making us uncomfortable," he said.

"Why?" I asked.

"Because if we offer someone tea and they refuse it, it is because they are angry with us. They are showing us that they are unhappy."

"Oh," I said. "Well, I'm not angry at all, and I certainly don't want you to be upset. I was just hot and tired and didn't think I wanted tea right now. But . . ." I learned my lesson and drank my tea.

Thinking back, I realized I'd witnessed something earlier that should have clued me in regarding this offer of tea. Five and a half months earlier, just before fall migration, when we had accompanied Shir Ali, Qoli, their families, and numerous other Komachi to Kerman to shop prior to migration, we had witnessed sizzling family quarrels, one between Qoli and Nesrat, the other between Shir Ali and his two school-age sons, Sohrab and Dorab. Nesrat, Sohrab, and Dorab (who all thought of themselves as the aggrieved parties in these disputes) each sat surrounded by others, refusing to eat or drink or to say much more than "I will not eat or drink." It had been apparent then that this withdrawal from hospitality and sociability had deeply upset those around them. I could now see how powerful the convention was.

This convention was not peculiar to the Komachi. Preparing this book, I found a passage in Bishop's writings in which she recounts how, after having used her medical skills to save a child's life, she could not accept an invitation to tea at the father's house. This upset the father greatly, for he felt she "must be enraged with him" (Bishop 1891, 1:310).

The only other gifts of food that we could successfully make were fresh fruit and vegetables. People loved them, but they were available only in towns, were expensive, and were not all regularly found in the market. In winter quarters, where several of the wealthier Komachi owned part shares in gardens, people had some access to oranges, lemons, and limes. They also planted watermelons as a cash crop, and toward the end of the season, the camp was nearly inundated by watermelon. At first, it was a treat and people gobbled it. By the end of the season even the children were no longer excited by it, and they ate more of the seeds than the flesh. In summer quarters fruit was both more and less available. Shirinak and the surrounding villages all had groves of apricot trees. Most were owned by landlords in Kerman city or from nearby towns, though some local people owned shares of the gardens. Still, the fruit was not sold locally, and we did not see people eating it. Instead, it was shipped to the towns or Kerman city, where the landowners sold or ate it.

Two occasions on which we had local fruit stand out in my mind. Once we were taken to a garden for a picnic. Our friends shook fresh apricots from the trees, and we ate as many as we wanted. They were extraordinarily sweet, the best apricots I have ever eaten. Interestingly, our Komachi friends ate the fruit, but they also cracked the pits for the almondlike center. They seemed to enjoy that more than the fruit itself. On the second occasion, we were taking a trip to Kerman City and decided to take the minibus from Qaryeitalarab. It had a semiregular schedule, and we used it as the means for getting into town. On this trip the driver was having trouble with the bus, and so it was delayed. Embarrassed at the delay, he invited us to his home for tea while we waited. While we were there, he presented us with several huge, perfect apples. We had never seen any like them in the local stores. When we asked him, he told us they came from the gardens at the edge of the town, owned by an absentee landlord. We had frequently driven by the gardens, but because they were surrounded by high mud-brick walls, we had never seen anything other than the very tops of the trees. The driver explained that he transported some of the fruit into town for the landlord, and that was how he got the apples.

Vegetables such as tomatoes and cucumbers, as well as herbs, were equally scarce. As a result, whenever we went into Kerman, or even into Qaryeitalarab, we would buy fruits and vegetables and distribute them in our camp, or take them to people in other camps if we had a visit planned. Although some Komachi men went to Kerman fairly frequently and Qaryeitalarab even more frequently, and although they would buy things in the bazaar for their wives and children, they did not seem to buy fruits and vegetables. The only man who I know bought them was Amon Ali, because once when we gave him a lift from Qaryeitalarab to Shirinak, he was carrying a large, rather sticky, leaking package of fruit that he had bought in the Kerman bazaar for his wife and children.

Accepting hospitality also had nuances that we did not always appreciate. When we visited people whom we saw irregularly because they lived some distance from the main body of the Komachi or were members of neighboring tribes, we were almost always fed a meat meal. Sometimes, particularly when we were traveling with other Komachi, this form of hospitality became frustrating. Our hosts would prepare a comfortable place for us and serve us tea; then, leaving us to sit in leisure like honored guests, our host and often the people we had traveled with would melt away. This might happen before or after we did some set-piece anthropology, such as doing a camp census and taking genealogies if we were visiting someplace new. Since we were often really more interested in hearing people talk—finding out why our friends wanted to make a trip to distant camps, hearing gossip about politics, marriage, or whatever—we did not want to sit by ourselves. If and when we started wandering about, people would become uncomfortable because they feared *we* were uncomfortable—which, of course, we were, but not in the way they thought. We would try to explain, but usually only time solved the problem. It was only after we had visited frequently enough that we could be "informal" guests.

One of the most difficult things about these situations was the fact that we knew our discomfort made others uncomfortable. That, certainly, was being a bad guest, and it was not something we wished. Sometimes, though, we just could not help it. We missed the signs. Once we visited Ahmad Shah Mirza. The second most important Komachi, he and his brothers lived at the very edge of Komachi summer quarters. Their winter quarters were miles and miles of very bad road away from where we camped, so although he was someone we enjoyed visiting and generally wanted to know better, we did not see as much of Ahmad and his family as we wished. Near the very end of our stay, we made arrangements to drive up and visit his camp and more or less say goodbye. We got there relatively early in the morning, talked the morning away, ate a meat meal for lunch, and stayed talking until midafternoon. Then, feeling the press of other things not done, we began, as politely as we could, to thank them for the meal and indicate that we would depart. Ahmad's wife began to urge us to remain, to stay the night. We had not expected that, and, feeling pressed for time, we refused as politely as we could. It very quickly became apparent that she was really upset. She turned to Ahmad and said, in effect, "We have served them a meal, they should stay."

"They are strangers, they don't really understand," we heard him say to her quietly, and then he swept us up into appropriate goodbyes. We left sadly, both because we felt we had messed up and because it was so rare to talk with someone who in practice recognized how little we knew.

15

MEDICINE AND RECIPROCITY

From the beginning of our stay with the Komachi, we entered into modest exchanges of goods and services with them. Early on, our greatest gift was transportation; we used our jeep to take people and goods here and there. We also received requests for medicines and medical treatment. While we were willing to hand out the odd aspirin tablet to whoever requested it, and were equally willing to give Khanom, Shir Ali's widowed sister, as much masking tape as she wanted to tape her wrists and elbows while she worked, Ann and I resisted the idea of playing doctor. We had some limited medical supplies and a first-aid book, but we had neither the material nor the knowledge to supply medical care. Thus initially, if a request came, we were much more likely to volunteer to drive the patient to a clinic than to intervene more directly. However, in this area, as in many others, our intentions were subverted by circumstance.

TAJ ALI, OR I BECOME A DOCTOR

Shir Ali was a wealthy man, owning over eight hundred sheep and goats. Still, when early in our stay in the lowlands one of his ewes fell sick, he made a great effort to save its life. Culled from the herd, it was kept near the tents and given special rations. Often, in a joke that played on his own ambivalence, Shir Ali would look at the animal longingly and say, "I'm hungry. Maybe it will become really sick, perhaps it will get ready to die. Then we can eat meat." Shir Ali's reluctance to abandon this ewe to its fate drove home to us the degree to which the Komachi valued animals as capital.

But day by day the ewe got scrawnier and uglier; patches of hair fell out, and it developed a kind of mange as it slowly wasted away. One day, attracted by the sound of loud bleating, I went out one day and saw Shir Ali standing over the ewe. He had a syringe in one hand and a vial of veterinary tetracycline in the other and, having wrestled the ewe down, was trying to give it a shot. I went over and held the ewe steady while Shir Ali filled the syringe. Then he plunged the needle in at the ewe's knee. There was no flesh for the needle to penetrate, and when Shir Ali let go of its leg, the animal kicked and the tetracycline (which was visible as a kind of blister under the thin skin) shot back out the needle hole. Shir Ali was frustrated; unable to control myself, I laughed out loud.

Not surprisingly, Shir Ali challenged me, "Do you think you can do it better?"

I had never injected anyone or anything with a hypodermic needle. Still, I felt I couldn't do any worse than Shir Ali. I knew that a knee was a poor location to give a shot. I wasn't particularly concerned about the ewe's feelings, and I thought it might be interesting to try, to experience the particular and peculiar kind of opportunity fieldwork provides to do something one never gets to do at home. So I filled the syringe, stuck the needle in the ewe's thigh, and pushed the plunger. The tetracycline went in and the animal protested mightily, but when we let her up, the medicine stayed in. I felt rather proud of myself but affected a kind of "aw shucks" modesty as we went off to have tea in Shir Ali's tent. I was soon to pay for my vanity.

At about the same time that Shir Ali and I were giving his ewe the injection, a group of Komachi men set off to buy wheat in the Hamum Jazmurian, a swampy lowland area about sixty or seventy miles from our camps around Jaghin and Manujan. Since they planned to pack the grain out on camelback, one of the men who went along was Taj Ali, the camel herder from our camp. He was the only member of our camp to go.

In his early to mid-fifties, Taj Ali was an interesting man. Like many of the poorer tribesmen who worked for other men, Taj Ali was not a "native" Komachi. His long-deceased father had been an itinerant mullah who came to the tribe to teach the sons of wealthier men the rudiments of reading and Islam. The mullah must have been a good teacher, for one thing that surprised us was the degree of literacy we found in the tribe. Shir Ali, one of the mullah's students, could read and write, and so could several of his contemporaries. Ironically, Taj Ali, the mullah's son, was illiterate. Having been left little by his father, he had worked for years as a camel herder, slowly building a herd of goats. He had married late; indeed, he had married his brother's widow, and now took care of her, her children, and his own widowed mother. Years of herding camels had baked Taj Ali into a thin, leathery fellow. As did many older Komachi, he hennaed his gray hair, and with his lean face, large melancholy eyes, hangdog expression, and bright orange temples, Taj Ali occasionally bore a striking resemblance to Emmett Kelly in costume. We came to like Taj Ali and his family a great deal.

The group of men who went off to the Hamum Jazmurian were, predominantly but not exclusively, poorer men. They had heard that wheat prices were particularly low in the Hamum Jazmurian. Since they could travel with camels, they felt this was a good chance to buy needed grain cheaply. The men were gone for several weeks, long enough to excite some comment and concern.

Shortly after his return, we were called to Taj Ali's tent. He was sick, running a high fever, which within the Persian system of medical humors was diagnosed as a "cold" fever (rather than a "hot" one). We found Taj Ali lying on the floor of his tent, wrapped in the skin of a freshly slaughtered goat, looking awful. In strident and agitated tones, Hajji, his wife, told us that many of the travelers had gotten sick and that Taj Ali felt that he was likely to die. Clearly there was only one thing to do. Taj Ali was bundled into the back of our jeep and, with other men from our camp showing the way, we set out for the town of Rudan and the nearest clinic.

Rudan was about twenty miles away over one of the worst roads in the area. The route had once been graded, but neglect, abuse, and flood had turned it into washboard all the way. There were, we had learned, basically three ways to drive these roads. One could drive them very, very slowly, grinding along at five miles an hour in low gear. Doing that meant that it took forever to get anywhere, and so it wasn't a viable choice for a trip of any length. A second choice was to drive at moderate speed. For some reason, doing this ensured that you got the maximum jolt out of every bump, and made the trip an agonizing endurance contest that neither we nor our jeep seemed likely to survive. The third choice was to grab the wheel tightly, put the pedal down, and attempt to skip along on the tops of the bumps. This provided the illusion of smoothing out the road. It made the trip more comfortable for the driver and the passengers, but the constant small vibration rattled loose everything on the car that could rattle loose, stressed the metal, and generally tore the car apart. All the drivers we had met drove this way, and so did we.

The trip was horrid: the roads worse than expected, the jouncing almost unbearable. Nonetheless, we arrived at Rudan more or less in one piece, and we found the clinic. After much, much waiting, much ringing of the bell, and much talking, protesting, cajoling, and pleading when someone did appear at the gate, we finally got Taj Ali in to see the doctor. He examined Taj Ali, confirmed that he had a high fever, gave him a massive dose of penicillin, and said that he should get additional shots of penicillin twice a day for the next five days.

Getting Taj Ali to the clinic each of the five following days posed a problem. There wasn't anyplace in Rudan for Taj Ali to stay; Rudan wasn't a place the Komachi frequented, and neither Taj Ali nor any of the men who accompanied us knew anyone there. It did not seem reasonable to follow one of the aide's suggestions, which was to leave Taj Ali to sleep outside the clinic walls. It also seemed likely that driving the round trip every day would destroy the jeep, if not Taj Ali.

The conversation kept coming back to the shots, and the doctor finally said, "Isn't there anyone who can give him shots?" I didn't know, so I said nothing. One of my companions answered, "Yes, there is." The doctor thereupon gave us ampules of distilled water and dry penicillin, and off we went.

As we were driving home I began asking myself who would give the shots. I thought that perhaps Reza, who had been trained as the tribe's veterinary assistant, would do it. The more I thought, the more I assumed that, since doctors were always scarce, some people must just have learned to give others shots.

Next morning when Arab, Taj Ali's daughter, came to get me, was I surprised to learn that the person who could give shots was *me*. "I don't know anything about giving shots," I protested. But we had syringes, people pointed out. Yes, I allowed, we did have syringes, in case we were stopped at a roadblock for cholera shots, but I had never given a shot. I was reminded that I had given a shot to the ewe, and it had survived. I could therefore give a shot to Taj Ali.

I did not want to give Taj Ali his shot. I did not at all equate him with a dumb, mangy ewe that I'd rather hoped would die anyway, and I was not convinced that my vast experience qualified me to practice medicine. To be honest, I was scared. I was afraid that I would make a mistake, that I would hurt (or worse, kill) Taj Ali, and I did not like at all the idea of sticking a needle through someone else's skin. On the other hand, I recognized that if I gave the shots, the needles would at least be sterile and that, with some care, I could probably be certain that I was not injecting Taj Ali full of air bubbles. In short, there seemed no one more qualified; Taj Ali needed the shots; and people expected me to do it. With much trepidation, and without much skill, I managed to mix the water and the penicillin. I can also report that Taj Ali's buttocks, if they were not literally callused from years of sitting on the ground, were like leather. His skin was far tougher than the sheep's.

I sat with him for a while after his first injection, to make sure he was all right, and as we talked Taj Ali showed me his tent furnishings. Unlike Shir Ali, he had only one carpet, and it was a thin one; he also had only one glass for tea. His supply of sugar, which he got from his employer, Shir Ali, as part of his shepherd's wage, was the cheap caramelized variety, not the crystalline white kind consumed by wealthier Komachi.

Twice a day for the next few days, I went to Taj Ali's tent and gave him his shots. He didn't die from my ministrations, and he ultimately recovered. To this day, I do not know what he had, although the skin on his palms and the soles of his feet blistered and scaled off. Since it happened to all the other men who got sick, too, I assume this was typical of the disease.

My going out of my way for Taj Ali—giving him his shots, helping him— paid great benefits for Ann and me. It seemed to show that we were not just the friends and guests of wealthy and powerful Komachi such as Shir Ali, but were interested in them all. That they might have assumed we would be uninterested in helping those who were poor or powerless was, I think, a significant reflection on the nature of their world and their social experience. Our unwitting action helped break down this potential barrier and made our work much richer and fuller. Several times we visited other camps with Arab as our guide. With her we met and spoke with poorer Komachi, often her kin, in ways that would have been impossible had we been traveling with a member of a wealthier family.

Alas, my helping Taj Ali had one other side effect. It was now absolutely, certifiably clear that I could successfully give people injections. There was now someone in the tribe who could give medicine, and it was me. Given this un- deniable ability, I gave many injections, not all with the same easy results I achieved with Taj Ali.

I GIVE ALI A SHOT

Toward the middle of our second summer in Shirinak, Ann and I moved into the empty school building. It had a single large room, and by shifting around the benches and tables, we were able to make ourselves comfortable. Shir Ali's compound was immediately next door, so, of course, we often spent time there.

Shir Ali and his family seemed to know everyone in the mountainous sum- mer quarters valley. They knew the nomads, they knew the smaller landlords, and they knew the peasants. One of the peasants who came round frequently was Ali, a younger man who lived in the neighboring village, Sarzeh, about half a mile down the valley, and who had fairly extensive business dealings with Shir Ali. We got to know him—not well, as we were frantically trying to tie up all the loose ends of things we still wanted to know about the tribe, but we knew who he was and where he lived, and occasionally we listened in on his conversations with Shir Ali and Sekine.

Although they talked of many things, including crops and prices, one subject dominated these conversations: Ali's health. His leg hurt. It ached, it throbbed, there were shooting pains. It made it hard for him to work, standing up to the middle of his thighs in the cold mud of an irrigated field; it made it hard for him to walk.

We did not find Ali's complaints unusual. Even before I gave Taj Ali his shots, people had listed for us their aches and pains. Since then, there had been a constant slow stream of people coming to our tent, holding out vials and ampules of medicine and telling us of their medical problems. Thus we had come to know very well that people ached and hurt and that when people hurt they let everyone know about it. There were other reasons Ali's complaints seemed natural. We had seen him and other peasants at work. Although tractors now did the main plowing in both Shirinak and Sarzeh, the rest of the work was done by hand. The fields were flooded with water coming from bitterly cold mountain streams. Ali and the other peasants, sunk in above their knees in the cold, muddy soil, prepared the field with heavy, awkward hoes. The toll on legs and lower back must have been brutal.

Thus I was not at all surprised when one day Ali announced that he had been to the clinic in Qaryeitalarab, where he had been prescribed medicine, and asked me if I would please give him his injections. I told him that I would, and we made a date for him to come back later.

Ann and I had long since discovered that not only could we walk into a pharmacy and simply ask for any drugs we wanted, without prescriptions, but most medicines came packaged with a little brochure in English listing all the particulars about the drug: indications, contraindications, side effects, test results, and so on. This, I might add, was often very interesting reading. It was so interesting and seemed so important that I started insisting that people bring me the literature along with the medicine. Ali did. His medicine was phenylbutylzoladine, and as I read the package insert I became more and more disturbed. It was immediately clear that this was an extremely powerful medication with quite devastating potential side effects. It was also potentially dangerous to administer. Unlike penicillin or some of the other drugs that had been prescribed to people for immediate relief of simple symptoms, this was really strong stuff. It was not at all the sort of thing that I should be shooting into someone in a small village in the middle of nowhere. Moreover, I was pretty certain that in any case this wasn't the kind of medicine that a not-quite-real doctor should have been prescribing for rural patients to have administered God knew how far from real medical attention.

So, when I got through reading the literature that came with the phenylbutylzoladine, I told Ali that I did not think I could give him the shots. I told him that the medicine was dangerous; that I thought it could hurt him; that if I gave it to him the wrong way, I might hurt him. Ali was upset. Ali was insistent. He didn't care; he would take the risk. Round and round we went. I really did not want to give him the shots, and he really wanted them.

As we argued on, several things became clearer. First, Ali assured me that he had been given a shot of phenylbutylzoladine at the doctor's office and that he had had no reaction to it. Second, it became apparent that the argument that the medicine might do him long-term damage was a nonstarter. He was in pain, and because he was sure the medicine would help, he wanted the shot. Third, I found out that Ali had paid a pretty penny for the medication. He believed that he would not be able to get his money back, and so he was determined to get his money's worth. Fourth and finally, it was clear that he believed all of the above so strongly that he was determined to find someone to give him the shots—if not me, then someone else.

Faced with this barrage of argument, afraid that if I (who could read the directions) did not give him the medicine, he would get his shot from someone else (who could not), I relented, though with deep and unremitting misgivings.[1] The directions called for injecting the medicine very slowly and intramuscularly, and so with Ali standing, I plunged the needle into his buttock and very, very slowly injected the phenylbutylzoladine. Ali stood still for the injection; then, as I finished and withdrew the needle, he began to collapse. In front of my horror-stricken eyes he went white under his deep tan. The effect was to turn him a sickly yellow; his eyes rolled, and he began to simultaneously stagger over to the door and collapse to the floor. As I grabbed him I felt all the thousands of fractured shards of first aid I had ever learned go whirling about my brain. I wondered if he should be placed head up or head down, and whether I should cover him; I tried to recall what the contraindications and cautions were; and I wondered what the penalty for killing a peasant with a hypodermic was likely to be. Ann flew next door and called for Sekine, who came running. Seeing Ali collapsed, she grabbed a large pail of water standing next to the well in the yard. Before I could say or do anything, she threw it full in Ali's face. Whether because of the water or simply because of having his head down, Ali began to recover. Ann and I stood anxiously around, ready to minister to whatever need he expressed.

Not Sekine! Standing with her hands on her hips, she lit into him. "Look at how you scared Mr. Daniel and Mrs. Ann. Get up, get out of here. You're not sick. Go on; don't trouble people who are trying to help you."

Faced with this tirade, Ali staggered to his feet. Ann and I were aghast, but Ali dragged himself off to Sekine's. Assuring us that he was all right, he drank several cups of strong tea and left for home.

Ann and I spent the afternoon in a state of near collapse. Back at Sekine's later that afternoon, however, we were treated to Sekine's account of our adventure as, with tears of laughter rolling down her face, she told Shir Ali how we and Ali had looked, and what she had told him.

The next day Ali returned. He brought a half dozen eggs wrapped in a handkerchief as thanks for our trouble. Assuring us that he was fine and that the medicine was working, he brought out the next ampule and asked if I could give him his next shot.

LAYARD'S ACCOUNT

As I reread the travel literature, I was surprised to find that it was filled with discussions of travelers giving medical care, and I was struck by the many parallels between their accounts and mine. In an extended discussion of his curing the son of Mohammed Taqi Khan, at that time perhaps the most powerful of the Bakhtiyari leaders, Henry Layard describes a situation that shares similarities with both my account of how curing Taj Ali helped us establish rapport and my account of the dire consequences I feared when Ali collapsed.

> My reputation as a Frank physician had preceded me, and I had scarcely arrived at the castle when I was surrounded by men and women asking for medicines. They were principally suffering from intermittent fevers, which prevail in all parts of the mountains during the autumn. Shortly afterwards the chief's principal wife sent to ask me to see her son, who, I was told, was dangerously ill, and I was taken to a large booth built of boughs of trees, in which she was living. . . . The lady sat unveiled in a corner, watching over her child, a boy of ten years of age, and about her stood several young women, her attendants. . . . As I entered she rose to meet me, and I was at once captivated by her sweet and kindly expression. She welcomed me in the name of her husband to Kala Tul, and then described to me how her son had been ill for some time from fever, and how the two noted physicians whom I had seen in the lamerdoun had been sent for from a great distance to prescribe for him, but had failed to effect a cure. She entreated me, with tears, to save the boy, as he was her eldest son, and greatly beloved by his father. I found the child in a very weak state from a severe attack of intermittent fever. I had suffered so much myself during my wanderings from this malady that I had acquired some experience in its treatment. I promised the mother some medicine and told her how it was to be administered. Returning to the castle I sent her some doses of quinine; but before giving them to the child she thought it expedient to consult the two physicians who had been summoned to Kala Tul. Fearing that if their patient passed into my hands they would lose the presents they expected, they advised that it would be dangerous to try my remedies. Their opinion was confirmed by a mulla, who,

upon all such important occasions, was employed to consult the Koran in the usual way by opening the leaves at random. The oracle was unfavourable, and my medicine was put aside. . . . The condition of the boy, however, became so alarming that his father was sent for. Soon afterwards Mehemet Taki Khan arrived at the castle. . . . He had scarcely entered the enderun of the castle, to which his wife had removed, than he sent for me. I found him sobbing and in deep distress. His wife and her women were making that mournful wail which denotes that some great misfortune has happened or is impending. The child was believed to be at the point of death. The father appealed to me in heart rending terms, offering me gifts of horses and anything I might desire if only I would save the life of his son. The skilful physicians, he said, for whom he had sent, had now declared that they could do nothing more for the boy, and his only hope was me.

I could not resist Mehemet Taki Khan's entreaties, and after reminding him that the medicines I had already prescribed had not been given, I consented to do all in my power to save the child's life, on condition that the native doctors were not allowed to interfere. Although he was willing to agree to all I required, he could not, as a good Musulman, allow the boy to take my remedies until the mulla, who resided in the castle and acted as secretary and chaplain to the chief, could consult the Koran and his beads. The omen was favourable, and I was authorised to administer my medicines, but they were to be mixed with water which had served to wash off from the cup a text from the Koran—a ceremony upon which the mulla insisted.

The child was in a high fever, which I hoped might yield to Dover's powder and quinine.[2] I administered a dose of the former at once, and prepared to pass the night in watching its effect. I was naturally in great anxiety as to the result. If the boy recovered I had every reason to hope that I should secure the gratitude of his father, and be able to carry out my plan of visiting the ruins and monuments which were said to exist in the Bakhtiyari Mountains. . . . If, on the other hand, he were to die, his death would be laid at my door, and the consequences might prove very serious, as I should be accused by my rivals . . . of having poisoned the child. About midnight, to my great relief, he broke out into a violent perspiration, which all the remedies hitherto given him had failed to produce. On the following day he was better, I began to administer the quinine, and in a short time he was pronounced out of danger, and on the way to recovery. (Layard 1841, 1:368–78)

In the Bakhtiyari hills in 1841, the value of Western medicine was not yet clear. By the 1890s, when Bishop traveled through the same region, she was constantly besieged by requests to provide medical care.

We camped outside the village [of Chahar Mahal, primary estate of the *ilkhani,* the state-appointed supreme chief of the Bakhtiyari confederation]. . . . The servants are in the habit of calling me the *Hakim,* and the report of a Frank *Hakim* having arrived soon brought a crowd of sick people, who were introduced and their ailments described by a blue horseman, one of the escort. His own child was so dangerously ill of pneumonia that I went to his house, put on a mustard poultice, and administered some Dover's powder. . . . It was in vain that I explained to them that I am not a doctor, scarcely even a nurse. The fame of Burroughes and Wellcome's medicine chest has spread far and wide and they think its possessor *must* be a *Hakim.* (Bishop 1891, 1:309–10).

Elsewhere she writes, "Sick people come all day long and the medicine chest is in hourly requisition. . . . The fame of the 'tabloids' has been widely spread" (Bishop 1891, 1:336). Later, in yet another camp, she notes, "When I opened the tent I found the crowd seated in rows five deep, waiting for medicines, chiefly eye-lotion, quinine and cough medicine" (Bishop 1891, 1:357).

While the Komachi did not sit in rows five deep outside our tent to wait for Dover's powder, they made considerable efforts to gain access to Western medicine, and quite consciously used us as the vehicle for its delivery. We, for our part, were sometimes willing, sometimes quite unwilling participants in this process. Like Layard and Bishop, we found that providing access to medicine, through transportation or injection, was a way of building rapport. At the beginning, it also seemed to us that providing access to medicine helped establish a kind of reciprocity, a way of repaying people for the bother we caused by asking them countless foolish questions, and for the meals we ate, which their canons of hospitality required them to prepare for us.

But here we learned our calculus was wrong. As guests, we really could not pay back hospitality—that was outside the bounds of exchange. Thus, driving people to the clinic or giving someone an injection did not balance the equation *help with health care = hospitality and information;* rather, it created a new and unbalanced equation, *help with health care = x,* the latter an unknown that had to be appropriately provided. Our protestations that we did not want or need anything for our services were not happily received. Local entrepreneurs charged for transportation, and when health care workers came to camps to provide medical care, they charged very high fees. Ultimately, people hit on a successful compromise; they realized that we valued fresh eggs (which permitted us to occasionally make treats for ourselves ranging from sunny-side-up to fresh mayonnaise and things that could be made with it). So, to balance our contribution, they gave and we accepted eggs. They always apologized for the fact that their eggs were not an adequate compensation for the trouble they had caused us, though the conventions of politeness would have dictated saying that regardless of their feelings. Our feelings were equally complex, for while we were delighted to get the eggs, we also wished we could figure a way to come out even in our calculations. Fortunately, one thing did seem to work out exactly as we hoped, in that giving shots and helping people reach the clinic did help establish rapport. In addition, it allowed us to see aspects of Komachi life and relations to the outside world that we otherwise might have missed.

One of the things we came to learn was not particularly pleasant: the peculiar distribution of Western medicine. I have already described how by the time of Bishop's travels Western medicines were highly valued even in remote corners of Iran. In this, Iranians' responses to Western drugs seem typical of the pattern for their role when they are introduced into societies lacking modern medicines, namely that Western medicines are "one of the most effective tools of Euro-expansionism . . . one of Europe's points of leverage—with the Islamic world in particular, whose rulers often summoned European physicians to tend them" (Pratt 1992, 83).

What Ann and I found disturbing was not the flow of Western medicine into rural Iran. It was clear that drugs, particularly antibiotics, saved lives. However, it often seemed to us that relatively minor complaints were being treated with extremely powerful drugs. People suffered from chronic aches and pains associated with long, hard physical labor. I have described how phenylbutylzoladine was prescribed for Ali's complaints. Others, generally women and shepherds, came to me bringing bottles of other powerful medicines, including cortisone, that seemed casually prescribed for aching shoulders or knees. What we saw seemed a massive effort to dump—there seems no other word for it— huge quantities of powerful, potent medications into an area in which they could not be reasonably or safely administered. Even though it was quite apparent that there was great local demand for drugs that promised quick relief of people's symptoms and that demand drove some of the use of medicine, we felt queasy about our participation in the process and even more queasy about the process itself.

Providing people some access to medicine not only let us see what kind of medical care they were getting and some of the problems attendant on it, it also let us understand some aspects of the social construction of sickness and disease among the Komachi. For example, we became aware of differences in the way people used medical care. We noted that women and shepherds, who were poorer working men, came to us far more frequently than wealthy men. We also noted that the vast majority of their complaints were not fevers, coughs, or other acute conditions, but rather chronic problems such as aching legs, sore shoulders, or painful wrists. At one level, this seemed natural. Most wealthy men did very little physical labor, and it was not surprising that the work entailed in clambering up and down mountainsides following a herd of sheep or goats, or sloshing a churn filled with sour milk back and forth for hours until butter formed, or the hours of weaving spent tamping the weft of tent panels or woven bags generated more complaints of muscular aches and pains than did sitting around a fire talking about prices over endless cups of tea. But we saw more than that.

We saw that whenever people passed a clinic, most conspicuously during migration but at other times as well, women poured out to use its services. The pattern we observed was strikingly like the one Sheil described for the mid-nineteenth century: women using a trip to the doctor as a social occasion.

> April.—My residence here has thoroughly dissipated my English ideas of the seclusion and servitude in which Persian women are supposed to live. . . . Whenever I pass the door of the physician to the Mission . . . the doctor's door and house are crowded with women, of all ages and of all ranks, from princesses downwards, who come to him to recount their ailments. It seems their applications for succour are often founded on most frivolous motives; gossip rather than physic being frequently their object. Sometimes, on the other hand, they seem to think all the diseases of Pandora's box are concentrated in their persons, when in reality they are perfectly well, but still insist on being treated. (Sheil 1856, 212–13)

During spring migration we were struck when, in response to their blandishments, we took women from our camp to the clinic and found that it was filled with Komachi women who had not seen each other for the months their camps had been separated in winter quarters. In one view, the women visited the clinic primarily for medical treatment; alternatively, one might argue that the need for medical care was secondary, and that it was an excuse that sanctioned the women's taking time out from the work of migration and provided a legitimate time and place to meet. Looked at in this fashion, Sheil's point that women "insist on being treated" even though they are "perfectly well" takes on a new light. Her discussion makes it sound as though this desire for medical care was whimsical, but the comparable claim for medical care by Komachi women seems to have been something else—an undeniable claim of the right to go to a clinic during migration, which, given the always crowded conditions at the clinic, promised them a legitimate way to meet and talk over the events of the winter.

Sheil is right to say that "in extenuation of the freedom allowed to themselves by Persian women in their medical visits . . . a physician is a privileged person in Persia" (Sheil 1856, 213). What she missed, but what our Komachi experience showed, was that women fastened on the position of privilege as a means of legitimating both a desire for rest and a desire for social interaction that was most commonly the province of wealthy men. Women's and shepherds' claims of aches and pains not only provided the occasional opportunity for seeing others like themselves at clinics, but also were effective weapons in regulating the amount of labor that could be drawn from them by those with some legitimate or semilegitimate claim to that labor. In the final analysis, women and poor men constantly put forward the claim "I hurt" because it ultimately legitimated one of the few weapons they could effectively command in their struggle to protect themselves against socially sanctioned demands for their labor. The fact that at certain points in time and space women proclaimed the need to get medical treatment and that women and poor men constantly complained of the kinds of aches and pains that (might) make work impossible provided insights into the workings of gender and class relations among the Komachi.

The process of our noting the ways that gender and class shaped people's claims of health and sickness involved both an accumulation of small, virtually inconspicuous events and two striking events that crystallized and foregrounded them. The constant demands for medical attention, ranging from Khanom's daily requests for tape and liniment to periodic requests to give people injections of medicine received from clinics or doctors, were largely inconspicuous events. Ali's collapse foregrounded the problem of the kinds of drugs people were receiving. The renegotiation of Mohammed Darvish's shepherding contract with Shir Ali crystallized our realization of who was coming for medical attention and why. I have described Mohammed's negotiations in detail elsewhere (see Bradburd 1990, 117–18). One striking feature of them was that Mohammed spent more time discussing the pain in his leg and the degree to which it did or did not interfere with his work than in negotiating salary or other demands. This jarred us into recalling his previous complaints, and then considering who had and had not complained, and what they had complained about. Seen in the context of Mohammed's case, the broader pattern of claims of illness jumped out. It is not quite so clear, however, that the pattern would have been visible if we had not been deeply, if unintentionally, involved in the process.

Thus, helping provide medical care not only helped us build rapport, acquire eggs, and learn more about our place in the Komachi scheme of things, it also helped reveal the nature of their relations with the world of modernizing Iran even as it provided an additional lens through which we could examine key relations within Komachi society. I came to learn a great deal from giving a single shot to a sick ewe.

Chapter

16

FARYAB

In late October and early November, the tribe migrated by truck from summer quarters in and around Shirinak to winter quarters near the towns of Manujan and Jaghin, near the southern border of Kerman province. When we arrived in the lowland winter quarters, we discovered that it was much harder to get gasoline there than in Shirinak. Often the local state-franchised dealer had no gasoline, so we had to scrounge around looking for black-market dealers who sold gas at an inflated price. Sometimes even these dealers didn't have gas. We adapted to this as best we could. Whenever we drove into Bandar Abbas, we filled the back of the jeep with twenty-liter jerricans even though they were heavy, hard to carry, and leaked if they weren't packed perfectly as we bounced on washboard roads. By doing this, we were able to build up a small store of gas.

The shortage of gasoline meant that we could not travel between camps as much as we wished, and since winter camps were much farther apart than those in Shirinak, we did not visit as widely as we had hoped. Nonetheless, we got around some. In mid-November, about three weeks after we arrived in winter quarters, we made it to Shiri Khabar's camp. In his early thirties, Shiri was the elder brother of our neighbor Qoli. He was young, energetic, and intelligent. Also, most unusually for a wealthy herd owner, he had married a shepherd's daughter. In any event, we liked Shiri, his wife, Malike, and many of the other people in his camp. So when, after driving to Manujan to see the locations of other lowlands camps, we got an invitation to come visit, we readily agreed.

Shortly after we arrived, one reason for the invitation became apparent. Shiri and Malike's youngest son was sick, and so was Malike's brother's child; people hoped that we would transport them to a doctor.

Getting medical care was a serious problem for the Komachi. Although several people had motorcycles, including Shiri, that was clearly not the best way to transport sick children to a clinic. Moreover, the nearest government clinic was in Rudan, which was an even longer drive from Manujan than it was from our camp. Having driven it once with Taj Ali, I did not look forward to driving there again.

"No problem," we were assured. "There is a doctor at Sarras, and you can take the children there." Sarras was the local headquarters for the Mohlavi construction company, a joint venture with Kampsax (a large Danish construction firm, which had the concession for road building in southern Iran). Sarras was a huge encampment. The road crews lived and worked there. There were barracks, mess halls, a huge machine shop for maintaining the road equipment, offices for the engineers, and more. The site covered acres and must have been home to several hundred men. It also had its own doctor.

We were assured that we could easily drive to Sarras; that the doctor—for a steep fee—would see the children; and that we would be back in a few hours.

By now, we had been in Iran over a year. We did not believe that it would be easy; we did not believe that it would take only two hours. I am not even sure we believed that the doctor would be there. Piling Malike, two of her children, her brother Hossein, his wife, and their child in the jeep, we set off to Sarras. When we got there, I was not surprised to find that the doctor was not in, that he had gone to Bandar Abbas, or Shiraz, or Isfahan, or Tehran, and would not be back in any amount of time that we could wait. I do remember being annoyed, in fact very annoyed, at Shiri and the others who had assured us the doctor would be in, even as I acknowledged to myself that they could not have known and I should not be angered at the outcome.

We were upset at being inconvenienced, but the children were really sick. So as we returned to Shiri's camp, stopping to let Malike visit some Baluch women along the way, we quietly cursed the world in general and the doctor in particular (in English) and asked each other what we should do.

Shiri was not in camp when we returned, but later, discussing what to do, he announced, "I am certain that there will be a doctor at Faryab."

"What and where is Faryab?" we asked.

After much discussion, we realized that Faryab was the chromite mine we had heard about. Shiri and Hossein, who was to be our guide, assured us that the mine was not too far and that the roads were good. Resigned to our fate, believing the trip would be neither short nor easy, we set out. It did not take us long to realize that our fears were justified. The road was washboard, its bumps jarring our teeth and rattling the very frame of the car to pieces. The road went on and on and up and up. Dust seeped in through every one of the hundred holes, rips, and spaces in the jeep's canvas; somehow, no fresh air came with it, and the jeep was not only dusty but stuffy and brutally hot. After a number of repeated assurances that the mine was just ahead, Ann and I settled into a game to ward off despair. We started fantasizing about what we wanted: a cool shower, an ice cream soda, an air conditioner, but mostly cold beer. The longer we drove on the seemingly interminable trip to a place we hardly believed we would find, the more fixed in my vision that beer became. Like the proverbial cartoon character crawling through the desert led on by the ever-just-out-of-reach vision of a pool of clear, cold water, I drove on imagining a tall, frosty glass of beer.

Ultimately, we came to a gate across the road. We had arrived at the mine. After a great deal of conversation with the guard, most of it entailing Hossein's describing our impressive credentials—which must have been immediately contradicted by our sweaty, dust-coated appearance—we passed through the gate and drove farther down the road. The mine itself was a great hole in the mountain off in the middle distance. But before we got to the mine, the road passed through a most extraordinary place, a kind of Oz in the desert. The mine had been developed by the British, and the houses of the engineers and senior staff, plus the mess and recreation hall for the senior staff, were wonderful British bungalows, each surrounded by a neat white fence, green lawn, and beds of flowers. As we poured out of the jeep, a pair of Iranians, alerted by a phone call from the gate, came up to greet us. They announced that the doctor was busy, that he couldn't see people now, but he would later. One of them led our friends away toward what we later discovered was the clinic. The other politely ushered Ann and me toward what I would have to call a club room cum mess hall. As we entered that building, still marveling at its architecture and the wonder of it all, we were greeted by an Iranian engineer. He wore blue jeans, a broad leather belt, and a wonderfully clean and pressed cotton shirt. His smile was broad, he spoke very nice, British-accented English, and as he led us into the room, chatting politely and telling us where we could go to freshen up, he turned to us and said, "You look hot. I bet what you could use right now would be a nice cold beer." Sometimes one must assume that there is a god who looks after fools.

Our friends did get to see the doctor, who injected their children with all kinds of antibiotics. Later the doctor showed us his enormous collection of huge, loathsome black scorpions, packed in jars of alcohol; he spoke with feeling of the difficulties of living in a place so far from everywhere. We washed our hands and faces with hot and cold running water; we drank very cold, very refreshing beers, which we had along with some lovely iced melons. It is not a combination I had ever had before, nor is it one I have had since, but I can say for certain that it was the best hot-weather snack I have ever had. We spent part of the afternoon speaking with the engineers, who were, like virtually every Iranian we met, warm and hospitable. They told us about the mine and what it was like to work there; they filled our gas tank to the brim at the company pump; and as they bid us farewell, they urged us to come back to see the mine and them. I deeply regret never returning to see the mine itself.

The journey home, downhill and into a cooling dusk, seemed much shorter and smoother than the trip out. It might have been the time of day; it might have been that we knew where we were going and what we would find when we got there. But I think the trip back was short because the day was magical. It was certainly one of the very few days I can remember, in Iran or elsewhere, where, against all odds and expectations, I got what I really wanted.

At the same time, our trip to Faryab helped sharpen our understanding of Komachi relations with nontribal Iranians, even as it brought into relief the incredible cultural discontinuities of Iran in the oil boom.

Over and over we were struck by the degree to which the Komachi and groups like them were marginalized by settled Iranian society. The clinic that should have been open was not; the doctor or physician's assistant who should have been supplying medical care to an isolated, rural population had found the isolation too much and taken off for the city, leaving the people without access to medical care. But, as James Scott has noted, though they may be poor and powerless, people do not acquiesce to their mistreatment. With access to the legitimate clinic blocked, the Komachi, and I am sure others like them, sought alternative access to the treatment they desired. If clinics serving the rural poor were not manned, clinics at mines were constantly staffed to serve the foreign or foreign-trained, highly skilled, not politically impotent professionals, and the Komachi would attempt to use those clinics. Indeed, they would use us to use them.

But even when they managed to gain access to the mine and ultimately to the doctor, their access and ours differed. We were swept off to be engaged and entertained. The engineers and doctor welcomed our visit—at the very least we were a kind of *divertissement,* and the invitation to return seemed sincere. The Komachi were set aside—literally sitting beside the clinic—while we were entertained. Our friends had to wait until the doctor was ready to see them. To the staff of the mine, we, as foreigners, were exotic and interesting. Our tribal friends, exotic and interesting to us, were to the mine staff merely backward. At the mine we were asked, as we were nearly every time we met an urban Iranian in the countryside or described to Iranians in a city what we were doing, "How can you stand it out here? It is so dull, there are no movies or restaurants. There is nothing to do. Don't you get terribly bored?"

To the urban Iranians we met, the countryside was a place one visited. It was quaint, one could get good clarified butter there, and there were generally people whose hospitality could be imposed upon.[1] But they considered the charms of the countryside, and particularly those of the rural population, limited.

At the same time, if the rapidly modernizing world was at best indifferent to them, the Komachi approached it as an environment that could be mined for things they valued. If state plans for environmental controls and cooperative herding groups seemed to threaten pastoralism, the physical plant and institutions of modernization could be cautiously manipulated to Komachi ends. Using traditional methods of building links with external benefactors through exchanges and favors, the Komachi attempted to create the same kinds of ties with doctors, mine and road engineers, and government technocrats that they had formerly made with local landlords and merchants in the bazaar. While their ability to turn these new external relations into effective assets seemed limited, it is hard to see the expenditure of effort, energy, and resources as a mistake; it was a calculated attempt to create islands of potential security within a hostile and indifferent external world and to build tiny beachheads through which, cautiously, the goods and services of the modern world could be appropriated.

I would stress that *cautiously* is a key word in my description of Komachi dealings with the outside world. The Komachi were fully aware of most settled Iranians' attitudes towards them. As a result, they generally avoided unmediated interaction with people they did not know, as the story of Qoli's trunk illustrates.

QOLI'S TRUNK

A few weeks earlier, we had been preparing for the fall migration, and pandemonium reigned. Unlike spring migration, for which the Komachi packed their households goods onto their own camels, fall migration proceeded in rented trucks and buses, for the camels had long since returned to winter quarters. As our camp was nearly the last to leave summer quarters, we had for days watched as large Mercedes-Benz trucks pulled into Shirinak or Giborj. There, all the possessions of a camp were jammed on board. All the trucks were overloaded. To call them filled to the top is to understate the case. At the front and rear ends of a truck, heaps of black goat-hair tent panels rose far above the wooden sides of the truck. These piles were in turn topped by rolls of reed tent siding, domed baskets of chickens, and everything else. The distribution of the material into high peaks at each end of the truck was deliberate; it created a well in the middle into which men, women, and children climbed just before the truck set off. With these illegally oversized loads, the trucks often made the migration on back roads, moving along a path that paralleled the migration route for camels rather than the highway we took in our jeep.

Finally our camp's truck appeared. The drivers, who were the owner and his cousin, were pleasant young men from Shiraz. They were themselves settled Basseri tribesmen who had bought a truck on credit and were attempting to make a living both by hauling other people's cargo from place to place and by buying, shipping, and selling goods on their own. Since I had become fascinated with the nature of this combined trucking/small-scale merchant capital industry, and since they were interested in the two Persian-speaking foreigners they unexpectedly found in the middle of nowhere, I spent a pleasant two hours chatting with them while the truck was being loaded. During the conversation, they gave us their phone number and address in Shiraz, and urged us to visit should we pass through the city.

Ann and I had planned to leave early, traveling on the highway directly to Bandar Abbas, then cutting over east to Jaghin, where Shir Ali would pitch his winter camp. We planned to take along Shir Ali, Sekine, their two married daughters, Nesrat and Esmat, and their three youngest daughters. To make room for them, our belongings were packed on the truck. Meanwhile, the truck was to travel from Shirinak to Lalehzar, where it would pick up Agha Hossein and the members of his camp, and then take whatever route the drivers chose to reach Jaghin.

Much to our chagrin, we did not leave early, and it turned out that Shir Ali needed, or at least wanted, to go to Lalehzar. Ann, who hoped to get mail in Bandar Abbas, was furious and showed it, so we were both crowded and tense as we set out. Moreover, though we did not know it then, other problems were developing that would ultimately involve Qoli and us.

Qoli was an active, intelligent young man. Like Shir Ali, who was his father's brother's son as well as his father-in-law, Qoli came from one of the central, wealthy herd-owning families in the tribe. Unlike most men (especially the older ones) from these families, who attempted to build their herds as their source of wealth, Qoli was taking a somewhat different tack. Married for three years when we met him, he had sold off some of the flock he had inherited, keeping just over one hundred head. One hundred animals was not a small herd; it produced a yield that easily supported a household consisting of only Qoli and his wife. But while other men might have spent time supervising the care of their animals or otherwise working to build their herd, Qoli was attempting to get rich through wheeling and dealing, buying cheap and selling dear. For days and weeks on end, Qoli would be off on his motorcycle, buying animals in out-of-the-way places, arranging their transport to Kerman city, trying to make money on the difference in price between the town and the country. He and his partners did the same with lowlands produce, attempting to buy dates, watermelons, cucumbers, and tomatoes in the extreme south of the province and ship them to Kerman city in the north. The goal of this activity was to make a quick killing, to find a difference in price big enough to come out ahead, but the game itself had a fascination. Qoli and his friends tried to use their mobility to get an edge on the market in every transaction. Sometimes they succeeded, but frequently the people they were buying from or selling to were richer, more powerful, had better information, or otherwise controlled the market. Often the financial reward for a great deal of time, effort, and maneuvering was tiny; not infrequently the partners shared a loss. As we mulled over Qoli's involvement in these deals, we began to get the feeling that he tried too hard to give himself an edge in every situation. That certainly seemed to be the case in the affair of Qoli's trunk.

As I noted above, Ann and I, Shir Ali, Sekine, and their five daughters migrated in our jeep, driving down the highway to reach Bandar Abbas. Unfortunately the trip provided the opportunity for another of our automotive disasters, so we reached winter quarters well after the unloaded truck had set off for its next destination. Even for nomads, moving was always somewhat dislocating, and the scene at our first winter camp was hectic. It was brutally hot; those members of the camp who had set off weeks earlier with the animals were nowhere in sight; Qoli and several other young men had gone ahead of the truck to see what deals they could make. But the worst was that as soon as we arrived, Nesrat became frantic. She could not find Qoli's small metal chest.

As nomads, the Komachi traveled light compared with most settled people. However, they had some valuable possessions. To protect them from both damage and theft, many Komachi kept their valuables in small metal chests that could be locked—not real strongboxes, because they weren't particularly strong. Nesrat could not find Qoli's chest, and she was beside herself. It contained some jewelry and a small amount of money, but it also contained their marriage certificate, their identity cards, and some other papers. She looked high and low. All the piles of all the goods from everyone's tents were gone through. It was nowhere to be found. Almost at once, suspicion turned to the truck drivers. But, of course, they were gone.

When Qoli himself finally arrived, part of the mystery was solved. Because the trunk was valuable, and because he had wanted to protect it, Qoli had not packed it with all the other things in the body of the truck. Instead he had placed it in the bin built over the truck's cab, where the driver's belongings and tools for the truck were kept. Too clever by half, Qoli had hidden his trunk to protect it, but he had then gone off to wheel and deal without telling anyone what he had done. Since no one had known that the trunk was someplace special, no one had looked for it. Now the truck and the trunk were gone.

As soon as Ann and I understood the problem, we stepped forward with what we assumed was the solution: the truck driver's name and address. We thought that one day soon, Qoli, either alone or with someone, would get on his motorcycle, or a bus or a truck, and head for Shiraz. There he would look up the truck's owner and pick up his trunk, and the problem would be solved. That did not happen. Although there was a good deal of discussion, complaint, and grousing about the missing trunk, nothing seemed to happen. No trip was planned, no action was taken. As far as I could tell, the most concrete action Qoli or any other Komachi undertook was to visit the trucking depot in Kerman to ask its boss to keep a lookout for the truck and driver. Whenever Ann and I raised the subject of the trunk, we were given a list of excuses why it was not the right time, or not otherwise possible, to go to Shiraz. What surprised us most was that Qoli, who spent so much of his time dashing around Kerman cutting deals, seemed so uncomfortable at the thought of traveling to Shiraz.

Months later, during a lull in activity, Ann and I planned to travel to Shiraz to visit Anne Betteridge, who was then doing fieldwork there. No sooner had we announced our intention than Qoli came visiting us, reminding us of his trunk. We received additional reminders from his wife and mother-in-law. In Shiraz, the address and phone number proved more than adequate. We contacted the driver, and we were able to pick up the trunk with no difficulty. At his house, we were told how very upset they had been to find the trunk, and they assured us, "The trunk was safe here. It would have been safe for one hundred years." We told them that we knew that was true, and we thanked them profusely. When we returned to the tribe, we returned the trunk. True to the driver's word, it was secure and unopened.

Qoli was one of the young men in the tribe who were aggressively attempting to take advantage of Iran's modernization. He owned a motorcycle, traveled widely through the region trying to arrange deals, and had a vast network of friends and acquaintances, *ashna* and *refiq,* whom he used to identify and arrange his deals. He was apparently one of the most sophisticated members of the tribe. Faced with a situation in which he had to deal with strangers in the absence of known mediators, however, he was virtually paralyzed. While a modernizing Iran was a resource the Komachi sought to exploit, their accumulated experience suggested it was filled with people who were at best indifferent to and often contemptuous of them. Nontribal Iran was a world to be approached cautiously, generally through known mediators.

AGHA HOSSEIN AND THE CIGARETTE SCANDAL

Agha Hossein was one of the Komachi we came to know best. He was another of Shir Ali's first cousins, like Qoli a father's brother's son. His younger brother was married to Shir Ali's sister. In winter quarters, his camp was closest to ours; during migration, he and his brother traveled along with Shir Ali and our camp. In addition, one of his sisters was married to Sekine's brother Asghar. Given that knot of ties, we came to see quite a bit of him. In an odd way, we saw even more of him than we otherwise might. Because Agha Hossein's summer quarters camp was just outside the village of Lalehzar, about twenty miles farther west in the valley, he would often spend a good deal of time at Shir Ali's or at Asghar's when he came to Shirinak. As a result, we probably saw him more often than we would have if he had camped in the vicinity.

Although he was not as well-off as Shir Ali, Agha Hossein was among the wealthiest Komachi. Still, in his relationship with Shir Ali, he was clearly the junior partner, turning to Shir Ali for advice.

Agha Hossein said he camped near Lalehzar, far away from other Komachi, because he needed more pasture for his large herd of sheep than he could find in the eastern end of the valley. But if the advantage of Lalehzar was open pasture, the disadvantage was isolation, and Agha Hossein paid for that isolation.

Early one morning, Shir Ali came to our tent and asked me if I would drive him to Lalehzar. He had just opened a carton of cigarettes that Agha Hossein had given him, and he had discovered that Agha Hossein had been swindled.

When we arrived at Agha Hossein's tent, I quickly discovered what the trouble was. In Iran at that time, all cigarette prices were nominally controlled. American cigarettes, which were considered much better than the various brands of Iranian cigarettes, were also much more expensive. These assumptions of quality, which may or may not have had a legitimate base, were so salient to the Komachi that at an *eizh,* guests of different ranks got different kinds of cigarettes: Wealthy and important men got Winstons or Marlboros, less important men were given some of the better kinds of Iranian cigarettes, and shepherds got the cheapest Iranian smokes.

Given this, when a traveling peddler came to his camp selling cartons of Winstons at a cut-rate price, Agha Hossein had jumped at the chance. As in all swindles, the con artist took advantage of the victim's greed. And, as a con game, the deal seemed rather clever. The peddler told Agha Hossein that the cigarettes he was selling had been smuggled in from the Persian Gulf, so he could sell them really cheaply. He could indeed sell them cheaply, but not because they were smuggled. As Agha Hossein told the tale, the man had opened a cellophane-wrapped carton and shaken out several packs of Winstons to show his wares. Perhaps he had done this with more than one carton; I don't recall. Unfortunately for Agha Hossein, well after the peddler had gone, he had shaken the carton to get another pack of cigarettes, only to discover as the packs tumbled out that just the first two or three in each carton were Winstons—the rest of the carton was filled with the cheapest Iranian cigarettes. All the cartons of "Winstons" had the same composition. Instead of buying Winstons very cheaply, Agha Hossein had bought the cheapest Iranian cigarettes very dearly.

Shir Ali and Agha Hossein discussed what could be done. Agha Hossein had already gone to the gendarmes, and they said they would look for the peddler. Shir Ali said that he would tell everyone in our end of the valley, and if the peddler came there, he would certainly be caught.

Then, after examining the cartons and the packs of cigarettes minutely, Shir Ali declared that he would never have been tricked. Holding up the packs of cigarettes, he showed that the cheap Iranian brand was slightly shorter than the pack of Winstons. Sliding all of them back in the carton and closing it, with the Winstons near the open end, he shook the carton.

"Listen," he said. "The shorter cigarettes don't fill the carton as tightly as the Winstons. They rattle around." And it was true that by listening carefully, we could discern a slight rattle as the shorter cigarette packs shifted within the carton. After ascertaining that we could hear the difference, Shir Ali boldly proclaimed, "If the peddler had tried to trick me, I would have heard the cheap cigarettes rattling in the carton, and I never would have bought them. He wouldn't have fooled me." This was, I thought, rather cold comfort for Agha Hossein.

In a different way, Shir Ali's claim reminded me of our experience with an American friend in Bandar Abbas. Whenever we saw him, he invariably served us the reddest, ripest, juiciest, most delicious watermelon. Having never had more than random luck ourselves, we finally broke down and asked him what was the trick of selecting such perfect melons.

"It's easy," he answered. "You just listen for the sound of a ripe one."

"Oh," Ann asked, "do you thump it?"

"No," he answered, "you listen for the juiciness." And when we asked him how he did that, he showed us. He picked up the whole watermelon, held it to his ear, and, closing fingers the size of bananas around it, squeezed and released the melon. He held it up to our ears, and I could hear the *schlllllsshhhhh* of the juice as he relaxed the pressure. I could see that it would be an infallible technique. Unfortunately, it also seemed a limited one. I have fairly large and strong hands; I can palm a basketball. But I can't use his technique, because I can't get enough compression on the melon. The only way I can find out what's inside is to open it. I suppose Shir Ali might have been able to shake a carton of cigarettes and tell from the sound and feel whether it was correctly filled or not. In any event, the only solace Shir Ali gave Agha Hossein was his description of how he would not have been fooled, and after eating a meal, we returned to Shirinak.

While his greed certainly played a role in the matter, Agha Hossein's isolation was also largely responsible for his being swindled. It would have been far harder for the peddler to play this trick in a more populated area, where many Komachi would have been around to examine the peddler's wares and question him. Agha Hossein's isolation cost him in other ways as well. Like many of the wealthier men in the tribe, Agha Hossein bought a motorcycle. Made in the Soviet Union, these were large, heavy machines that were excellent for traveling the dirt roads and tracks of Kerman province. Although they were recent acquisitions—no Komachi had owned one for more than three years—several of the younger Komachi had become very skilled at servicing them. I saw one group of young men pull the piston, change the rings, and put the engine back together again—this with relatively simple tools in a mountain valley with no garage for miles. Agha Hossein was a recent buyer, having purchased his motorcycle the summer we arrived. Unfortunately for him, his son, who drove the motorcycle, was not yet among the mechanically skilled. Thus one day when the motorcycle battery ran down, they turned for advice to a man in Lalehzar, who told them they could charge the battery by filling it with motor oil.

According to Agha Hossein, the resulting explosion was rather spectacular. Fortunately, neither he nor his son was seriously burned, and the only lasting harm was the cost of replacing the totally destroyed battery. Again, when Agha Hossein told the story, his audience's response was less than completely sympathetic. While many expressed anger toward the purveyor of malicious advice, others also boldly asserted that they would never have put oil in a battery. Rather, as they instructed Agha Hossein over and over, "The only thing you put in a battery is distilled water. The battery has acid in it; that is what caused the explosion." And while Agha Hossein strongly defended his son, arguing that he was just a young man and that, living in the country, he did not know anything about motorcycles or machines, I think in this case the members of his audience were more correct in asserting that this was advice they would not have taken, and had Agha Hossein been living among other Komachi, he probably would have found his way to one of these mechanically savvy young men.

Nonetheless, both cases show why the Komachi approached the outside world with caution. Whenever Ann and I asked ourselves why Qoli did not simply rush off to Shiraz, or others asked us why Komachi shepherds did not leave the isolation of the tribe to try to earn higher salaries working out of the area, we would recall how the nomads had been treated at Faryab, and the story of Agha Hossein's cigarettes.

Chapter

17

TRAVELING WITH THE KOMACHI

Whenever we entered a new area for any time, we reported our presence to the nearest gendarme post. Early on in our stay, we had introduced ourselves at the regional gendarmerie in Kerman city, and thereafter any local post we arrived at could refer back to a filed message sent out by headquarters. Our appearance was never a total surprise, and most of the time it also excited virtually no interest.

Shortly after we arrived in winter quarters we drove from Shir Ali's camp in Jaghin over to Manujan, about fifteen miles, to introduce ourselves to the gendarmes there. What was most striking about that meeting was not the way the post commander, a young lieutenant, treated us—which was a combination of the usual urban Iranian's shock that anyone would voluntarily choose to live in the middle of nowhere, coupled with very modest interest in our being in his district—but a conversation we overheard in the post.

The lieutenant was talking with a local about a dispute, and he was telling him to return the next morning, using the standard Persian word for "tomorrow," *farda*. Then he paused and went on, "I mean *sobh farda*, not *pas farda*, understand?"

The lieutenant came in to see me still muttering about *sobh* and *farda*, and I had to laugh. While *farda* might be standard Persian for "tomorrow," all Komachi used *sobh*, standard Persian for "early morning," to mean "tomorrow," and *farda*, "tomorrow," to mean "the day after tomorrow." We found it confusing; the lieutenant clearly found it annoying. Judging from his admonition, people had played a *sobh/farda* shuffle on him more than once, and he had caught on.

Based on past experience, I had assumed that my one brief but pleasant visit to the gendarme post in Manujan would take care of my dealings with official-dom in the area. I was wrong. One day a gendarme truck pulled up in front of Shir Ali's tent. Shortly thereafter, Ann and I were called over. When we got there, we found a gendarme whom we had met several times before. In the past, his conversations had always focused on how we were doing and whether we had any problems. Indeed, he had seemed less concerned with what we were actually doing than with how people were treating us. We were uncertain whether that was because part of his brief was to make sure that the resident foreigners weren't being damaged in some way or other, or whether he was worried that something might happen on his watch and he was just checking to make sure we were alive and not doing anything particularly stupid; either way his visits had seemed to present no problem.

This time, however, there was a problem. It was true that we had registered with the gendarmes in Manujan. But Manujan was in Kerman province, whereas Jaghin was in the coastal province whose capital was Bandar Abbas. Therefore, the gendarme said, the district chief (roughly the equivalent of a county executive) in Rudan wanted to see us and find out what we were doing.

I had no desire to drive to Rudan. It was roughly halfway to Bandar Abbas, but it was the bad half. I had taken Taj Ali to the clinic there when he was sick, and all I could think of were the incredible ruts, which had nearly rattled the jeep apart on the way. Moreover, aside from the district chief's office and the clinic, there was nothing I wanted to do or see in Rudan. However, when the gendarme mentioned Rudan and the district chief, Shir Ali perked up and said that he would go, too.

When the gendarme left, I learned that Shir Ali had another motive: obtaining grazing permits. In summer quarters, he had grazing permits, theoretically guaranteeing him the right to graze his animals on open range, which, by law, was government land. Neither Shir Ali nor any other Komachi had equivalent permits or guaranteed rights for pasture in their winter quarters, and he very much wanted them. Shir Ali apparently felt that approaching the district chief would be a good way to begin his quest for the permits, hence his desire to make the trip.

Since I took the request to speak to the district chief as a command and Shir Ali really wanted to see him, we planned to go to Rudan as soon as possible.

Our jeep really didn't seat more than two people in comfort, so Ann and I decided that she would stay behind while Shir Ali and I went to Rudan. My drive there was everything I had remembered and—with the passage of time, some winter rain, and more traffic on the roads—worse. We arrived in Rudan early in the afternoon, tired, dusty, and well shaken. I was also angry, for early afternoon was not a good time to arrive at any Iranian office. As in much of the Mediterranean world, offices opened early, remained open until about noon, and then, in theory, reopened in the late afternoon and early evening. Whether or not they would reopen, offices were punctilious about their afternoon closing. Arriving in early afternoon always meant a long wait, and if the office did not reopen, a fruitless one. Knowing that, I had intended to leave camp early in the morning so I could be certain of finding the office open. Shir Ali, however, had other things to do, and so we did not get away from camp until a morning arrival in Rudan was impossible.

As I expected, when we arrived in Rudan, the district chief's office was closed, and so was the town. The streets were deserted; since we knew no one in town, and since nothing was open, Shir Ali and I simply sat and waited. We talked a bit, but unlike his wife, Sekine, Shir Ali had little interest in answering questions or telling stories. Conversation was desultory. At one point, some scraps of newspaper blew across the dirt and got caught up against the jeep. For nearly an hour, Shir Ali read bits of the news; I tried to nap.

At about four o'clock I decided to try the district chief's office. It remained tightly shut and looked deserted. However, a local passing by said he thought the chief might be in, so I went around the building, found a gate with a doorbell, and rang it over and over again. Just as I was about to give up, the gate swung open.

When we finally met the district chief, I didn't know whether to feel sorrier for him or for myself. As he came into the room yawning and buttoning his trousers over his *shalvar,* it was apparent that we had awakened him from his afternoon nap. It also rapidly became apparent that if he had ever wanted to see me to find out what I was doing in his district, he certainly didn't want to see me that afternoon. He gave the various documents I had brought with me, primarily a research permit from the Ministry of Education and Culture, a most cursory glance while he and I drank tea and thanked each other for the courtesy of the visit and the reception.

During this interchange, Shir Ali sat silently by, being treated as though he were not really there. He was not, for example, offered tea, and remembering the circuslike effect I had generated in Manujan by deferring to Shir Ali while my nontribal host deferred to me, this time I did not pass him the tea served me. However, when Shir Ali judged that my business was done he sat up very straight, rocked back on his heels, and, holding his hat on his lap in a clear posture of supplication, launched into his request for a grazing permit. The chief listened for a few moments with obvious impatience and boredom and then, uncharacteristically for an Iranian, dismissed Shir Ali by saying, "I can't do anything about that."

Our audience was over. We returned to the jeep and bounced our way back to Jaghin. There, in the village, we stopped a few times. First Shir Ali visited with an *ashna,* an acquaintance, one of the many non-Komachi with whom Shir Ali, like most wealthy Komachi, had cultivated a mutually advantageous relationship. Then we stopped at some of the village stores, where Shir Ali priced goods to buy and sell. Finally, quite late, we returned to camp, where I wrote down my closing thought on the day: *"When you travel with the Komachi, you travel like the Komachi."*

My note to myself meant many things. One, certainly, was that over time I had come to feel that whatever I expected to be a simple, straightforward endeavor—a trip with a goal—would, in the company of the Komachi, become an extended operation. A trip to here invariably entailed a trip to there as well, generally with a long wait somewhere. I have already recounted how our visit to Shiri's camp turned into an expedition to Sarras and ultimately Faryab, and I have noted how, to our surprise, the start of fall migration took us to Lalehzar before we started to Bandar Abbas. Perhaps the most striking instance of being hung up like this occurred when we all waited for Abbas Tavakoli.

This encounter began on October 15, when we went to Kerman with Shir Ali and almost all of his family, planning to spend a brief time in town. They were taking care of their final financial arrangements and making their last purchases before the migration to winter quarters; we were doing more or less the same. We truly hoped the trip would be short, because we wanted to watch the other camps setting off on their migration. Still, we began with no great expectation that the trip would be as short as we wanted. We knew that Id Fetr, the holy day marking the end of Ramadan, was two days away, and if we were still in Kerman then, we would be further delayed. Since so many from Shir Ali's family were going, we decided to take the minibus from Qaryeitalarab rather than drive all the way into Kerman overloaded with people and goods.

When we arrived in Kerman, we discovered that almost everyone else in the tribe was also there, doing their last-minute shopping, and that an incredible number of things were going on. In some ways, the days we ultimately spent in Kerman were among the most intense and event-filled of our time among the Komachi. That was just as well, because there were plenty of them.

On our first evening in town, Shir Ali told me that he had met Abbas Tavakoli, and without asking us had made an arrangement for us to drive Abbas Tavakoli (in his car) to his country house in Lalehzar the next day. I was not thrilled, but told him I would be happy to do so. I had met Abbas Tavakoli several times before, and I found him interesting. He was one of Shir Ali's most important economic patrons, and just then Shir Ali was trying to get him to buy notes and postdated checks from the various butchers and merchants to whom

Shir Ali had sold goods. I had seen Abbas Tavakoli attempting to mediate a dispute over who had rights to (illegally collected) wild licorice roots; I had watched him attempt to help Shir Ali negotiate a marriage between his son and Ma'adi's daughter; I had seen his most impressive old country home in the village of Lalehzar. I knew he was important to Shir Ali and the Komachi, and so I felt that the more I learned about him, the more I would learn about them. Driving him to his country home seemed an excellent way to accomplish this.

Alas, for some reason we could not set out as planned on the sixteenth. The next day was Id Fetr, and we were still in Kerman. The morning of October 18, after Id Fetr, Shir Ali and I went to Abbas Tavakoli's house, expecting to find him there ready to leave. He wasn't there, and through a scratchy intercom, we had a short, garbled, and very unsatisfactory discussion with a disembodied female voice who suggested that we come back the next morning. Angered, and upset by the thought of not seeing other camps leave for winter quarters, I told Shir Ali that next morning Ann and I were leaving, with Abbas Tavakoli or without him.

Late in the afternoon of the eighteenth, Shir Ali returned to the rooms in which we were all staying, telling me that he had met Abbas Tavakoli in the bazaar and that we were invited to his house that evening to arrange the trip. We went. After much tea and polite conversation, I heard Shir Ali and Abbas Tavakoli discussing going to Lalehzar "*farda*." As I noted earlier, *farda* was used ambiguously in Kerman; sometimes, as in standard Persian, it meant "tomorrow," and sometimes it meant "the day after tomorrow." It was only when all the plans had been proposed, formalized, and finished that I thought to ask which *farda* they meant. Sure enough, it was the day after, the twentieth. While I attempted to gather my thoughts and words to effectively protest, Shir Ali and Abbas Tavakoli finished their business, and the twentieth it was.

We made it through the nineteenth, watching and listening as three or four different small dramas unfolded in the crowded rooms. That night, people began to pack, getting ready to leave, and they urged us to be ready to go early the next morning. "Fine," we answered, "because if Abbas Tavakoli is not ready, we are getting on the bus first thing and we will be gone." The morning of October 20 came, and there was no Abbas Tavakoli—and no bus. Ann and I then began making earnest plans to go back on the afternoon bus. Later in the day Shir Ali came back and said he had again seen Abbas Tavakoli and had arranged for us to leave that evening, after the bus would have departed. At that point, seeing the possibility of even more delay, I finally blew up, saying, "No, not now; not ever!" Shir Ali seemed surprised. That afternoon Ann and I left on the world's most overloaded minibus. Everyone who had been in town was on it, and they all had everything they had bought. It did not seem likely that the bus would be able to move. Fortunately, it did, and on the night of the twentieth we were back in Shirinak.

Accounts of similar delays are found in most of the early travelers. Bishop, for example, writes of a time among the Bakhtiyari when,

> having accepted an invitation from the Ilbegi to visit him at Naghun . . . we were ready at seven, the hour appointed, as the day promised to be very hot. Eight o'clock came, nine o'clock, half-past nine, and on sending to see if the young Khans were coming, the servants replied that they had "no orders to wake them." So we Europeans broiled three hours in the sun at the pleasure of "barbarians"! (Bishop 1891, 1:330)

Layard records a far, far longer delay.

> Although Shefi'a Khan assured me that he was about to leave Isfahan at once, the days passed by without any sign of his departure. I was continually going to and fro to the caravanserai. . . . He always had some excuse ready to explain the delay in his departure. . . . As my patience was now almost exhausted by these delays, I applied to the Matamet to allow me to proceed to the mountains. . . . But he now alleged that the condition of the Bakhtiyari tribes was such that I could not travel amongst them. . . . There was nothing to be done but resign myself to this detention, which lasted for nearly five weeks. . . .
>
> On September 22 Shefi'a Khan sent to tell me that everything was ready for his departure . . . and that he intended to leave Isfahan that very evening for the mountains. . . . He proposed that I should meet him at sunset in the garden of the ruined palace of Heft-Desht, near the Shiraz bridge. I was there by the appointed time. Instead of finding, as I expected, the Khan and his companions ready to start, I saw that they had evidently settled down for the night. . . . Shefi'a Khan apologised for the delay, throwing the blame for it on an officer of the Matamet. . . . There was nothing to be done but to picket my horse, and to spread my carpet as near to it as possible. (Layard 1841, 1:323–25, 336)

Even at this remove in time, I am conscious that there is an edge to my account of the frustrations, delays, and inconveniences of traveling with the Komachi. I am also aware that this tone is the very cooled-down aftereffect of what I felt as the events were unfolding, when, I fear, I would have sounded far more like Bishop than like Layard. At the time I wrote it, a large portion of my note, *"When you travel with the Komachi, you travel like the Komachi,"* reflected frustration. That frustration was not, I think, simply a response to a lack of punctuality. It was much more frustration over losing autonomous control of my time, of being unable to do what I wanted when I wanted. The irony, of course, is that my frustration arose from being treated, through the Komachi, like the Komachi. By traveling with them, I came to be treated as they were treated by the larger Iranian society, which held them up, delayed them, incon-

venienced them, and promised them one thing after another with little or no regard for their needs or concerns. Their response to this, as I have suggested
above, was to develop a pattern of passive decision making that centered on
doing something when it was possible, not when it was best for them. Traveling with them, being forced to make my decisions the same way, brought me
to the boiling point. If I have read the earlier travelers accurately, similar types
of events had the same effect on them. The anger that I, Isabella Bishop, or
Henry Layard felt at the delays suggests that being middle-class (or in Layard's
case, something better) in Western society entails an expectation that we will
be treated with dignity and our wants and needs taken care of. Traveling with
the Komachi taught me that those expectations are not universal. My anger
then was sorely misdirected.

Chapter

18

TANHO

Sometimes a single unexpected or striking event called our attention to an aspect of Komachi life, but there were also fundamental elements of Komachi life that, by their very constancy, were almost unmarked. To borrow the image of the growth of a coral reef that James Scott develops in *Weapons of the Weak,* here anthropological awareness emerges not as the result of a single event but from the slow accretion of many otherwise unremarkable events. Komachi feelings about people being alone fall into this category.

In the beginning, we clearly missed important markers indicating how the Komachi felt about being alone, though looking back, they were there. In truth, I think we first noticed their concern over people being alone with regard to ourselves. It emerged in several ways. During conversations with the Komachi, from nearly our first day with them until the last, one topic that came up over and over again was the degree to which we were heartsick, *deltang,* because we missed our families, and our parents in particular. At one point I thought that this was just a form of making conversation—sort of, "What can we talk about with the foreigners? I know, how lonely they must be." It was usually followed by a heartfelt recommendation to have children.

But in whatever guise, the concern with social isolation was there. For example, Ann soon noticed that whenever I went away, leaving her behind in camp, Sekine either invited her into their tent or sent one of her daughters to keep Ann company. As the pattern with Ann became clear, other things we hadn't really noticed or understood fell into place.

Qoli was deeply involved in countless economic deals. As a result, he was often out of camp for days at a time, and occasionally weeks on end, leaving his wife, Nesrat, who was Shir Ali and Sekine's daughter, alone. And just as frequently as he went out of camp, one of Nesrat's younger sisters was sent next door. When we first joined Shir Ali's camp, Nesrat had just had a miscarriage, losing her first child. If we noticed the visiting pattern, and I am not sure we did, we would have assumed that this was an attempt to keep Nesrat cheerful and otherwise help with her recovery. After Ann had been on the receiving end of enough visits, the reason for Sekine's sending other daughters to visit Nesrat—who, like Ann, was in a tent no more than twenty yards away—became more apparent.

Once we became somewhat attuned to notions of loneliness and concerns with being alone, we noticed that it appeared as a theme. When the Komachi described people in an awful state, one phrase that we heard over and over was "*tanho, gharib, bi-kess*" (alone, a stranger, without anyone), a condition that seemed their nightmare. On one hand, the scourge of loneliness was illustrated by the frequent discussions Komachi had with us in which we were urged to have children or in which our condition, alone and away from our families, was noted as "not good." On the other hand, the problem of loneliness and isolation was also revealed in accounts of the virtue of togetherness.

Probably the most striking and unexpected example of the value placed on togetherness came during our second spring migration. It rained for several days, and we spent much time huddled in one tent or another, trying to keep warm and dry. Sitting by the fire on one of those days, Sekine idly noted, "Mullah died here."

"Who?" we asked.

"Mullah, Taj Ali's father." We grunted "hunh" to indicate that we understood, and Sekine continued her story.

"They were on migration and Mullah became sick, and he knew that he was going to die. When he knew that, he asked for his children. His wife and those who were living with him gathered around him. All his family was there, except Taj Ali, who was away with the camels. So he was sent for. Meanwhile everyone was around Mullah as he lay there."

Sekine's eyes nearly shone as she described this, drawing pictures with her hands to sharpen the image of the old man surrounded by all his family, slowly slipping away.

"Finally, when it was clear that Taj Ali would not be able to come in time, Shir Ali came and said Mullah's name. 'Taj Ali?' Mullah asked, thinking that his son had come. 'Yes,' Shir Ali said. And then Mullah died happy."

Sekine's story about Mullah's death illustrates the importance that the Komachi placed on people being together in times of need or crisis. But this story merely exemplifies a vital feature of Komachi life: a truly powerful sense of living with each other. In ritualized form, the community was proclaimed in the assertions "We are all one" and "There are no strangers here." In practice, this being part of something was enacted through people's taking care that other members of the community were not isolated. Being alone was bad, because being in the community was not just living among people but living with them. The sharpest mark of anger—setting aside Mard Ali's curses—was not arguing with people or shouting at or about them; it was withdrawal, refusal to eat or drink, refusal to talk or participate, refusal to be with people.

The wish to be alone is one that our culture recognizes. People's claim that they need some time to and for themselves is, if sometimes difficult to achieve, culturally sanctioned here. We feel that we can be fulfilled alone. Among the Komachi, such claims for time and space were seen as evidence of ruptures in the social fabric. Being with people—interacting with them, exchanging with them, fighting with them—built a social world in which there were no strangers. The Komachi tribe lacked hard and fast boundaries and was not set off from the other neighboring groups by dramatic cultural differences. In its way, the tribe was constructed and reconstructed every day through social intercourse. Given that, being apart was not valued, and aloneness was a thing to prevent rather than to promote.

19

CRAZY FOR LOVE

As was often the case with gossip, we first heard about it from Nesrat while we were visiting in her parents' tent.

"Have you heard?" she said. "Maraste has gone mad." We hadn't heard, and didn't really know the girl, and so our first response was a sort of jumble of questions about who, how, what, why, and when. Nesrat explained that Maraste was a daughter of Bur Ahmad, whose family lived in the camp with Janallah (commonly known as Jani), Moqtar, and Isau. That gave us a rough idea of who she was, though at that point we still did not really know her personally. Nesrat continued to insist that Maraste had recently gone mad, and was still mad. Indeed, it soon became clear that part of the discussion was an attempt to get us to agree to take Sekine over to see the girl, a suggestion we jumped at. It seemed that her madness essentially involved her walking around shouting and screaming and being abusive to others, which alternated with her sitting around doing nothing. Moreover, she wouldn't eat, she wouldn't drink, and she would do no work. And finally, Nesrat asserted, she had gone mad because she loved Rostam, Zolf Ali's son, but couldn't marry him because he was promised to someone else. Thwarted love was driving her mad.

During migration, we did indeed drive over to Janallah's camp. We saw a young woman sitting still and alone in front of a tent. Nesrat and Sekine came home with an elaborated version, detailing how bad and difficult and painful it was, how resistant to help the girl was, and how hopeless her case seemed.

Time went by, and in the crunch of all the other things to do and see, we temporarily lost track of Maraste and her problem. We had, however, been alerted to the linkage of romantic love with being crazy and with marriage.

Since we had come to be tremendously interested in Komachi matchmaking, we resolved to return to the issue.

Our chance came months later, when we were again visiting Shir Ali and Sekine. Discussions of Maraste and Rostam's plans to get married had started to float around, and Ann and I began to suspect that, whatever else it might be, becoming mad might be a strategy through which young Komachi men and women exerted some control over who their potential marriage partners were. With that thought in mind, we asked Sekine, who did most of the talking, whether Maraste was unique, or if there was anyone else who had gone mad from love. Right away she responded with the sharp, nasalized grunt "hunh," which signified an emphatic yes, and said, "Jani."

"Who?" we said, wanting to be sure.

"Jani Darvish."

Jani Darvish! We were stunned. Darvish had been one of the most important men in the tribe, a central figure in Komachi accounts of their history. Jani and his brothers were still prominent men, heads of camp. Jani's wife, moreover, was a daughter of Reza—Qoli's father, Shir Ali's father's brother, Agha Hossein's father's brother, and one of the most prominent men of his generation. Their match linked the tribe's most important families, and it appeared to us to be an eminently intelligible political marriage, almost a paradigmatically perfect one.

"Jani and Kokab?" we asked, making sure that Jani's "madness" was indeed associated with his wife, not someone else.

"Yes, yes," Sekine said. And then Shir Ali, laughing so hard that he almost cried, started in. "Yes, Jani. He walked around holding his head, crying, and moaning. 'Oooooh,' he'd cry." Shir Ali demonstrated, letting loose a hideously pitiful, long, moanful cry as he held his head in his hands. He did this several times, his imitation of Jani's sad moans punctuated by sputters and snorts as he broke into uncontrollable gales of laughter at the memory of Jani's behavior.

"What made Jani crazy?" we asked, attempting to pursue the point.

"*Eshk,*" Sekine replied.

"*Eshk?* What do you mean?" we asked.

"He was crazy because he wanted to marry Kokab, but the girl's mother said she wouldn't give her to him. So he became crazy."

"You mean that he really loved her, and was so unhappy when he heard he couldn't have her that he became crazy?"

"That's right."

"Well," Ann asked, "do married couples usually have *eshk* for each other?"

Shir Ali and Sekine looked a bit sheepish and didn't immediately answer. "Yes, usually they have much *dust,*" they finally answered, using the word that signified warmth, affection, comfort, and deep feeling, rather than *eshk,* which signified passionate, romantic love.

"But do married couples have *eshk* for each other? Do you and Shir Ali have *eshk* for each other?"

"No. That's for young people. Old people don't have *eshk* for each other. They live together and work together and have children, and then after a time they have *dust* for each other."

"So you and Shir Ali have *dust* for each other, but you don't have *eshk* for each other?"

"Yes."

"Do most couples have *eshk* for each other when they marry?"

"No. After time they have *dust* for each other."

"Did you and Shir Ali have *eshk* for each other when you were young and got married?"

"No, no. We didn't have *eshk* for each other," Sekine said dismissively. "I told you, having *eshk* is crazy."

Having *eshk* might be crazy. But toward the end of our stay we visited Rostam and his new wife. She was sitting in a room, dressed in a bride's finery, speaking with us and others as though there had been nothing peculiar about her courtship and marriage. It was as hard for us to imagine that she had been crazy as it was to imagine Jani Darvish's madness. Moreover, her madness had permitted her to marry the man she wanted and—given the impoverished state of both their families—had let them get married without the expense of a large wedding celebration. Given the outcome in both cases, one wonders if madness for love was not a bit like Hamlet's.

In any event, reflecting on madness and marriage once again forced us to recognize that cultures provide many ways to a given end. In *Ambiguous Relations* I analyzed Komachi marriages to show that not only were there rules or norms for whom one should marry and how it should be done, but that people used appeals to those very rules to bring about outcomes more diverse than the formal structure might appear to permit. The successful marriages of Maraste and Jani Darvish suggested that in addition to the formally sanctioned ways of making a match, a parallel, culturally defined way of totally avoiding the formal rules also existed. Successful members of a culture not only know the rules and how to manipulate them, they also know the rules for completely avoiding the rules. It is no wonder that it takes a long time in the field to figure out what is going on.

Chapter

20

SELLING THE JEEP

Getting rid of our jeep was the event that most deeply embedded us in Iranian life, and to a substantial degree Ko-machi life, because it moved us over the line from doing participant observation to being active, if not always willing, participants in the Iranian economy.

When we bought our jeep in Tehran, we had planned to sell it there as well. However, the longer we stayed in Kerman, where it repeatedly broke down, the more uncomfortable we became at the thought of driving back to Tehran. Our trip from Tehran to Kerman had been an adventure; then, after substantial repairs, the main bearings had burned out during our second big survey with Mr. Abusaidi; we had replaced the generator or its bearings three times; we had had a cracked motor mount rewelded, and numerous other small things had gone wrong as well. In short, the jeep had broken down on virtually every long trip we had taken. We didn't trust it, and the thought of breaking down again, loaded up with all our things, was not a comforting one. Moreover, we had built the jeep's resale value into our budget. It had cost us about $2,500, and we needed the money to pay our way home. We didn't have cash to spare and were worried about the cost of another major repair.

There were other reasons we wanted to get rid of the Jeep. During migration and the longer survey trips we took early in our stay, or when we had wanted to go to Kerman or Bandar Abbas and pick up mail or supplies, the jeep's extended bed was very useful for carrying large loads. It was essential for long trips. But there were many places, particularly in the mountainous summer quarters, that were too rocky or too narrow for the jeep. And once we finished the 1975 spring migration, the inconvenience and limitations of the jeep out-weighed its advantages.

Many of the wealthier families in the tribe had motorcycles, which could go almost anywhere a horse or mule could. It seemed to us that a motorcycle would give us the freedom of movement we wanted without the burden of the jeep. If we had been rich, we would have kept the jeep and bought a motorcy-cle too. We couldn't afford that, so we began to think of selling the jeep and buying a motorcycle.

Other people's thoughts were running parallel to our own. As our departure approached, several wealthier Komachi began to ask vague questions about what we planned to do with the jeep and how much we were likely to ask for it. One of the local settled landlords began asking similar questions. Our initial responses to these feelers were mixed. Our own wish to sell the jeep was largely motivated by fears that it wouldn't make the trip to Tehran or that it would suffer a major and costly breakdown before we could get it sold. Selling it to people we knew and liked seemed to be taking advantage of them. Selling it to the landlord seemed a better idea; we really didn't like him much. But be-fore we could explore these options, we got a nearly irresistible offer from Mo-hammed, the village chief of Shirinak.

Mohammed did not migrate with the Komachi but was very closely tied to them. While his father, who had also been the village chief, was not a nomad, his mother was Komachi. His eldest sister was our neighbor Sekine, and his two elder brothers headed their own camps. Mohammed lived by endless hus-tling: he owned some agricultural land and some gardens whose produce he consumed or sold; he managed several carpet shops in which he was junior partner to entrepreneurs from larger towns; he worked as a broker, putting to-gether herds of animals to sell for commission, and he was a key member of numerous speculative partnerships. These were modest ventures in which Mo-hammed and his partners put up money to buy commodities such as animals, fruit, nuts, or grain cheaply in an out-of-the-way part of the province, then ship the goods to places where they could be sold at a higher price, the potential profit depending on the difference in price rising from regional variation. Since he owned some land, had good ties with both the Komachi and more important people in the local settled world, and hustled all the time, Mohammed lived fairly well. Mohammed also worked hard. In addition, because he was almost constantly using his capital to make a deal, pay his weavers, buy some wool, or what have you, Mohammed very rarely had much cash on hand. He did have a motorcycle, a real desire for the jeep, and a willingness to deal.

Mohammed's deal was simple. He wanted the jeep. He knew we had paid

about 17,000 tomans for it and hoped to get that as our price. He offered to buy
it by giving us the motorcycle immediately, which was worth, in his estimation,
about 11,000 tomans, and 6,000 tomans cash, some of which he would pay us
right away, paying the rest as he could over the next few months. To sweeten the
deal even more, by making sure we couldn't lose, he promised us that should
we wish it, he would buy the motorcycle back from us when we left.

Mohammed's offer was great. We would get just about what we wanted for
our car, plus we would also get a motorcycle with no hassle, and we were
pretty sure that Mohammed would be good for the money over the next few
months. We also checked around about the motorcycle; it seemed that his eval-
uation of it was fair and that we could sell it at close to that price. Our one big
concern remained selling the jeep to someone we knew. We catalogued all its
problems. Mohammed dismissed them. He had spoken to people; he knew all
the problems. They didn't bother him. He had a mechanic in Kerman who
could fix them.

Slowly it dawned on us. Mohammed *really* wanted our jeep. He saw himself
able to use it to transport grain, wool, carpets, and other items he dealt in. He
also saw it as a real marker of status. Mohammed would be the only person in
that part of the valley to own a vehicle other than a motorcycle. Moreover, Mohammed really wanted *our* jeep. The kind of deal he could offer us, part cash,
part motorcycle, and part payment over time, was one that fit in perfectly with
his economic situation and would allow him to be the registered, legal owner
of a jeep. There was no other way he could do it, and our jeep aside, he was unlikely to get many opportunities to purchase one in that fashion. Drawn by our
own desire to get rid of the jeep and pushed by Mohammed's constant pressure, we agreed to sell it to him.

So off he and I set to Kerman city to register the sale. As we approached the
city Mohammed began speaking to me very slowly, very carefully, and much
more formally than he had ever done before.

"When we go to register the sale," he said, "the man will ask you if I have
given you the full price of the car, the seventeen thousand tomans."

"Okay," I said.

"When he asks you that, you have to tell him yes. You have to tell him that
I have given you the full seventeen thousand tomans."

"Okay. When he asks me, I will have to tell him that you have given me the
full seventeen thousand tomans."

"Yes, even though I haven't. You will have to tell him that I have given you
the full seventeen thousand tomans."

"Okay. Even though you haven't given me the full seventeen thousand tomans, when he asks me, I will tell him that you have," I said. "But can you explain why I have to tell him that?"

"Because otherwise it is not a legal sale."

Later, in Kerman, Mohammed led me through the maze of offices in which we had papers filled out, signed, and affixed with various tax stamps that we bought. Finally we came to the office in which the purchase was to be registered. After some brief, polite discussion, the clerk went over the papers, checking our stamps, seals, and signatures. At one point he paused, turned to me, and asked, "Has he paid you the full seventeen thousand tomans?"

"Yes," said Mohammed, who looked as though he wanted to nudge me in the ribs to be sure I remembered what to say.

"Yes," I said.

"Okay," said the clerk, who went on to check the rest of our stamps and seals, took additional signatures, and recorded the transaction in one of the enormous ledgers used in public offices all over Iran.

Shortly thereafter we left the office, Mohammed the proud owner of a somewhat battered 1963 (at least parts of it) extended-body Willys-Overland jeep, and me the proud owner of a used motorcycle and a handwritten promissory note guaranteeing that Mohammed would pay me six thousand tomans. We both were quite happy.

Our motorcycle was Russian, as were most of the motorcycles in Kerman. It looked as though it had been modeled on an old Harley-Davidson, with lots of chrome and big shock absorbers. Actually, it was wonderful for rural areas. It had one cylinder, displaced 350 cc, had a huge and heavy frame, and was practically indestructible. Ann and I rode it back and forth to camps all over the summer quarters. Often we would have an additional passenger, and except on the steepest hills, we would chug along three in a row. The cycle never broke down, and it did make local traveling much easier.

Mohammed was not as lucky. He too did a lot of driving, and he carried enormous loads of goods and people. Finally the jeep broke down, and he had to have it towed to town by a tractor. Mohammed told me the story rather sheepishly, because I had warned him about hauling too much, or too many people. Still, I knew the breakdown—a blown head gasket—wasn't really his fault. For months before I sold it, the jeep had been boiling over in tough driving. Indeed, I had had the head gasket replaced not all that long before I sold it. That helped a bit, but going over mountain passes or running heavily loaded made the jeep run too hot. I suspected that the head needed to be milled, but I couldn't even imagine where I was going to get that done in Kerman. My mechanic's solution was more practical: carry lots of water and loosen the radiator cap when you're climbing a high pass. I had told Mohammed all of this, warned him about it before I sold him the jeep, and he told me the story of his breakdown with a laugh. Still, I felt some guilt, and so I split the cost of the repair with him.

Meanwhile, Mohammed made payments on the jeep, and part two of our plan, selling the motorcycle, seemed no problem. Hardly a week went by without someone offering to buy the motorcycle. Some offered cash on the barrel, some half down and the rest when we left; many just stopped by to say, "When you want to sell your motorcycle, call me first." We noted who made the offers, were gratified that there seemed so many that selling out couldn't be a problem, and threw ourselves into studying the last round of marriage negotiations, celebrations, and things we wanted to focus on before we left.

Our plans were shattered on August 8, 1975, by the announcement of the government's new "antiprofiteering" program. As with all government moves, it formed the lead story on the radio news broadcasts that were our hosts' main source of information on the outside world: "*Diruz Shahanshah-ye Aryeh Mehr elam-kard ke . . .*" ("Yesterday the King of Kings, Light of the Aryans, announced that . . ."). In this case the shah announced that he was mandating wage and price controls. This would solve the problem of inflation by attacking those venal individuals—mostly bazaar merchants and middlemen—who were pushing up prices and causing inflation by buying and selling on speculation. Moreover, in an effort to rectify the wrongs caused by previous price gouging, he was rolling back all prices by 40 percent immediately. At least that was how the announcement was interpreted and implemented in the villages and camps in the mountain valleys south of Kerman.

The announcement of the antiprofiteering measure was, in fact, a stunning development, and it had a substantial impact on both the Komachi and us. One might think that the members of a small-scale, rural population such as the Komachi would have benefited from a price freeze and/or rollback. But many Komachi were devastated by the measure. First, the primary goods the Komachi produced were meat (on the hoof), wool, and a variety of dairy products. The prices of meat and dairy products, for which the buoyant oil economy had fostered great demand, had risen far more rapidly than the prices of other commodities, particularly wheat, the main element in the Komachi diet. Thus, all Komachi, rich or poor, stood to lose by the implementation of any law that rolled back meat prices by 40 percent. Second, like Mohammed, many Komachi, generally neither the richest nor the poorest, attempted to exploit their annual movement between the northern and southern ends of the province by making money as petty brokers and dealers. Strict price controls, which in part focused on profit margins, almost automatically made this kind of merchant capitalism illegal, unprofitable, or both. Coupled with a rollback of meat and dairy prices, the antiprofiteering measure threatened the standard of living of many Komachi. Finally, because many Komachi were working as dealers or brokers, the dramatic and immediate price controls and rollbacks caught many of them in an economically extended position. They had bought commodities such as animals, dates, or wheat in anticipation of being able to market them at the higher prices in Kerman City. The 40 percent rollback meant that if they sold the items they had already purchased, Komachi dealers would suffer a substantial loss of their limited capital.

Of course, it was not only the prices of meat and dairy goods that got rolled back. Particular attention was paid to the prices of imported commodities, whose dealers, often with a government-granted monopoly, were alleged to have been engaged in price gouging. Imported motorcycles were one of the items targeted for price controls, and so, on or about August 8, 1975, the price of a brand-new Russian motorcycle plunged nearly 50 percent, dropping well below the 11,000 to 12,000 tomans I had calculated as the trade value of Mohammed's (now my) used Russian motorcycle. Put another way, my motorcycle went from having a resale value of about 12,000 tomans to having a resale value of about 6,000 tomans. Overnight, I had lost about $900.

Of course, I didn't feel the loss overnight. Like the Komachi, it took me weeks to fully realize the implications of the antiprofiteering measure. And when I did, my response was pure rage. Suddenly, and through no apparent fault of my own, the government of Iran had reached out and arbitrarily taken $900 from my pocket. I was livid. I did not feel less upset when several of our Komachi friends, people who knew we were leaving, came around and, by way of making an indirect offer for the motorcycle, began telling us what (really, how little) it was worth.

My response to the dramatic drop in my motorcycle's value was largely irrational. I told people I didn't much care what the motorcycle was worth. I told them I was so angry that I had pretty well decided that rather than sell it for 6,000 tomans less than I'd paid for it, I was going to set it out in front of camp, put a match in the gas tank, and burn the whole thing up. It was not my finest hour. My Komachi friends and Ann all counseled me against doing something so stupid, and as our time in Iran grew shorter and shorter, we began an earnest search for someone to buy our motorcycle.

Even at its reduced price, however, the continuing impact of the antiprofiteering measure made the motorcycle difficult to sell. Our problem was not an absence of willing buyers; many people wanted the motorcycle, recognizing that buying it at 6,000 tomans was a great deal. Our problem was the Komachi's problem. As I noted above, many Komachi were involved in ventures as dealers and brokers, and, like Mohammed, they had most of their capital tied up in goods that were now worth 40 percent less than they had cost. Cash was scarce and people were economically pinched. Moreover, the people who were most pinched were precisely those who were most likely to want a motorcycle: individuals who wanted mobility in order to travel and deal. In effect, people whose lifestyles made them want a motorcycle couldn't afford one, whereas other people either didn't want a motorcycle or already had one.

I finally sold the motorcycle to Ma'adi Yarbok. Ma'adi was one of the very few recently settled Komachi. A former head of camp, and the oldest son of one of the most important men in tribal history, Ma'adi made his living by brokering, dealing, and being partners in a carpet workshop whose primary employees were his children, nieces, and nephews.

Ma'adi paid me in an interesting way. He gave me about half the motorcycle's price in cash, and then he got the remaining 3,000 tomans from his economic patron, Hajji Nasrollah, one of the butchers in Kerman. Ma'adi and I closed the deal in Shirinak. Then, some days later, Ma'adi and I rode into Kerman. Once there, we went to Hajji's shop on the traffic circle at one end of city's main street. When we got there, Ma'adi requested the cash from his patron. But it readily became apparent that Hajji did not have it to hand, perhaps in part because he too had bought sheep at their old price. In any event what he did have was an open butcher shop, and for much of the day, I sat around it, drinking tea, watching the yellow jackets hover around the meat, and listening to conversations as Hajji sold meat, his cash drawer filled, and he came closer and closer to having enough money to pay off his client's debt. Finally, in the late afternoon, we drank a final cup of tea, he gave me the cash, and I was out of the automobile/motorcycle business.

Many aspects of this set of transactions seem noteworthy. In the larger course of events, perhaps the most important is the degree to which it shows how the Pahlavi regime's attempts to control Iran's economy jeopardized the well-being of ordinary people. Measures that were intended to control prices by putting pressure on large-scale profiteers damaged little people involved in penny capitalism through speculative ventures. Large numbers of Komachi, people of modest means as well as people who were relatively wealthy for the Komachi, suffered serious losses in the antiprofiteering campaign. Since the Komachi were hardly alone in their participation in such ventures, it seems likely that the campaign destroyed much of the accumulated capital of millions of Iranians of modest means. In short, far from protecting the weak from wealthy predators, the campaign damaged them profoundly. It was not an effective way to build popular support for a regime lacking other forms of legitimation.

The impact of the antiprofiteering campaign was made far greater by another aspect of the Iranian economy that this anecdote illustrates. Not only were people engaged in *momale* ventures—brokering, buying cheap and selling dear—in a search for petty profits, but much of the dealing was done on credit. Moreover, the credit was peculiarly extended. The common situation in the United States is that large institutions—banks or corporations—extend credit to individuals, who then buy things by going into debt. But in Iran the pyramid of debt was reversed. Tribesmen in the interior of the province gave animals to the Komachi, their brokers, who in turn sold them either to other brokers or to butchers, who themselves did not and could not pay off until the animals were retailed as meat, in part because they had debts for trucks, meat grinders, and trips to Mecca. Most exchanges were based on credit of a kind, but it was credit extended by poorer people to wealthier people who in turn extended it to people wealthier still when they gave them their goods in exchange for future payment. I hasten to add that this pyramid of credit was not simply an artifact of Islamic injunctions against collecting interest. Interest was paid and collected in prerevolutionary Iran. This was a structuring of financial relations that worked to the advantage of the wealthy rather than the poor.

In addition to our dealings over the jeep, we encountered this pyramiding of credit in another, equally uncomfortable experience. Although the Komachi did not weave carpets, women did various kinds of flat weaving, making bags and cloths of different kinds. One type of cloth was *sofreh nun*, a brightly colored, very tightly woven, heavy wool cloth that women used as a surface for kneading bread. As we watched families putting together their daughters' trousseaus, we became aware that some of them hired other women in the tribe to weave these bags and cloths for them. We also learned that Senne, Kawki's wife, was one of the women who wove *sofreh nun*. Early in our second summer, with some trepidation, Ann and I asked her to weave us one. We spoke generally about the cost but did not negotiate an exact price. As the summer wore on and turned to fall, we were aware that Senne had not yet begun our cloth. Not wishing to press, we didn't say much. Finally she started, and one day, very close to the end of our stay, she finished the piece.

In the intervening time, we had collected far more information on marriages, preparations for marriages, and preparations for setting up new households. As a result, we now had a pretty good idea that the "price" of a *sofreh nun* was about 200 tomans, roughly $30. Shortly before Senne was finished weaving the *sofreh nun,* she and Kawki invited us to dinner. We sat and talked of many things, and inevitably the *sofreh nun* and its price came up.

In a pretty straightforward fashion we asked how much it would cost. We expected one of two answers that seemed common within the tribe, either a straightforward declaration of a price close to the commonly accepted one within the community, or the more polite version, "Whatever you think it's worth," which again led to people paying the commonly accepted price. In anticipation of that, we had checked with several people to make sure that our estimates of what people were paying were correct.

But instead, Kawki launched into an enormous sales pitch. He described the difficulty of the labor; he claimed that the wool was dyed with *"rang rashti,"* presumably special high-quality colors from the city of Rasht in northern Iran. Ann and I were taken aback, and when we asked again, he named a price far higher than we had expected or others paid.

We were nonplussed. In fact we were deeply upset and left without the matter's being settled. Several things seemed to be going wrong. First, Kawki's reaction severed any illusion that we might have sustained that we were one of the group. We were being treated like strangers. Second, like strangers, we were being set up as a source of profit. Disturbed by this, we turned to Sekine and asked what we should do. Her answer was even more disturbing.

"It's only worth two hundred tomans," she said, "and they have already paid for the wool. Tell them you don't want it. After a while they'll be glad to take the two hundred tomans."

In that disturbing response, the pyramiding of credit and the absence of noblesse oblige combined, crystallizing a vivid picture of Iranian life.

One might be inclined to see this pyramiding of debt and willingness to pressure those at the bottom as an effect of the oil boom of the early 1970s, or even as a result of Iran's place in the world market. To some extent, it might be. But it is not recent. Over 120 years before we observed this riot of debt, Sheil noted:

> February 15th.—This is decidedly an odd people. The entire nation seems to be in debt, commencing with the Shah, who is in debt to the Emperor of Russia, and ending with the humblest muleteer. The marvel is who are those that lend the money; they, it may be conjectured, being out of debt. Every man of rank one hears seems to be in the same predicament, though it is to be suspected this poverty is often feigned to escape from the weighty hand of exaction. (Sheil 1856, 141)

This seemed an equally accurate description of things in 1975, except that booming oil revenues had freed the shah from debt, and that the question of who extended credit was easy: everyone. In *Ambiguous Relations* I noted evidence of brokers buying and selling on credit as early as 1727. Thus it seems that at the very least one has to see this question of credit as having a long history. I can only add that when we were caught in the collapse triggered by the antiprofiteering measures, we were outraged. If we were not vastly deceived, the Komachi and those they dealt with were outraged as well. At the time these events struck us more emotionally than intellectually, but when the shah's regime fell in an overwhelming flow of popular discontent, the antiprofiteering campaign, the pyramid of credit, and the willingness to squeeze people who had already made a cash outlay immediately came to mind.

Chapter

21

LOOKING BACK

            At about noon on October 15, 1975, the minibus that Ann and I had hired to take us into Kerman arrived in Shirinak. We had been saying our goodbyes for several days, and the pattern was almost always the same. With the farewells and exchanges of last little gifts, we would always assure people that this wasn't forever and that we would be back. I, an optimist, said we would be back in a year or two; Ann, more pessimistic, usually said we would be back in five years. The Komachi never said when, and their constant reply to our hopeful promises was *"ensha'allah."* It is now 1998; we left over twenty years ago, a revolution has intervened, and we have not yet returned. For a few years we corresponded sporadically. Then even that stopped. In the early 1990s I began corresponding with an Iranian anthropologist who was working with the Komachi. From him, we learned that Shir Ali and Sekine were still well, and that Shir Ali and almost all the other men in the tribe had sold their camels, so the Komachi now migrate by truck. And we received a list of all the marriages that had taken place since we left. I sent him copies of all of my work on the Komachi and of other recent work on Iranian pastoralists. I have not heard from him recently.

As I was preparing this text, several points struck me. The first is typified by the contrast between Komachi caution and my casual assumption that we would soon return. In some of the preceding chapters, I have tried to describe how that caution was typical of the Komachi, and I have tried to show what triggered it. What of my lack of caution? Many things may have contributed to it, but one certainly was my youth.

As I read over these chapters and the field materials on which they are based, I was constantly struck by the disjunction between my field experience and my life experience. I was twenty-eight when I went off to Iran. I had been married and divorced, but other than that all I had ever done was go to school. I had no children; to the degree that I had lived on a budget, it was as a graduate student. Beyond paying rent and tuition, I had few responsibilities. I had experienced the death of no one closer to me than a grandparent; the great crises of my life were the war in Vietnam (which I successfully avoided), passing my exams, and getting funding to go to Iran. And there I was, studying people's lives, trying to come to some understanding of how people responded to the very real pressures of having and losing children, of providing for those children, of making sure that their household was economically solvent or at least viable. I, who had never faced any of these problems in my own life, was trying to understand people trying to live their real lives in a rapidly changing world. At twenty-eight, twenty-nine, and thirty I was amazed at how cautious the Komachi were in facing the world and how contingent their plans seemed. At fifty I have learned a lot about plans for the future, contingency, and responsibility. I now realize that I was looking at the Komachi through two filters: that of my culture and that of my own inexperience. Since I suspect that much modern ethnography is based on people's doctoral research—after all, when else can one so easily abandon the responsibilities of life here to live for an extended period there?—much of it, too, must be based on materials colored by that same filter of callow youth.

In my mid-forties, I spent a summer doing fieldwork with pastoral peasants in Sardinia. I felt then that age brings a fieldworker greater empathy and an ability to learn through discussion of shared rather than vicariously apprehended life experience. Still, being young and being on a very limited budget permitted us, and in some ways forced us, to try to efface ourselves. We could not live as middle-class Americans tourists. As much as we sometimes wished it, we were not able to conduct our fieldwork from an air-conditioned Winnebago or easily escape the field. As younger, foreign students with our very ambiguous status, it was easy to defer to Shir Ali and others within the tribe. In either way, our youth certainly shaped our vision and our understanding.

Our culture was our second filter, and I have attempted to make explicit those previously invisible aspects of our culture that living with the Komachi made manifest. In reading through my text, it seems clear that adapting to and understanding the risk-aversive, contingent way the Komachi lived was the most difficult aspect of their life for me to participate in. While my awareness of contingency was spurred primarily through the accumulation of situations such as the one described in my discussion of traveling with the Komachi, my consciousness was also raised by living with our jeep, for, as I have noted, the jeep imposed its own contingencies on us and made us live with uncertainties and a lack of control that we would not have experienced with a new Land Rover.

My frustration and anger at not having control, not knowing how things would turn out, and not having the expected happen when I expected it to, along with my discovery that earlier travelers had experienced similar feelings and responses, suggest to me that one great difference between Komachi culture and bourgeois Euro-American culture is that we expect to live with order and control far more than they. Or perhaps more bluntly, we expect things to come out as we wish, while they do not. Now, having had and raised children of my own, I would argue that these different expectations are inculcated from earliest childhood.

Among the Komachi the three days after childbirth are highly ritualized. Charms and rites protect both mother and child from fairies and other harmful things. They were striking, and Ann observed them with fascination. One rite she found particularly disturbing: The newborn infant was not nursed until the mother's colostrum had passed. Moreover, feeding did not seem a matter of urgency. When the baby cried, possible reasons were discussed. Aches, pains, winds, and humors were raised and dismissed, until finally women considered the possibility that the child should be fed. *Considered* is the operative word here. For as the baby cried and became more upset, a discussion was carried on. Then, once the decision to feed the child had been reached, its food had to be prepared. Food for the infant was a special preparation, *godoxteh,* a mixture of melted butter, sugar, and herbs. Before the baby could be fed, a tiny spoonful at a time, the mixture had to be heated, cooked, and cooled. Thus in their first days of life Komachi children were not fed on demand, and generally were fed only after they were shrieking with rage.[1] This contrasts sharply with what occurred when our children were born and what we have seen occur with friends and family. Here great effort is spent on helping a baby to nurse as soon as possible, and in my observation it is often the mother who is frustrated because the baby does not know how to suck. If the baby is frustrated, it is not because adults are not rushing to feed it.

Indeed, among the Komachi, frustration seemed a part of being a child. We saw this for the first time at Shiri Khabar's, when a group of adults, including his father, were playing with his young son. But, in fact, they were not playing with the child, they were teasing him. They told him to be brave, then they pretended to give him an injection. People pretended that they were going to hit him, that they were going to cut off his ear. Things were given him, and then they were taken away. Needless to say, the child would get upset; he was comforted, often by his father, and then the round of threat and teasing would start again. We often saw this pattern repeated elsewhere.

A fascinating letter sent by Mustafa Khan (son of a very important official in late Qajar Iran) to his brother-in-law, instructing the latter on how to care for Mustafa Khan's family and estate during his absence for a trip, permits us to compare Komachi child-rearing practices to the dramatically different expectations commanded by Mustafa Khan for his son, who was still young enough to be cared for by a wet nurse (Gurney 1983, 155ff.). Mustafa Khan commands that the child should be examined by a doctor once every two or three days, and woman servants should take turns looking after him "so that he is not left unattended, even for a single moment" (Gurney 1983, 156). The child should never be allowed to become upset or to "fuss or mope"; "every day something fresh must be brought or sewn for him, so that he may be thrilled"; "every other day . . . [his] clothes must be entirely changed" (Gurney 1983, 157). Mustafa Khan charges that his son can only be handled by four people, and commands that anyone else who picks him up "be immediately punished and unexceptionally beaten." The father asks that the nurse commence weaning in early spring, but commands that if his son frets, the weaning be put off until he returns. He also commands that whatever food the doctor orders for his son and the wet nurse be provided "with abundance" and "not stinted."

I will not belabor the contrast with the Komachi, but I would stress that while young Komachi children were constantly frustrated, Mustafa Khan explicitly commanded that his son's pleasures be indulged lest he "fret" or be "upset." To that degree, Mustapha Khan's instructions seem to be an extreme form of child-rearing practices often found in America today. In contrast to the teasing and the proffering and removal of playthings and of security among the Komachi, when children in middle-class American families want things, they get them. Far from taking things from children, parents here work at helping children learn to share and not to take things from playmates, and in so doing assure children of the security of their possessions. Age may disabuse us of the notion that we will always get what we want when we want it, but my observations of myself and my friends, family, colleagues, and students suggest that the implicit expectation that we will live ordered lives and get what we want when we want it is a powerful element of our culture. In this context, Euro-American comments on the fatalism of Iranians (and Muslims in general) reveal more about the nature of our culture than of theirs.

My major goal in this work has been to show how we came to understand significant elements of Komachi culture through both the cumulative process of becoming aware of the import of apparently insignificant events and through the dramatically different process of having serendipitous, unexpected, perhaps peculiar encounters and events open our eyes to aspects of Komachi life. I have also attempted to show how these events and understandings made us aware of elements of our own culture that had previously been invisible to us. Finally, I have tried to suggest how this double process of gaining awareness of their culture and ours, in turn, shaped our understanding of the nature of culture and of social life. In keeping with the maxim I quoted in my introduction, I will refrain from reviewing how particular events shaped our understandings. If I have not yet succeeded in showing that, this book has failed.

I will close with two final points. Throughout this text, I have periodically cut in passages from earlier writers' accounts of tribal Iran. Initially, they attracted my attention because they seemed to describe situations and feelings that paralleled ours. Taken as a whole, I think they illustrate both the changes and the continuities in Iranian culture, or at least Iranian culture as it was encountered by British and American visitors over the past 150 years. Examination of the similarities in their responses and ours helps bring into sharper relief those elements of our own bourgeois Euro-American culture that become visible in contrast to Iranian culture. Setting aside the obvious differences that can be accounted for by changed circumstance, the greatest difference between those accounts and my own seems to lie in their tone. Modern ethnography presses on its authors a relativism that precludes the harsher, wholesale judgments of people contained in the earlier texts: I worried over how to represent Taqi Arbab! Thus when we describe the same kinds of events, I note that where they evaluate, I seek to contextualize and explain. There is a second difference in tone. Layard waxes romantic about the Bakhtiyari leader Mohammed Taqi Khan. His is a participant's account of a political struggle with clear heroes and villains. Bishop casts a much colder eye on Iranians, but is nearly as romantic about Christian missionaries in Iran. Wilson's descriptions of Sir Percy Cox, British Resident in the Persian Gulf, and the work of Cox and the agents of the Anglo-Iranian Oil Company also are suffused with a rosy glow. Modern ethnography tends to scrub that out as well. Open partisanship, like open contempt, makes the text suspect.

Finally, a last attempt to contextualize this work: As I noted at the outset, it arose largely in response to my feeling that the twin babies of fieldwork and ethnography were being thrown out with the bathwater of a rejected simple empiricism. To that end, the central purpose of the book is not to reveal aspects of Komachi culture, of Iranian culture, of our own culture, or of culture in general. My central goal has been to show the relationship between event and understanding and through that to reconfirm the simple, central importance of being there.

22

EXPERIENCE AND UNDERSTANDING

The
Theory
of
Being There

My goal in this book has been to show how the accumulation of unexpected experience shaped my understanding of the Komachi. I have identified and described situations and events that affected my view. I have also attempted to clarify how my understandings differed from those found in the earlier, nonethnographic accounts of Mary Leonora Sheil, Isabella Bishop, Henry Layard, and Arnold T. Wilson. While I shall touch on these points again, in this chapter I will attempt to show why my reflections on the relationship of fieldwork to understanding have led me to reject the post-modernist criticism of ethnography (and, implicitly, of the anthropological project) that has dominated anthropological discourse since the mid-1980s. Because it is relevant to my attitude toward this critique, I will begin by explaining, as well as I can, why I was first attracted to anthropology. I then turn to a discussion of the postmodernist criticism of the anthropological project, responding to aspects of this criticism that seem misguided.

I came to anthropology as an undergraduate at Columbia University, where I bounced around courses in many other disciplines as I searched for a major. Unfortunately, I did not keep "field notes" of the period; at the time I doubt I could have fully articulated the reasons for my attraction to anthropology and my ambivalence about other disciplines, though some now seem apparent. Mulling over my memories of my feelings, I conclude that I found the idea of being an anthropologist attractive because I liked the idea of traveling to far-away places and I was captivated by the thought of a career in which someone would pay for me to live in some odd corner of the world. I was thus attracted by a romantic vision that conflated the anthropologist and the adventurous traveler. Beyond those rather foolish reasons, I now realize, I was drawn to anthropology because it was more concerned with and attached to real life than any other discipline I encountered, and real life was what interested me.

Reasons of temperament and rebellion against a parental role model precluded serious engagement with the hard sciences. When I took psychology, presumably to learn about people, I got to spend hours in subterranean gloom alternately torturing and being tortured by a white rat whose behavior and conditioning were, my professor assured me, little different from mine. While I was perfectly willing to accept that there was little difference between the rat and the professor, I found the existence of a caged rat a poor substitute for real life; I loathed psychology. Sociology presented the grand abstractions of Parsons and Merton, which seemed to bleed humans of all humanity. Political science, largely political theory at the introductory level, also seemed detached from the primary political event in my life: the Vietnam War and the mad political circumstances that spawned it. Religion, both Western and other, held a deep fascination, but as soon as I began to consider it from a comparative perspective, there seemed little reason not to consider it anthropologically. I do not know why I did not connect with history; it is ironic, since much of my work for the last fifteen years has had a strong historical bent.

If I found some subjects not fully attractive, I really did not like literary criticism. I enjoyed the texts, but I was made uncomfortable by the critical practice put in play to engage them. I often felt that I was watching a shell game of symbolic manipulation in which wordplay and facility at wordplay dominated common sense. That distrust of slippery wordplay remains a prejudice that I have not completely overcome.

In contrast to the other disciplines, anthropology had real people. The texts we read, even where they no longer dealt with individuals, generally were not so abstract that life as people lived it disappeared. One could see through the abstractions to people doing things. Anthropology was also real at the level of its practitioners. My teachers recounted their field experience, and in so doing gave life to both the project and the people. I think I found that apparent grounding comfortable. Coupled with the romanticism of travel inherent in fieldwork, anthropology was formidably attractive.

Two elements of this personal history are significant to the text at hand: the attractions of anthropology ultimately account for my doing the fieldwork that produced this book, and my aversion to the game of symbolic manipulation that I associated with literary criticism almost certainly accounts for a good deal of my feeling about postmodernist criticism of ethnography. At the least, I was skeptical about that kind of criticism well before it was turned on anthropology. In short, I liked anthropology because word-game analysis was largely absent from it; thus I was not predisposed to embrace a postmodern anthropology emerging from literary criticism.

One powerful motivation for writing this book came from my feeling that postmodernist criticism of ethnography had become excessively negative, incorrectly calling into question the value of ethnography and ultimately the value (or rather, the possibility) of anthropology. The postmodernist arguments are densely interwoven, but they attack ethnography on a number of levels ranging from the political and/or ethical through various layers of intellectual, theoretical, or epistemological concerns.

At the political level, the argument seems to run as follows: Ethnography is a form of intellectual imperialism, closely akin to and allied with other projects of Western domination over indigenous peoples, such as wars of conquest, colonialism, and the creation of a modern transnational economic and cultural order. Within this context, doing fieldwork and writing accounts of it are themselves acts that express an asymmetry of power. In this asymmetrical relationship, the ethnographer oppresses those among whom he lives both through his intrusive presence and through the text that he creates.

There are at least two related arguments here. The first is that the Western ethnographer is by definition a member of a dominating group that has historically been oppressive; therefore his project, the collection of knowledge about others, is an integral part of the project of domination. The second argument is that classical ethnography is also problematic because ethnographers have traditionally reified the people that they have studied—for example, objectifying them as "the" Komachi, who think this and say that. In so doing, the argument goes, the ethnographer has created and deployed a single, allegedly homogeneous voice, which misrepresents the diversity of opinion of the individual members of the society even as it denies them the chance to speak for themselves. In the jargon of postmodernist criticism, traditional ethnography is problematic because it masks the "heteroglossia"—the rich variety of voices—that is the true condition of any society and because it is nondialogic in that it provides the members of the society no space to make counterclaims to the voice of the ethnographer.[1]

Let me for the moment duck the larger political question of ethnography as domination—though I don't know who has more consistently spoken for local interests than anthropologists—and speak first about whether we should see the ethnographer's presence among a group of people and his nondialogic representation of them as problematic. Put differently, I will try to answer the question of whether one can rationalize "the sheer inexplicability and unjustifiability of the ethnographer's presence from the standpoint of the other" (Pratt

1986, 42). Then, as a corollary, I will speak to the question of whose voice should represent people such as the Komachi.

I cannot deny that Ann's and my presence among the Komachi was fundamentally inexplicable to them. No matter how many times we told them what we thought we were doing—trying to understand the lives of people different from ourselves, collecting information, hoping to write books and articles—we could not help overhearing how they described us to other people. Boiled down, this was what we heard: "They live in a tent; they travel around; they ask questions like, 'Who lives in this tent?' or 'Who was your grandfather?'; they are on a *tafrih* [roughly, a pleasure trip to the country]."

Did the Komachi find our presence unjustifiable? I can only note that their characterization of us seemed benign, and that at least some Komachi seemed proud that we were with them rather than another tribe. Minimally, we were a source of humor and of local transportation even as we asked them boring questions or intruded ourselves into their daily lives.

What of the question of representation, or appropriate representation? The assumption that something is problematic about an alien ethnographer representing (in multiple senses) people who are different runs through postmodernist criticism of ethnography. To address this point, I would like to refer back to my discussion of the Komachi, and ask who should be their representative. This is no idle question. As I hope I have shown, Komachi relations with most Iranians were at best ambiguous. Most urban Iranians I saw treated the Komachi as objects of scorn. In my observation of their encounters with nontribal Iranians, the Komachi received little or no respect.[2] This is not surprising, for the Komachi were essentially peasants, and Iran was a most stratified society. In addition, government policy was that the Komachi and other pastoral nomads were anachronisms. More government effort was spent trying to change (often radically) their lives than to understand them or even to better them. While I know that there were Iranians whose attempt to understand the Komachi (or groups like them) and their circumstances was not shaped by the goal of settling them or forcing them into production cooperatives, such Iranians most often worked with larger, more important groups in areas considered more vital to national development.[3] With the exception of a few merchants and others who had long-term dealings with nomads, we did not meet many urban Iranians sympathetic to them.

Most Komachi knew how urban Iranians felt about them. Komachi experience in encounters with urban Iranians was sharp enough to permit them to generate a clear understanding of how they were seen. Thus, perhaps some Komachi felt that our seemingly inexplicable presence among them, our interest in their lives, and our willingness to be there, to migrate with them, and to share their experiences may have been a positive thing, so that our presence did not seem entirely unjustifiable.

Simply letting people such as the Komachi speak for themselves is also harder than it might seem. There were no Komachi educated enough to be ethnographers in conventional terms. Nor were there poets, bards, or recognized recorders of Komachi life. There were 550 Komachi, so, setting aside small children, there were 450 potential voices for the Komachi. Traditionally, Komachi interlocutors with the outside world were the tribe's wealthiest and most powerful men. But, as I hope I have successfully shown, even within a community of roughly a hundred households, there was significant variation and people had vastly different views of how the world did and should operate. I am certain that no single Komachi could have represented the voices of other Komachi effectively or even authentically for all areas of their lives.

Within critical anthropological theory, much of the discussion of heteroglossia and dialogue ignores questions of just whom the ethnographer selects as the other voice(s) and how this selection is made. In particular, these discussions seem to stand outside the real-time flow of fieldwork. In my experience, in a social world as small as that of the Komachi, it took a long time to figure out just whom I was speaking with. Far from being able to record material as representative of a particular voice or set of voices, I recorded material to figure out first the nature of the whole social universe I was encountering, then whom (in terms of that social universe) I was speaking with. Only then could I feel that my attempts to represent or contextualize other voices were modestly accurate. And as circumstances changed, so did the apparent position of the voice I was recording. Any attempt to write an ethnography containing representative voices of the Komachi or any other group is therefore contingent on the ethnographer's having done enough analysis to know who represents what, and it is the ethnographer who still controls the "dialogue." Whether this is a great danger is not clear. In her 1995 essay "Resistance and Ethnographic Refusal," Sherry Ortner argues that it is very hard to write people out of their ethnographies:

> The ethnographic stance holds that ethnography is never impossible. This is the case because people not only resist political domination; they resist textual domination as well. The notion that colonial or academic texts are able to completely distort or exclude the voices and perspectives of those being written about seems to me to endow these texts with far greater power than they have. Many things shape these texts, including, dare one say it, the point of view of those being written about. Nor does one need to resort to various forms of tex-

tual experimentation to allow this to happen. . . . It seems to me grotesque to insist on the notion that the text is always shaped by everything but the lived reality of the people whom the text claims to represent. (Ortner 1995, 188)[4]

Other reasons also make it difficult to choose whose voices will represent any
given group. All societies are divided by multiple internal conflicts of the variety illustrated in this book and my other work on the Komachi. Selecting any
single "other" voice to the exclusion of its rivals masks internal conflicts and
risks what Ortner calls "the reified and romanticized subject of many resistance
studies" (and, by extension, of ethnographic description) by identifying with
one side of a conflict to the exclusion of other points of view (Ortner 1995,
186). This approach is disingenuous because in claiming to represent the "true
story" by giving voice to, for example, the "powerless," it suppresses other
voices. What is at issue here is not whose words are in the text, but how completely the ethnographer describes the complexity of a society.

It is, I think, important to note that even the process of attempting to set up
a dialogue, of attempting to identify and quote counterposed views within a society, can be problematic. Conflict within a society often entails potential danger for those with less power. Thus, the full range of discourse in a society always contains what James Scott has called "hidden transcripts," the necessarily
private expression of discontents by the poor and powerless for themselves,
among themselves. In discussing the acts and expressions of "quiet resistance"
by the powerless, Scott has forcefully argued that they are possible on a continuing basis only because they are hidden from those with power. Honest discourse between the parties is politically impossible, and revelation of the "hidden transcript" by, for example, an ethnographer is ethically improper. In short,
recognition of internal conflict and the concomitant existence of hidden transcripts suggests that it is naive to assume that an ethnographer might easily
record a fully open and informed discussion representing the views of differently empowered members of a society.[5] To the degree that ethnographers are
aware of "hidden transcripts" and know what they are, juxtapositions of different positions—examples of heteroglossia, if one wishes to call them that—can
be created only by the ethnographer (or other party) who is outside the web of
local power relations, for others equally outside the web.

I have raised the topic of the "hidden transcript" and, at least implicitly, of
the audience for anthropological texts. This in turn raises further points relat-
ing to the questions of ethnographic presence, representation, and power. One
concern expressed in postmodernist critiques of anthropology is that representing someone or some group in a text, capturing them on paper, is a form of
domination. Ethnographies may misrepresent people in any number of ways,

but it seems to me that the worry that this is a significant form of domination is overblown. In fact, it seems an almost bizarre misreading of the nature of the modern world to argue that ethnographic representations are a form of domination or an exemplar of power. Most ethnographies are read by a tiny audience of regional specialists; the audience for articles in professional journals is comparably small. It is a peculiar form of ethnocentrism, with perhaps a bit of hubris thrown in, that permits academics to assume that their words have impact much beyond the walls of their own tiny community. Certainly since the late 1960s (which marks the start of my own involvement in anthropology) the harm done to people by having texts written about them has been minuscule compared with the havoc wreaked by other forces in the world.

This is not, of course, to claim that ethnographers can do no harm. They can and do, though I suspect far more harm occurs from carelessness during fieldwork than from the impact of what is written. The reason for this should be clear. There are differences of wealth, power, and position in most societies. Not everyone shares all the information that is available, and there are very good reasons why many people don't want their words, thoughts, or deeds shared with other members of their community. Ethnography requires learning what is going on; who is doing what; and, to the degree possible, why they are doing it. To find answers, the ethnographer has to ask questions. Since, at least at the outset, the ethnographer cannot begin to know what is public knowledge and what is not, he or she has plenty of opportunity for getting things wrong, asking the wrong question, or making public information that should be private. In doing this, the ethnographer may well damage people's interests, sometimes severely.

But compared to the evil done by those with real power—often people's own governments—the harm done in this way is modest. I think it is even possible that the harm anthropologists do is modest compared with the good that flows from ethnographers' generally sympathetic representations of others or from their supplying medicine and transportation to the people they live with. Calling attention to the damage that can be and is done is important; dramatizing it is self-aggrandizing.

If one thrust of the postmodernist critique of ethnography has been largely political, the second has been directed more at the intellectual roots of the ethnographic project. While various critics have developed their particular criticisms in different ways, what seems to underlie many of them is a radical skepticism about the ethnographer's ability to apprehend, understand, and convey the "subjective" experience that he or she encounters in the field. The bases for this skepticism cover a wide range. There is the modest position that because all knowledge is culturally constructed, what ethnographers see and learn in the field is more a reflection of who they are than whatever it is they have encountered. A more radical position is that since twentieth-century science and philosophy (usually taken as some combination of Einstein, Heisenberg, Gödel, and others) have shown that there are limits on what we can definitively know, we really don't know what we think we know. The most radical positions argue, for example, that the truth or falsity of assertions is a linguistically verifiable proposition rather than an empirically verifiable one—in effect, there is no "there" there.

What links these various skepticisms is the assumption that the observer, in this case the ethnographer, does not really see what he thinks he sees or know what he thinks he knows. Knowing, suspecting, or fearing this, the ethnographer is forced to find ways to make his questionably real experience acceptably real to the audience who will read his works. Postmodernist critics claim that the ethnographer accomplishes this by writing up his experience in a way that makes the experience seem more real. He creates textual markers of authority and authenticity, like the lab coats worn by actors portraying doctors in cold-remedy advertisements. Since it is often difficult to show convincingly in any specific case that the ethnographer's experiences are not what he or she thought they were, much postmodernist criticism of ethnography has, in practice, centered on generically questioning the link between experience and understanding, criticizing the textual representation, showing how it omits voices, and uncovering the devices that authors have used to create an aura of authority and authenticity. This often means discovering that the author has falsely taken a stance of being scientifically objective, or disclosing that he has been creating his authority by personalizing the account and privileging subjective experience, neatly catching the author in a double bind.

By now it should be apparent that I have come to regard this elaborated worrying of the question of how we know what we know as something close to obsessive behavior. Needless to say, others share my opinion. However, I have found most responses to postmodernist criticism to have been ineffectual. Anthropologists hostile not only to postmodernist criticism but to the intellectual tradition it springs from have written scathing attacks that, sharing no common ground, vent frustrations but create no dialogue. Some have suggested cures as bad as the disease. Anthropologists more sympathetic to the tradition from which the criticism springs have responded only weakly to its excesses. Thus, Clifford Geertz, whose advocacy of "interpretive anthropology" seems to have prepared the way for the postmodern anthropological project, diagnoses postmodern anthropologists as suffering "grave inner uncertainties, amounting almost to an epistemological hypochondria, concerning how one can know that anything one says about other forms of life is as a matter of fact so" (Geertz 1988, 71).[6] But Geertz's response is embedded within a text that ultimately offers only the weakest support for ethnography: "If there is any way to counter the conception that ethnography is an iniquitous act or an unplayable game, it would seem to involve owning up to the fact that, like quantum mechanics or the Italian opera, it is a work of imagination" (Geertz 1988, 140).

This minimalist vision may speak to criticisms such as Clifford's, which claim that "the present predicament [of ethnography] is linked to the breakup and redistribution of colonial power in the decades after 1950" or that "no sovereign scientific method or ethical stance can guarantee the truth of such [ethnographic] images . . . constituted . . . in specific historical relations of dominance and dialogue" (Clifford 1983:118–19)—which may or may not be as portentous as they were intended to be. But the minimalist position seems a poor response to the more extreme attacks that seem to deny the possibility of legitimately doing ethnography. Short of a retreat into scientism, is there no effective response to cleverly worded linkages of ethnography with fiction—as in Clifford's "fictive world," "ethnographic fiction," or "true fictions"? Have we no concrete response to the innuendo-laden views of the ethnographer as "Hermes-like"— that is, essentially untruthful (Crapanzano 1986)—or like the literal inquisitor whose records form the basis of Le Roy Ladurie's history of Montaillou (Rosaldo 1986, 97)? What difference, after all, is there between Clifford's assertions that ethnographies are "true fictions" and Geertz's claim that they are "work[s] of imagination"? Is ethnography really nothing more than "the representation of one sort of life in the categories of another" (Geertz 1988, 144)?

In the following discussion I seek a common-sense-based middle ground from which I will try to reassert the possibility of doing meaningful ethnography. In doing so I seriously engage Clifford's challenging question: "If ethnography produces cultural interpretations through intense research experiences, how is unruly experience transformed into an authoritative written account?" (Clifford 1983, 120). In doing so, I will suggest that recent postmodernist critiques expressing concern with the epistemological bases of ethnographic experience overstate the problem. I will argue that it is simply wrong to assume that because the fieldworker's experience is "subjective" rather than "objective," it is nondialogic. I will try to show how ethnographic "being there" differs from just plain "being there." And I will attempt to suggest why the insight gained from fieldwork is vital to any understanding of others.

To answer Clifford's question in a positive way, it will be useful to more or less follow his argument, noting where we agree and responding to his criticisms as they arise. I recognize that by quoting Clifford extensively, I change the tone of this text. However, Clifford's argument is complex, and I think it unfair to simply paraphrase it. Moreover, the quotes that follow are good examples of postmodernist criticism. Those who do not generally read this kind of theoretical writing can look upon these passages as a kind of field experience in reading.

I begin by noting that I fully agree with Clifford's suggestion that "it is more than ever crucial for people to form complex concrete images of one another . . . [and] the relationships of knowledge and power that connect them" (Clifford 1983, 119). I similarly agree that

> participant observation obliges its practitioners to experience, at a bodily as
> well as intellectual level, the vicissitudes of translation. . . . There is, of course,
> a myth of fieldwork. . . . But as a means for producing knowledge from an in
> tense intersubjective engagement, the practice of ethnography retains a certain
> exemplary status. (Clifford 1983, 119)

Put briefly, if you want to know what other people's lives are like, try living with them. Or, try doing it *without* living with them!

But of course it is not so simple. The problem, really the double problem, is establishing the authenticity of experience and then of textual representation. Clifford's "On Ethnographic Authority" still seems the clearest enumeration of these problems.

Regarding the questions of fieldwork and its translation into "authoritative" text, Clifford argues, "This peculiar amalgam of intense personal experience and scientific analysis . . . emerged as a method: participant observation . . . [which] remains the chief distinguishing feature of professional anthropology." According to Clifford, this method "serves as a shorthand for a continuous tacking . . . on the one hand grasping the sense of specific occurrences and gestures emphatically, on the other stepping back to situate these meanings in wider contexts" (Clifford 1983, 127). Put simply, one has experiences; one tries to understand them.

In his exposition of just what this process entails, Clifford further argues, "Fieldwork was . . . centered on the *experience* of the participant-observing scholar. . . . Experiential authority is based on a 'feel' for the foreign context" (Clifford 1983, 128). Thus, in some significant sense, the center of ethnography is the process of "being there" and then "bringing it home" for others. This then becomes the crux of at least one problem: What is ethnographic experience? What does "being there" mean?

Up till this point, I have only marginal disagreements with Clifford—certainly I agree that fieldwork is the chief, and largely positive, distinguishing feature of anthropology. But on the question of "experience," our paths diverge. Developing his theme, Clifford argues, "It is difficult to say very much about experience. Like 'intuition,' one has it or not, and its invocation often smacks of mystification" (Clifford 1983, 128). But it seems that the mystification—the feeling of being tricked—here lies in claiming that experience is like intuition, whose very existence is suspect. To me the field experience is far more like a sharp blow to the head or a large spoonful of horseradish; it is a process that marks those who have been through it.

More important, Clifford claims that experience is most strongly grounded through Dilthey's notion of *Verstehen,* or "understanding others . . . from the sheer fact of co-existence in a shared world." But he goes on to argue, "This experiential world . . . is precisely what is missing or problematic for an ethnographer entering another culture." Comparing anthropological experience to *Verstehen,* which is equated to shared experience, Clifford is able to argue that the ethnographer, lacking the shared experience, lacks understanding, and therefore his experience is as ephemeral as intuition. He then goes on to say that what happens through the fieldwork process is that "Dilthey's 'common sphere' must be established and re-established, building up a shared experiential world in relation to which all 'facts,' 'texts,' 'events,' and their interpretations will be constructed," and adds that this process is "always subjective in nature" (Clifford 1983, 128). Thus, "ethnographic 'experience' can be seen as the building-up of a common, meaningful world, drawing on intuitive styles of feeling, perception, and guesswork" (Clifford 1983, 129). Put slightly differently, we best understand others if we share their life experiences. But anthropologists entering new societies share little apparent common experience with the people they encounter, so they cannot understand them. Being there long enough, they come to share experiences and thus arrive at a common understanding with the people with whom they have lived.

But is ethnographic understanding really the process of building up the "common, meaningful world," or is it a process of building a meaningful world that may *not* be common to the ethnographer and the observed? Moreover, is the process simply built on "intuitive styles of feeling, perception, and guesswork," or is there more? In some sense this is the key question. If fieldwork is nothing more than being there and exercising our intuitions, nothing more than guesswork directed toward the process of building a common sphere with those whose cultures we study, of empathizing with them, then perhaps the postmodernist critics are right. I think, however, that it is more than that.

In the preceding chapters, I have attempted to show how my experiences among the Komachi shaped my understanding of them, and that part of field experience consists of a constant process of being brought up short, of having expectations confounded, of being forced to think very hard about what is happening, right now, with me and them, let alone the thinking and rethinking about those experiences when they have—sometimes mercifully—passed. If I have been able to effectively evoke what it was like to see Shir Ali treated with unexpected disdain by a district governor, or how Sekine treated Ali after he fainted, or what Taj Ali told me about his tent furnishings after I gave him penicillin, or how I responded to waiting for Abbas Tavakoli, then it seems to me that Clifford's claim that "because it is hard to pin down, 'experience' has served as an effective guarantee of ethnographic authority" (Clifford 1983, 130) is mistaken. Experience, though subjective, is not particularly furtive; striking experience is even less so. It can be described, and so can one's response and the larger context.

Indeed, on reflection, it seems to me that the greatest problem centered on experience and understanding lies not with having ethnographic experiences or even necessarily in writing them up or down in a way that is authentic and authoritative. The far greater problem involves helping others whose experience is only vicarious really understand what the anthropologist's own experience was all about. My account of the difficulties my Komachi listeners had in visualizing or understanding the realities of wheat production in the United States highlights the difficulty of helping others grasp what they have never seen. Put slightly differently, ethnographic experience—for example, learning about tents and pegs and flies and screens—is, if it is sharp enough or sufficiently cumulative, likely to create understanding. Having others understand that understanding is the trick. Providing a vivid and full account of ethnographic experience dramatically increases readers' chances of sharing in the ethnographer's understanding.

Clifford also argues that "experience evokes a participatory presence . . . and experience also suggests a cumulative deepening knowledge," points with which I would largely concur. But he goes on to argue that "this world when conceived as an experiential creation, is subjective, not dialogical or intersubjective" (Clifford 1983, 130). That is, because we encounter the world through our experience of it, we create our own private understanding of it. In some ultimate sense, this is certainly true. But Clifford seems to push the point, assuming a most peculiar relation between fieldworkers and the people among whom they live. Of course the fieldworker's vision of the "ethnographic world" is subjective, as are all our views of all our experiences. But there are other people there, and they are never silent. Again and again, I have tried to show that the project of understanding is fully dialogic and intersubjective. Ann and I had expectations, understandings, views of the Komachi and of the Iranian world. When we acted on them, others acted back. Their responses, the ways they shattered or confirmed our expectations, were precisely part of an experience that was constantly dialogic and intersubjective. We created our own understanding, but we had a lot of help doing it.

Again I stress that our ethnographic understanding was not, as Clifford suggests, necessarily the process of building a common, meaningful world. We were not trying to become Komachi. Rather, coming to ethnographic understanding was the process of building *our* meaningful model of the Komachi world through a process in which the model was constantly being corrected as the result of the actions of others and of encounters with them. The process could hardly be more dialogic.

It also seems that part of the problem with the notion of experience lies in the imprecise use of the term. In some sense—I am certain that I too am guilty of this—there is a tendency to conflate "fieldwork" with "field experience" or just plain "experience." While the conflation is partly reasonable, it is not fully so.

First, and it must be said, while it is probably true that everyone who has been "in the field" has had "field experience," it is by no means true that everyone who has been "in the field" has done "fieldwork." An obvious and significant distinction separates ethnographers from travelers, castaways, captives, or others who have "been there" but haven't done fieldwork. As I noted in my introduction, this is a distinction that Mary Louise Pratt has called into question, and I shall turn to her argument shortly.

Second, one might distinguish between good (or at least adequate) and bad fieldwork. In *Works and Lives,* writing of writing ethnography, Geertz says:

> "Being There" authorially, palpably on the page, is in any case as difficult a trick to bring off as "being there" personally, which after all demands at the minimum hardly more than a travel booking and permission to land; a willingness to endure a certain amount of loneliness, invasion of privacy, and physical discomfort; a relaxed way with odd growths and unexplained fevers; a capacity to stand still for artistic insults, and the sort of patience that can support an endless search for invisible needles in infinite haystacks. (Geertz 1988, 23–24)

But can we say that this kind of experience—"been there, saw that, ate that, got sick, came home"—is field*work?* In a recent essay, Ortner notes that ethnography

> minimally . . . has always meant the attempt to understand another life world using the self—as much of it as possible—as the instrument of knowing. . . . Classically, this kind of understanding has been closely linked with fieldwork, in which the whole self physically and in every other way enters the space of the world the researcher seeks to understand. (Ortner 1995, 173–74)

Still, what does this mean? How does the self become the "instrument of knowing"? How does one move from "being there" to apprehending the "thickness . . . producing understanding through richness, texture, and detail . . . (with

traces of both exhaustiveness and holism)" that Ortner argues—and I concur—
is "at the heart of the ethnographic stance" (Ortner 1995, 174)?

Reflecting on my experience, and making no claims that my fieldwork was
anything more than adequate, several answers seem to emerge. First, field*work*
is just that; it is not simply field experience. Some parts of the work entail all
the obvious things: watching, listening, surveys, censuses, measuring, counting, questioning, kinship charts, and, to some limited extent, doing. But given
the role of census takers, extension workers, tribal liaison officers, and community workers—not to mention home-grown and exogenous spies, secret police, and what have you—simply watching, asking, or even writing it down is
not what distinguishes ethnographic fieldwork. Rather, ethnographic fieldwork
is totally dialogic, in that it involves the constant questioning of experience and
encounter as part of the creation of an understanding of the other—that is,
model building. Each noted event, each happening, that is lived through, seen,
experienced as either participant or observer is examined for what it means,
how it fits in, how it changes, and how it amplifies or confirms the ethnographer's understanding. Experience is played off against other experience, against
models in the literature, against theory, against the anthropologist's own provisional models. It is precisely the constant attempt to use experiences as elements of an understanding that is at once incomplete and impossible to complete, but also wonderfully capable of being improved, that makes fieldwork
experience different from just experience and turns it into doing ethnography.

Reflecting on my own fieldwork, I would argue that my encounter with experience was always part of a triangular conversation in which experience represented one point and Ann and I the other two. It is hard to estimate what portion
of our time was spent discussing what we had seen and heard, then attempting
to determine what we would need to know and whom we would need to ask. If
we did not agree, we had to decide how we could determine which of our views
was more reasonable (and stubborn people with no arbiter may go to great
lengths) or, if neither of us was happy with our understanding, what we could
do to arrive at an understanding that either (and ideally both) of us considered
reasonable. Our field notes are filled with comments such as "find out,"
"check," "must check," and with references back to events now better explained
or understood by an encounter with additional information or a later experience.

The point here is that one really does agonize over the relationship of experience and understanding. As much as possible, and recognizing everything
that constrains its happening, one simply wants to get things as right as one
can. This starts with experience and understanding, and then is followed by the
problem of trying to communicate that understanding as well and as honestly
as possible (and the *writing* of ethnography is as much, if not more, the focus

of much postmodernist criticism). The phrases that Ortner uses to describe aspects of the ethnographic project—that it entails "the *obligation* to engage with reality," and that it is such that "the anthropologist and the historian are *charged* with representing the lives of people who are living or who once lived" (Ortner 1995, 189, emphasis added)—appropriately suggest just how important this is.

The "charge" to get things right derives from a number of things. Unlike texts that can be read and reread, what ethnographers see is ephemeral. There is no simple way to check any anthropologist's claim to have seen something. Ethnographers have an obligation to each other to get it as right as possible. They also have an obligation to the people whose lives they enter to represent them as honestly as possible, to carefully link experience and understanding. Moreover, these obligations are not simply based on a notion of being professional—although that is an element of it. To the degree that there is a moral agenda to anthropology, it is one of promoting the appreciation and understanding of difference in a world in which very significant and powerful forces encourage (and thrive on) the politicization and demonization of difference. In undertaking to struggle against that most dangerous position, it is vital to have one's "facts" as well marshaled, accurate, and honest as one can.

This constant attempt to "get it right" is not limited to description. While Ann and I tried to make sure we had things "right," and we used each other as fact checkers, our work, even in the field, was by no means just an attempt to record what we had seen. Rather, the dialogue was an attempt at understanding, at putting the single pieces and events into a larger, fuller context: a vision of the Komachi world in which theory (or at least a model) and experience coincided. That this understanding was limited, incomplete, and in some cases quite likely wrong goes almost without saying. There were more than a few times that Ann and I wished there were yet a third fieldworker, a true metaethnographer, doing the ethnography of us and the Komachi, someone whom we could turn to as an arbiter and ask, "We think it's this way, are we right?"[7]

Sometimes our attempt to "get things right" evolved into a quasi technique. Our work on the politics of hiring shepherds and marrying off children was based on a continuous process of observation, discussion, and follow-up. We would observe negotiations, disputes, and Komachi retellings of these events; we would attempt to analyze, contextualize, and understand what we had seen and heard; then we would seek out informants, either to try to gather additional information that would clarify the situation or to check our analyses. Whatever else it was, the translation of experience into understanding was far closer to Clifford's tacking between "grasping the sense of specific occurrences and gestures emphatically . . . [and] stepping back to situate these meanings in wider contexts" (Clifford 1983, 127) than a process of "feeling and intuition." Here and in the preceding chapters, I hope I have been able to some degree to make explicit the process of that tacking, of forming the link between occurrence, context, and understanding.

I have already quoted Clifford's claim that the experience of fieldwork is "the chief distinguishing feature of professional anthropology" (Clifford 1983, 127). I agree with this view, and I think it is precisely this intense grounding of understanding in practical experience that makes anthropology so distinct and so important—hence much of the preceding discussion of understanding and reaffirming the importance of the fieldwork experience, of "being there." However, I have also suggested that with regard to fieldwork, "being there" doesn't mean just the passage of time and the willingness to endure the discomforts enumerated by Geertz. Rather, the ethnographic process of being there minimally entails a kind of work directed at explicitly understanding those one lives among. However, the consideration of other kinds of fieldwork undertaken toward different ends suggests that as a definition of fieldwork, "working there" is also too minimal. In attempting to distinguish ethnographic fieldwork from other forms of "being there," I will set my answer against the works of two authors. One, again, is James Clifford; the second is Mary Louise Pratt, who in a series of works has trenchantly asked what distinguishes ethnography from other forms of writing about "being there"—for example, from travel writing or captives' tales (Pratt 1986; 1991).

My inclusion within this text of excerpts from other, earlier authors can be taken as evidence of my interest in their works. This interest is twofold. When I use their texts as historical sources, I am interested in the specifics of what they have to say. However, I am also interested in how to understand the similarities and differences in feeling or attitude I find in their work and my own; that is my primary concern here.

In "On Ethnographic Authority," James Clifford recalls for us the dialogue between Bronislaw Malinowski—one of the founding giants of fieldwork-based anthropology—and Alex Rentoul, a colonial magistrate who had the "temerity" to question some of Malinowski's views on Trobriand paternity and to suggest that on occasion a magistrate "might be in a more advantageous position than would a visiting anthropologist, however gifted" (Rentoul 1931).[8] Writing of this encounter and the early period of ethnography, Clifford reminds us that "at the close of the nineteenth century nothing guaranteed, *a priori,* the ethnographer's status as the best interpreter of native life—as opposed to the traveler, and especially the missionary and the administrator" (Clifford 1983, 121).

There are reasons for this, some of which Clifford enumerates—for example, length of stay and linguistic competence (both generally favoring the missionary or administrator)—and others he does not. While this is not the place for details, my reading of numerous reports, notebooks, memos, letters, and diaries of late-nineteenth-century and early-twentieth-century British travelers and officials in Iran reveals that those who were conscientious worked hard at learning languages (often spending hours a day with tutors), spent time on local customs, and had some access to collections of earlier reports and documents. The number of printed and bound reports of journeys and reconnaissances is staggering, suggesting that individuals were interested not only in providing appropriate background information for effective administration but also in getting their name in print, and that getting in print was a good thing. Some of the discussions of these materials, published or otherwise, by others with similar expertise—for example, at meetings of the Royal Geographical Society and other venues—suggests that the collection and transmission of knowledge were taken very seriously indeed.[9]

Thus whatever it was that distinguished ethnographic fieldwork and ethnographic knowledge from that collected by the British working in Iran (and by extension, I believe, other colonial officials), it was not that ethnographers had greater training, greater local knowledge, or greater dedication to getting information. Much of what we now gloss as travel literature was collected by men and women whose primary reasons for traveling and collecting information were serious enough to merit great attention to the material at hand.

Mary Louise Pratt has argued that "the authority of the ethnographer over the 'mere traveler' rests chiefly on the idea that the traveler just passes through, whereas the ethnographer lives with the group under study" (Pratt 1986, 38). But as I have suggested, this is only sometimes true. Of the four authors whose accounts I have presented, Wilson spent over a decade in Iran, Sheil spent nearly four years there, Bishop spent roughly two years in Iran, and Layard over eighteen months in Iran and more than ten with the Bakhtiyari. By contrast, Barth spent fewer than six months with the Basseri. Thus, while it may be the case that in (many) earlier ethnographies, "dull-looking figures called 'mere travelers' or 'casual observers' show up from time to time, only to have their superficial perceptions either corrected or corroborated by the serious scientist" (Pratt 1986, 27), it is hardly the superficiality of their perception that distinguishes the observations of earlier writers from Ann's and my own.

Pratt has also suggested, and I generally concur, that much travel literature can be characterized as "sentimental." She argues that "sentimental writing explicitly anchors what is being expressed in the sensory experience . . . in the authenticity of somebody's felt experience" (Pratt 1992, 76). It may be that this distinguishes some travel literature from some highly formal ethnography, though, as Pratt suggests, personal narratives are a part of almost every ethnography. But to the degree that a narrative of personal experience forms the core of this work, it is clear that "sentimentality" alone does not distinguish travel literature from ethnography.

One key to explaining this may perhaps be found in Pratt's description of Mungo Park, whose works are exemplars of sentimental travel literature. Of Park she notes, "He made himself the protagonist and central figure of his own account, which takes the form of an epic series of trials, challenges, and encounters with the unpredictable" (Pratt 1992, 75). Bishop and, to a somewhat lesser extent, Layard did make themselves the "central figures" of their works. This seems less true for either Sheil or Wilson; until recently this focus on one's self was absent from most ethnography.[10] One salient difference between travel writing and ethnography lies in the shift of focus from the author as central figure and protagonist to a focus on providing a representation of the "other people" as revealed by the experience of the ethnographer. Significantly, I do not think that this shift of focus from author to other is necessarily the same as the shift that Pratt identifies as the move from sentimentality to its "opposite," the "bureaucratic/scientific practices of objectivism," where "the authority of . . . discourse resides in the detachment of what is said from the subjectivity of both the speaker and the experiencer" (Pratt 1992, 76). What is significant is not the visible presence or absence of the ethnographer, but what she or he is trying to help us see and understand. Ethnography is precisely concerned with *not* being detached from the subjectivity of the speaker and the experiencer.

If the distinguishing characteristic of the ethnographic observer is not greater specific knowledge, greater accuracy in observation, greater subtlety of interpretation, or "bureaucratic/scientific objectivism," what is it? To the degree that the nonethnographic texts I have chosen are representative of nonethnographic writing, the greatest differences lie in what ethnographers attempt to do with their "data." Ethnographers make a serious and significant attempt to contextualize the encounter, event, and observation and to place them within a framework that facilitates understanding of the encounter even as the encounter shapes and changes the framework. Ethnographers attempt to observe and understand with moral judgment reserved (not suspended), generally by assuming that what is observed cannot be judged as an isolated instance but takes place within a system of meaning generally glossed as "culture." Ethnographers operate with the quixotic and peculiar assumption that the goal of knowledge gained is neither some practical outcome—for example, the opening of a new trade route to the interior of Iran—nor a justification for some larger moral project of transforming others. Rather, the aim is just to learn about those others.

In the end, the ethnographic project comes down to the attempt to *under-*

stand, as best as possible, what people are doing and why they are doing it, if only through situating what people are doing within the quasi system of rules and interpretations that anthropologists call culture.[11] At least implicitly, that understanding often has a comparative basis, setting the particular culture in question against others that are similar or different. It is this attempt to understand that distinguishes ethnography from travel writing and, as far as I can tell, from spying too.

Perhaps I can illustrate this distinction by providing an example, in this case part of an intelligence report written by W. Baring in 1882.

> The Bakhtiyari hills [under Hossain Kuli Khan] are safe enough. . . . At his death however, it will be strange indeed if more than one candidate does not spring up and contend for the post. The Persian government, *more suo,* will confer it on the man who pays the largest sum down, or who offers to squeeze the most revenue out of the people. Factions will be formed and disturbances will take place. (Baring 1882, 4)

Baring here uses the notion of culture or custom, using the Latin term *more,* partly to explain the political turmoil he predicts but primarily in an ironic mode to diminish the moral authority of the Persian government. Baring's use of culture to denigrate its bearers is vastly different from the ethnographic deployment of the concept of culture, which, because it is directed at understanding, stresses the commonality of people(s) instead of concretizing differences between them.

Fieldwork provides the experiences and the encounters that by their force and intensity demand that the ethnographer try to understand them. It is the combination of the ethnographer's desire to understand and the experiences' demand to be understood that drives the ethnographic project. Fieldwork—being there and working through the experience—is not the only way to achieve ethnographic understanding, but because of the number, kinds, and intensity of the encounters it entails, it is the most important and effective way; it provides the basis for the kind of "thickness" that lies at the heart of the ethnographic project.

This latter point may seem self-evident—it does to me. But it was a challenge to this very notion that impelled me to write this book. Mary Louise Pratt's examination of anthropologists' responses to a work by Florinda Donner (which many took to be a reworking of other people's experiences among the Yanomamo, so that her book was seen as an ethnographic account based on no ethnographic experience) seemed to directly attack the root of all ethnography: our ability to accept other ethnographers' works as, at the very least, good-faith descriptions of what they believe they have seen. Pratt asked why, if no one claimed that it contained ethnographic errors, anthropologists were upset about

Donner's book, suggesting that "what was at issue was not ethnographic accuracy, but a set of problematic links between ethnographic authority, personal experience, scientism, and originality of expression" (Pratt 1986, 29).

Earlier in this chapter I attempted to suggest that a number of the alleged problems in the link between experience and ethnographic authority are not as great as some claim. What is far more problematic is the argument that ethnographic authority does not rest on fieldwork experience. That fieldwork experience does not convey absolute authority goes without saying; that field experience alone does not make one an ethnographer I have conceded. What does seem problematic is the notion that there can be either ethnography or understanding of the other without the opportunity for observing the "thickness" that field experience supplies. Pratt's discussion of Florinda Donner seems to suggest that the problem of the link between "ethnographic authority [and] personal experience" is the same as the problem of claiming to have been in the field when one hasn't. In other words, for Pratt, fraudulently claiming to have done fieldwork is no more problematic than the vexed link of "ethnographic authority" to experience. Put this way, I hope it is clear why anthropologists became upset about Donner's work. Subjective as it is, experience—the forced encounter with that which demands to be understood or explained—is all there is. That experience, coupled with the will and the effort needed to understand it, is ethnography.

My goal in this chapter and in this book has been to illustrate the relation between experience and ethnographic understanding by examining the ways in which the cumulative effect of serendipitous, unexpected encounters and experiences shaped my understanding of the Komachi. In addressing those issues, I have spent some time discussing what distinguishes ethnographic fieldwork—"being there" as an anthropologist—from just "being there"; I have also mentioned, perhaps primarily in passing, the relationship of fieldwork to "ethnographic authority" (the question of why anyone should accept my account of the Komachi, or anyone else's account of the people they have worked with). I would like to close with two points.

In this book I have made a conscious effort to show a direct link between what I encountered and how I developed an understanding of both the event and the Komachi. If I have been moderately successful, most people reading this book will find most of the links I have drawn between my experiences and my understandings reasonable, and they will agree that my understandings provide an effective way of seeing the Komachi. Alternatively, readers may reject the validity of the experiences, the links, or the understanding. In doing so, they are testing my authorial (and indeed my ethnographic) authority. This testing of my authority, of the authenticity of my understanding, may or may not be easier to do to a text in this format than to a more conventional ethnography. However, having written both kinds of books, I would like to stress that in my opinion, the linkage between experience and understanding is in both cases identical. What distinguishes an anecdotal text such as this from a more formal work such as my earlier *Ambiguous Relations* is not the experience, the linkages, or the understandings, but the degree to which one or another of them is foregrounded. In the final analysis, the authority and authenticity of all ethnographic accounts rest on the integrity of the ethnographer's experience and subsequent mental labor. Thus, one can ask whether a text such as this really provides greater substantiation of ethnographic authority or authenticity than more formal work, or whether our judgment of authenticity rests on our critical reading of the integrity of the work regardless of its format. I think the answer is clear.

The preceding question leads directly to my second point. If texts such as this do not guarantee more authenticity than formal ones, why not stick to classic ethnographies? I would argue that one reason is to place in the public domain as much description of experience and encounter as possible. The purpose of doing so is not to buttress claims of authority; it is to provide current and future readers, whatever their backgrounds or interests, the greatest possible range of material to work with as they seek to understand the ways in which the lives of peoples of different cultures are similar to or different from their own. Earlier, I argued that the hard part of ethnography lies not in the ethnographer's turning her or his experience into understanding but in effectively communicating that understanding to an audience that does not share the experience. I am not certain that the more directly experience is conveyed, the more effectively understanding can be shared, but my teaching has made me suspect that this is so. Finally, we must remember that the description of experience, the attempt at understanding, is not static. The British consul who described the prospects for trade in Kerman province in the 1840s did not project my using his data to explain the development of classes among the Komachi. Who knows what anyone in the future will make of my account or my analysis in this work or any other? But if we believe in any accumulation of knowledge and increase in understanding in the human sciences, it seems clear that description and portrayal of direct experience, appropriately contextualized, is the basis of both present and future understanding of others. And that is not a bad thing.

NOTES

Introduction

1. Sir Justin Sheil had in fact served earlier as an advisor to the Persian army; overall he remained in Iran for nearly twenty years (Wright 1977, 22).

2. As I noted above, this text in a way emerges directly from my encounters with the literature on writing ethnography and, within that, on the relationship of ethnography to travel literature. To create a text that is readable and useful to a more general audience, I have chosen not to front-load this work with yet another iteration of the problem/nonproblem and the relationship of this work to it. Instead, in a separate chapter, following the conclusion of this narrative, I include a brief discussion of the relation of this work to some of the literature on fieldwork and writing ethnography.

3. "Being there" is a modest borrowing from Geertz's discussion. It is intended to stress the importance of a long-term, cumulative encounter. One aspect of my annoyance at postmodernist criticism of fieldwork and ethnography is that it has, rightly or wrongly, served to validate nonanthropological "multicultural" study based on flying visits, brief encounters, and highly selective readings. I do not see this as an effective way of advancing knowledge or understanding.

Chapter 3

1. I am not, of course, the only one who has noted or commented on the stereotypic aspect of accounts of trips to the field. See, for example, Pratt 1986 and 1992 for interesting comments on the nature and significance of journeys and arrivals in both ethnographic and travel literature.

Chapter 5

1. Traditionally Iranians ate sitting on the floor with their dishes of food spread on a woven cloth. By the 1970s these woven cloths had generally been replaced with

lengths of plastic sheeting, often covered with repetitive designs. *Chelow kebab* is the Iranian equivalent of fast food: thin slices of lamb are seasoned, threaded on skewers, grilled, and served over mounds of white rice. Restaurants and stands serving *chelow kebab* are found in cities throughout Iran and at stopping points along most highways. Good *chelow kebab* are truly delicious.

Chapter 9

1. There was, of course, considerable exchange of deliberate ethnic and religious insults, but those emerged later and were predicated on a clear control of group boundaries and membership.

2. There was much greater variety in women's names. Some were religious in origin, but others came from names for flowers or abstract qualities.

3. They are, in fact, one and the same person, the Imam Hossein's half-brother, slaughtered with him at Kerbala (see pages 55ff. in this chapter).

Chapter 13

1. Although Moqtar was Janallah's older brother, and although both were from a very important Komachi family, Moqtar did not act like a prominent member of the tribe, nor was he considered one.

2. Not surprisingly, I get almost the same response when I ask my students why we put up trees at Christmas or give baskets of candy at Easter.

Chapter 15

1. There is, of course, no excuse for my behavior. I should not have given Ali the medicine, and though I can describe my rationalizations, they remain just that.

2. Dover's powder—given the Bakhtiyari by both Layard and Bishop—was a common nineteenth-century cure for respiratory problems. Its active ingredients were ten grains each of opium and ipecacuanha, mixed with eighty grains of milk sugar.

Chapter 16

1. Lois Beck (1991) describes urban Iranians descending on Qashqa'i nomads while partaking of a day in the country. We saw somewhat similar impositions among the Komachi, although the visitors were never the total strangers Beck describes.

Chapter 21

1. The behavior I describe here is one that Ann observed several times with different mothers, different babies, and different women in attendance. It was only when they were much, much older that children were nursed promptly.

Chapter 22

1. For example, James Clifford argues that "the words of ethnographic writing, then, cannot be construed as monologic, as the authoritative statement about, or interpretation of, an abstracted textualized reality. The language of ethnography is shot through with other subjectivities and specific contextual overtones. For all language,

in Bakhtin's view, is 'a concrete heteroglot conception of the world'" (Clifford 1983, 133). The following from Tyler seems a typical statement of the need for a new way of writing ethnography: "Post-modern ethnography privileges 'discourse' over 'text,' it foregrounds dialogue as opposed to monologue. . . . Polyphony is a means of perspectival relativity . . . the form itself should emerge out of the joint work of the ethnographer and his native partners" (Tyler 1986:126–27).

2. See, in particular, chapter 16, especially pp. 114, 115 and 121. This is a problem even where the external representative appears sympathetic. My more sensitive students are frequently disturbed by elite authors' creation of thoughts or feelings for the poor and oppressed, as, for example, in Nawaal el Saadawi's novel *God Dies by the Nile*.

3. In the case of tribal Iran, many of these individuals were themselves members of large political groups that had a history of opposition to the state.

4. The countering position can be found in Crapanzano's critique of Geertz, where he raises the problems of imputing to others a singular vision. "How," he asks, "can a whole people share a single subjectivity?" and he warns that summary statements about what the so-and-so think or feel risk being seen as "constructions of constructions of constructions . . . projections, or at least blurrings," conflating the ethnographer's point of view "with that of the native, or, more accurately, of the constructed native" (Crapanzano 1986, 74).

5. To use an example that we encountered, an ethnographer cannot ask a wealthy herd owner, "Your shepherd told me he will leave you because you don't treat him right. Do you think he will?" Indeed, in small-scale societies where ethnographers live shockingly public lives and people often know exactly whom one has spoken to and when, there are times when it even might not be appropriate to ask, "Do shepherds leave their employers if they say they are unhappy with them?" The following brief anecdote will make it clear how much people knew of our activities. About a year into our stay with in Iran, Ann received some small, inconspicuous silver earrings from her parents. Later, she lost one earring. Very shortly after that, when several young women commented on her changing her earrings, Ann mentioned losing the earring. Later still, when we visited another quite distant camp, the women there commented on Ann's new earrings and the loss of one of the old ones.

6. Geertz's comment on the result of this "hypochondria" is too telling to pass by: "What is at hand is a pervasive nervousness about the whole business of claiming to explain enigmatical others on the ground that you have gone about with them in their native habitat or combed the writings of those who have. This nervousness brings on, in turn, various responses, variously excited: deconstructive attacks on canonical works, and on the very idea of canonicity as such; *Ideologiekritik* unmaskings of anthropological writings as the continuation of imperialism by other means; clarion calls to reflexivity, dialogue, heteroglossia, linguistic play, rhetorical self-consciousness, performance translation, verbatim recording, and first-person narrative as forms of cure" (Geertz 1988, 131).

7. Of course, we also used whatever insights we could get from other anthropologists. The late Connie Cronin, whose fieldwork with elites in Tehran overlapped our

work in Kerman, always enjoyed laughingly describing our periodic arrivals in Tehran, claiming that no one could shut us up as we talked nonstop about our field experiences. But those nonstop descriptions ultimately led to long, useful conversations, as we were able to try our provisional models on living, critical respondents.

8. To the external observer, and indeed to Rentoul (1932, 274), Malinowski's response (1932, 33ff.) appears both disproportionate to the offense and unnecessarily harsh. It makes most sense to see it as a turf war: Malinowski was trying to establish the professional reputation of anthropologists vis-à-vis others working in colonial situations. Today those of us doing historical work are simply glad to find data we can use.

9. This feeling is, of course, magnified when one considers the mass of material printed in such vehicles as the *Journal of the Royal Geographical Society* and the *Journal of the Royal Central Asian Society,* not to mention the *Times* (London) and other newspapers and more popular magazines. One should also note the periodic compilation of material into gazetteers (some of which were formidable documents), the creation of bibliographies, and the publication of books, for example, Lord Curzon's *Persia and the Persian Question* or Sir Percy Sykes's various works on Iran, which refer extensively to both published works and British government documents. My more limited contact with Russian and French materials on Iran and other areas of the Middle East suggests an equivalent diligence and seriousness of purpose.

10. Again, perhaps it is Sheil's slightly self-mocking tone that decenters her as a sentimental heroine. How is one to deal with a description of a journey that begins, "I doubt if our hardships will excite the sympathy they deserve" (Sheil 1856, 99)? I must add that her book, which is divided into her own narrative and a series of "notes" by her husband, provides in itself a fascinating contrast of voices, hers more or less discursive, his far more clipped and factual. A good deal of Wilson's text shares this latter tone, which seems quite close to what Geertz, writing of the great British anthropologist E. E. Evans-Pritchard, calls "Akobo Realism" (Geertz 1988, 61) and Pratt calls "bureaucratic/scientific . . . objectivism" (Pratt 1992, 76). For what it is worth, having read more reports of "encounters" than I ever expected to, I believe that there is much more to this tone than a desire to buttress one's scientific credibility.

11. I take it as a given that placing events in their cultural context is not always a complete explanation. It is, however, a far better explanation than, for example, "Shit happens." Put in a Komachi context, I have already noted that Ann and I did not feel that "It is our custom" was a satisfying explanation for the Komachi doing things as they did. On the other hand, it was not an untrue answer. Moreover, the knowledge that events taking place were expected and appropriate is also significant to understanding what is taking place.

WORKS CITED AND SUGGESTED READINGS

Baring, W.
    1882   "A Report on a Journey to Shuster, Dizful, Behbehan, and Shiraz."
                India Office Records Library, London: V/27/69/24.
Barth, Fredrik
    1959   "The Land Use Pattern of Migratory Tribes of South Persia." *Norsk
                Geografisk Tidsskrift* 17:1–11 (Bobbs-Merrill Reprint No. A-11).
    1960   "Nomadism in the Mountain and Plateau Areas of Southwest Asia."
                In *Problems of the Arid Zone*. Paris: UNESCO.
    1961   *Nomads of South Persia*. Boston: Little, Brown.
Bates, Daniel, and Amal Rassam
    1983   *Peoples and Cultures of the Middle East*. Englewood Cliffs:
                Prentice-Hall.
Beck, Lois
    1986   *The Qashqa'i of Iran*. New Haven: Yale University Press.
    1991   *Nomad*. Berkeley: University of California Press.
Bishop, Mrs. Isabella Bird
    1891   *Journeys in Persia and Kurdistan*. New York: G. P. Putnam's Sons.
Black-Michaud, Jacob
    1986   *Sheep and Land*. Cambridge: Cambridge University Press.
Bradburd, Daniel
    1980   "Never Give a Shepherd an Even Break: Class and Labor Among the
                Komachi of Kerman Iran". *American Ethnologist* 7(4):604–20.
    1981   "Size and Success: Komachi Adaptation to a Changing Iran". In
                N. Keddie and M. Bonine, eds., *Modern Iran: The Dialectics of
                Continuity and Change*. Albany: State University of New York Press.
    1982   "Volatility of Animal Wealth Among Southwest Asian
                Pastoral Nomads". *Human Ecology* 10(1):85–106.

1983   "National Conditions and Local Level Political Structures: Patronage
          in Pre-Revolutionary Iran". *American Ethnologist* 10(1):23–40.

1984a   "Ritual and Southwest Asian Pastoralists: The Implications of the
          Komachi Case". *Journal of Anthropological Research* 40(3):380–93.

1984b   "The Rules and the Game: The Practice of Komachi
          Marriage". *American Ethnologist* 11(4):738–53.

1989   "Producing Their Fates: Why Poor Basseri Settled but Poor Komachi
          and Yomut Did Not". *American Ethnologist* 16(3):502–17.

1990   *Ambiguous Relations: Kin, Class, and Conflict Among Komachi
          Pastoralists*. Washington, D.C.: Smithsonian Institution Press.

1992   "Territoriality and Iranian Pastoralists: Looking Out from Kerman".
          In Michael Casimir and Aparna Rao, eds., *Mobility and Territoriality*.
          New York and Oxford: Berg.

1994   "Historical Bases of the Political Economy of Kermani Pastoralists:
          Tribe and World Market in the 19th and Early 20th Centuries". In
          C. Chang and H. Kostner, eds., *Pastoralists at the Periphery*. Tucson:
          University of Arizona Press.

Chardin, Sir John

1988   *Travels in Persia 1673–77.* [Original French edition, 1686; abridged
          English translation, 1927.] New York: Dover.

Clifford, James

1983   "On Ethnographic Authority." *Representations* 1(2):118–46.

1986   "Introduction: Partial Truths." In J. Clifford and G. Marcus, eds.,
          Writing Culture. Berkeley: University of California Press.

1988   *The Predicament of Culture*. Cambridge: Harvard University Press.

Clifford, James, and George Marcus, eds.

1986   *Writing Culture*. Berkeley: University of California Press.

Crapanzano, Vincent

1986   "Hermes' Dilemma: The Masking of Subversion in Ethnographic
          Description." In J. Clifford and G. Marcus, eds., *Writing Culture*.
          Berkeley: University of California Press.

Cronin, Vincent

1957   *The Last Migration*. London: Rupert Hart-Davis.

Curzon, Lord George N.

1966   *Persia and the Persian Question*. 2 vols. [Originally published 1892.]
          New York: Barnes and Noble.

1985   *Travels with a Most Superior Person*. Edited by Peter King. London:
          Sigwick and Jackson.

de Bode, Baron Clement

1845   *Travels in Luristan and Arabistan*. London: J. Madden.

Digard, Jean-Pierre

1981   *Techniques des nomades baxtyâri d'Iran*. Cambridge: Cambridge
          University Press.

Dillon, Robert
    1976   "Carpet Capitalization and Craft Involution in Kerman, Iran." Ph.D. dissertation, Department of Anthropology, Columbia University.
Doughty, Charles
    1921   *Travels in Arabia Deserta.* New York: Boni and Liveright.
Dunn, Ross
    1986   *The Adventures of Ibn Battuta.* Berkeley: University of California Press.
Ehmann, Dieter
    1975   *Bahtiyaren-Persiche Bergnomaden in Wandel der Zeit.* Tübinger Atlas des Vorderen Orients, no. 15. Wiesbaden: Dr. Ludwig Reichert Verlag.
Eickelman, Dale F.
    1989   *The Middle East: An Anthropological Approach.* Englewood Cliffs: Prentice-Hall.
el Saadawi, Nawal
    1985   *God Dies by the Nile.* London: Zed Books.
English, Paul W.
    1966   *City and Village in Iran.* Madison: University of Wisconsin Press.
Evans-Pritchard, E. E.
    1962   *Social Anthropology.* Glencoe, IL: Free Press.
Fox, Richard
    1991   *Recapturing Anthropology.* Sante Fe: School of American Research Press.
Fraser, Keath, ed.
    1991   *Bad Trips.* New York: Random House.
Friedl, Ericka
    1991   *Women of Deh Koh.* Washington, D.C.: Smithsonian Institution Press.
Garthwaite, Gene
    1983   *Khans and Shahs.* Cambridge: Cambridge University Press.
Geertz, Clifford
    1973a   "Deep Play: Notes on the Balinese Cockfight." In *The Interpretation of Cultures.* New York: Basic Books.
    1973b   *The Interpretation of Cultures.* New York: Basic Books.
    1988   *Works and Lives: The Anthropologist as Author.* Stanford: Stanford University Press.
Gurney, J. D.
    1983   "A Qajar Household and Its Estates." *Iranian Studies* 16:137–76.
Harvey, David
    1990   *The Condition of Postmodernity.* Oxford: Basil Blackwell.
Irons, William
    1975   *The Yomut Turkmen: A Study of Social Organization Among a Central Asian Turkic Speaking Population.* Ann Arbor, Michigan: Museum of Anthropology, University of Michigan.

Jameson, Fredric
    1991   *Postmodernism, or the Cultural Logic of Late Capitalism.* Durham:
            Duke University Press.
Keddie, Nikki
    1978   "Class Structure and Political Power in Iran Since 1796." *Iranian
            Studies* 11:305–30.
Lapidus, Ira
    1988   *A History of Islamic Societies.* Cambridge: Cambridge University
            Press.
Layard, Sir Henry
    1841   "Layard Said Behador Peiman." Handwritten diary. British Library
            Additional Manuscript 39083.
    1887   *Early Adventures in Persia, Susiana, and Babylonia.* New York:
            Longmans Green.
Lee, Richard
    1984   "Eating Christmas in the Kalahari." In *The Dobe !Kung.* New York:
            Holt, Rinehart and Winston.
Malinowski, Bronislaw
    1932   "Pigs, Papuans, and Police Court Perspective." *Man* 32:33–38.
Morier, Sir James
    1811   "Journal," vol. 2. British Library Additional Manuscript 33840.
    1812   *A Journey Through Persia, Armenia, and Asia Minor.* London:
            Longman, Hurst, Rees, Orme and Brown.
    1976   *The Adventures of Hajji Baba of Ispahan.* [Originally published
            1824.] New York: Hart and Co.
Mortensen, Inge Demant
    1993   *Nomads of Luristan.* New York: Thames and Hudson.
Musil, Alois
    1982   *The Manners and Customs of the Rwlala Bedouin.* New York:
            Charles Crane.
Ortner, Sherry
    1995   "Resistance and the Problem of Ethnographic Refusal." *Comparative
            Studies in History and Society* 37(1):173–93.
Pratt, Mary Louise
    1986   "Fieldwork in Common Places." In J. Clifford and G. Marcus, eds.,
            Writing Culture. Berkeley: University of California Press.
    1992   *Imperial Eyes.* London: Routledge.
Rentoul, Alex
    1932   "Papuans, Professors, and Platitudes." *Man* 32:274–76.
Reyna, Stephen
    1994   "Literary Anthropology and the Case Against Science." *Man*
            29:555–81.
Richard, Yann
    1995   *Shi'ite Islam.* Oxford: Blackwell.

Rosaldo, Renato
  1986   "From the Door of His Tent: The Fieldworker and the Inquisitor." In
          J. Clifford and G. Marcus, eds., *Writing Culture*. Berkeley: Univer-
          sity of California Press.
Scott, James
  1986   *Weapons of the Weak*. New Haven: Yale University Press.
Sheil, Lady Mary Leonora
  1856   *Glimpses of Life and Manners in Persia*. London: John Murray.
Smith, Anthony
  1953   *Blind White Fish in Persia*. New York: Dutton.
Spurr, David
  1993   *The Rhetoric of Empire*. Durham: Duke University Press.
Stöber, Georg
  1978   *Die Afshar Nomadismus im Raum Kerman*. Marburg: Geographis-
          chen Institutes der Universität Marburg.
Stark, Freya
  1934   *The Valley of the Assassins and Other Persian Travels*. London:
          John Murray.
Sykes, Major Percy
  1902   *Ten Thousand Miles in Persia*. London: John Murray.
Tapper, Richard
  1979   *Pasture and Politics*. London: Academic Press.
  1983   *The Conflict of Tribe and State in Iran and Afghanistan*. New York:
          St. Martin's Press.
Thesiger, Wilfred
  1959   *Arabian Sands*. London: Longmans, Green.
  1964   *The Marsh Arabs*. London: Longmans, Green.
Thomas, Nicholas
  1994   *Colonialism's Culture*. Princeton: Princeton University Press.
Tyler, Stephen A.
  1986   "Post-modern Ethnography: From Document of the Occult to Occult
          Document." In J. Clifford and G. Marcus, eds., *Writing Culture*.
          Berkeley: University of California Press.
Ullens de Schooten, Marie Thérèse
  1956   *Lords of the Mountains: South Persia and the Kashkai Tribe*.
          London: Chatto and Windus.
Wilson, Sir Arnold
  1941   *S.W. Persia: Letters and Diary of a Young Field Officer, 1907–1914*.
          London: Oxford University Press.
Woodcock, George
  1991   "My Worst Journeys." In K. Fraser, ed., *Bad Trips*. New York:
          Random House.
Wright, Sir Denis
  1977   *The English Amongst the Persians*. London: Heinemann.

INDEX

Library of Congress Cataloging-in-Publication Data

Bradburd, Daniel.
  Being there : the necessity of fieldwork / Daniel Bradburd.
      p.   cm. — (Smithsonian series in ethnographic inquiry)
  Includes bibliographical references and index.
  ISBN 1-56098-777-4 (cloth : alk. paper). — ISBN 1-56098-753-7 (pbk. : alk. paper)
    1. Komachi (Iranian people)—Social conditions.   2. Komachi (Iranian people)—Economic
conditions.   3. Shepherds—Iran—Kirmān (Iran : Province)   4. Social classes—Iran—Kirmān
(Province)   5. Social conflict—Iran—Kirmān (Province)   6. Kirmān (Iran : Province)—Social
life and customs.   7. Ethnology—Iran—Kirmān (Province)—Field work.   8. Ethnology—
Iran—Kirmān (Province)—Philosophy.   I. Title.   II. Series.
DS269.K65B75   1998
305.891'5—dc21   97-38155
                                                                                                  CIP

British Library Cataloguing-in-Publication Data is available

Manufactured in the United States of America
05 04 03 02 01 00 99 98   5 4 3 2 1

♾ ⊕ The recycled paper used in this publication meets the minimum requirements of the
American National Standard for Information Sciences—Permanence of Paper for Printed Library
Materials, ANSI Z39.48-1984.